Lough

THE NATION AS MOTHER

ALSO BY THE AUTHOR

Books

His Majesty's Opponent: Subhas Chandra Bose and India's Struggle against Empire

Agrarian Bengal: Economy, Social Structure and Politics, 1919–1947

Tagore: The World Voyager

South Asia and World Capitalism

Peasant Labour and Colonial Capital in the New Cambridge History of India series

Credit, Markets and the Agrarian Economy of Colonial India

Nationalism, Democracy and Development: State and Politics in India (joint editor with Ayesha Jalal)

Modern South Asia: History, Culture, Political Economy (joint author with Ayesha Jalal)

Netaji Subhas Chandra Bose, *Collected Works* (joint editor with Sisir Kumar Bose)

A Hundred Horizons: The Indian Ocean in the Age of Global Empire

Rabindranath Tagore, *Purabi: The East in Its Feminine Gender* (translated by Charu C. Chowdhuri, joint editor with Krishna Bose)

Cosmopolitan Thought Zones: South Asia and the Global Circulation of Ideas (joint editor with Kris Manjapra)

Documentary Films

Rebels against the Raj

Mandir, Masjid, Mandal and Marx

Netaji and India's Freedom

Recordings on CDs of Music and Translations of Poems and Songs

Amaar Rabindranath (My Tagore)

Visva Yatri Rabindranath (Tagore, the World Voyager, with Pramita Mallick)

Dandi March (Bapuji), linocut print on paper by Nandalal Bose, 1930

THE NATION AS MOTHER

and Other Visions of Nationhood

SUGATA BOSE

PENGUIN
VIKING
An imprint of Penguin Random House

VIKING

USA | Canada | UK | Ireland | Australia
New Zealand | India | South Africa | China

Viking is part of the Penguin Random House group of companies whose addresses can be found at global.penguinrandomhouse.com

Published by Penguin Random House India Pvt. Ltd
7th Floor, Infinity Tower C, DLF Cyber City,
Gurgaon 122 002, Haryana, India

First published in Viking by Penguin Random House India 2017

Copyright © Sugata Bose 2017

Page 253 is an extension of the copyright page

All rights reserved

10 9 8 7 6 5 4 3 2 1

The views and opinions expressed in this book are the author's own and the facts are as reported by him which have been verified to the extent possible, and the publishers are not in any way liable for the same.

ISBN 9780670090112

Typeset in Dante MT Std by Manipal Digital Systems, Manipal
Printed at Replika Press Pvt. Ltd, India

This book is sold subject to the condition that it shall not, by way of trade or otherwise, be lent, resold, hired out, or otherwise circulated without the publisher's prior consent in any form of binding or cover other than that in which it is published and without a similar condition including this condition being imposed on the subsequent purchaser.

www.penguin.co.in

For
students
who value freedom

CONTENTS

Introduction: Nationalism in India, 1917–2017   ix

The Nation as Mother   1

Nation, Reason and Religion: India's Independence in International Perspective   33

Instruments and Idioms of Colonial and National Development: India's Historical Experience in Comparative Perspective   61

The Spirit and Form of an Ethical Polity: A Meditation on Aurobindo's Thought   85

Different Universalisms, Colourful Cosmopolitanisms: The Global Imagination of the Colonized   107

Unity or Partition: Mahatma Gandhi's Last Stand, 1945–48   127

Why Jinnah Matters   149

Track Record of India's Democracy   153

Limits of Liberalism   159

Our National Anthem   167

SPEECHES IN THE LOK SABHA

The True Meaning of Bharatavarsha	175
Fiscal Federalism	181
The India–Bangladesh Border	187
Against Intolerance, towards Cultural Intimacy	195
Free Our Universities, Free Our Students	201
Kashmir: Crucible of Conflict, Cradle of Peace	209
Acknowledgements	217
Notes	219
Index	241

INTRODUCTION

Nationalism in India, 1917–2017

In 1917 Rabindranath Tagore's little book titled *Nationalism* was published by the Macmillan Company, New York. It consisted of three chapters, 'Nationalism in the West', 'Nationalism in Japan' and 'Nationalism in India'. The first was based on a series of lectures delivered in the fall and winter of 1916–17 during the poet's travels in the United States of America. The second drew on two lectures given in Japan in June and July 1916. The final chapter on his own country was composed in the United States late in 1916. Towards the end of this chapter Tagore recorded his conviction that 'my countrymen will gain truly their India by fighting against that education which teaches them that a country is greater than the ideals of humanity'.[1]

When I gave the G.M. Trevelyan Lecture in Cambridge on the occasion of the fiftieth anniversary of Indian Independence in 1997 on 'Nation, Reason and Religion', I ended with a few lines from the poem 'The Sunset of the Century' that Tagore had included as a conclusion to his book. I found myself seeking solace in those lines once more in a speech I gave in Parliament as I defended university students being branded as anti-national and charged with sedition in 2016. Seventy years after freedom the substance of Tagore's hundred-year-old critique of nationalism is more salient than ever before.

'Nationalism is a great menace,' Tagore had proclaimed. If Marx had once described religion as the opiate of the people, Tagore regarded 'the idea of the Nation' as 'one of the most powerful anesthetics that man has invented'.² Yet Tagore's views on British rule in India might be termed nationalistic. 'The newspapers of England,' he complained, 'in whose columns London street accidents are recorded with some decency of pathos, need but take the scantiest notice of calamities happening in India over areas of land sometimes larger than the British Isles.' In cataloguing the adverse economic consequences of colonial rule, he was not that different from Dadabhai Naoroji or Romesh Dutt. 'It must be remembered,' he insisted, 'that at the beginning of the British rule in India our industries were suppressed and since then we have not met with any real help or encouragement to enable us to make a stand against the monster commercial organizations of the world. The nations have decreed that we must remain purely an agricultural people, even forgetting the use of arms for all time to come.'³

'I do not for a moment suggest,' Tagore wrote, 'that Japan should be unmindful of acquiring modern weapons of self-protection. But this should never be allowed to go beyond her instinct of self-preservation.' He saw the war raging in Europe as 'the war of retribution'. 'Men, the fairest creations of God,' he lamented, 'came out of the National manufactory in huge numbers as war-making and money-making puppets, ludicrously vain of their pitiful perfection of mechanism.' It was the mechanical organization of the nation form that posed a danger to humanity. He bemoaned the spectacle of 'nations fearing each other like the prowling beasts of the night-time; shutting their doors of hospitality'. In India before the age of the nation-states the texture of governments was 'loosely woven, leaving big gaps through which our own life sent its threads and imposed its designs'.[4]

There were weaknesses in Tagore's analysis of Indian society in the time of 'no nation'. His criticism of caste appears tepid at best from the vantage point of 2017. 'In her caste regulations,' Tagore commented, 'India recognized differences, but not the mutability which is the law of life.'[5] But it was his thoroughgoing critique of nationalism that initially caused some concern among his Indian contemporaries. Having read excerpts in the *Modern Review* from Tagore's speeches in America, Deshbandhu Chittaranjan Das wondered in April 1917 whether 'Rabindranath of the swadeshi days who made the passionate pleas to God to bless the soil and water of Bengal has been turned into Sir Rabindranath now'. However, the Tagorean critique was absorbed by figures like Das and Bipin Chandra Pal in the years that followed, allowing for a more nuanced understanding of both the oppressive and liberating aspects of nationalism. Das insisted that Indian anti-colonial nationalism was not the same as the belligerent nationalisms of France or Germany. An intellectual effort was undertaken to ensure that a generous conception of nationalism underpinning India's freedom struggle was compatible with the spirit of universal humanism. As Pal put it in his 1917 essay titled 'Federalism: The New Need', '*Narayana*, or humanity is the whole, the different nations of the world are parts of that whole.'[6]

Even more important was the articulation of variations on the theme of the federal unity of India that respectfully accommodated the myriad internal differences of language, region and religion. Fully elaborated in my essay on Aurobindo in this book, this was a general characteristic of the most sophisticated political thought in

India during the early decades of the twentieth century. Sidelined at the moment of inheritance of the unitary sovereignty and centralized structure of the British Raj in 1947, the federal idea has acquired renewed urgency in 2017 as an alternative to religious majoritarianism. My essays in this volume owe an intellectual debt to a range of political and economic thinkers of the early twentieth century whose contributions have been overlooked in sterile debates on Gandhian localism and Nehruvian centralism.

Taking Tagore's critique of nationalism as its point of departure, this book of interconnected and inter-referential essays examines the relationship between nation, reason and religion in Indian political thought and practice. It does so through historical analyses of the legacy of precolonial patriotisms, rational and religious reforms, colonial modernity and anti-colonial nationalisms, visions of nationhood and forms of state power, colonial and national development, famine and partition, and postcolonial nationalisms both for and against the state.

A conceptual and comparative perspective is brought to bear on the history of nationalism in India. The book offers a subtle interpretation of the evocation of the nation as mother and examines the ways in which national identity has been imagined in relation to gender, class, language, region and religion. By adopting a theoretically informed and historically grounded approach, this book seeks to shed light on contemporary debates about nationalism and anti-nationalism. The historical experience of India is placed in a global context.

The Nation as Mother analyses the character of anti-colonial nationalisms both in terms of normative thought and political practice, including a special focus on reason and religion in Gandhi's nationalism and the structure and ideology of the postcolonial state. The aim is to enable readers to see the historical backdrop to official nationalisms relying on secularism or religious majoritarianism in defence of central state authority and anti-state nationalisms energizing a variety of regional political movements and insurgencies. The book brings to light alternative concepts of sovereignty in precolonial and anti-colonial thought and practice that were designed to accommodate difference, distinctiveness and multiple identities.

The essays were composed over a period of a quarter of a century. The ones that came out around the time of the fiftieth anniversary of Independence in 1997 were written in the shadow of the demolition of the Babri Masjid in 1992 and in the context of economic liberalization in India since 1991. However, they had a deeper historiographical purpose in seeking to move beyond the dead-end debates between secular statist and subaltern communitarian histories. The need to break out of the stranglehold of the false dichotomy between nationalism and communalism was announced most decisively in Ayesha Jalal's essay 'Exploding Communalism'.[7] My own essays 'Nation as Mother' and 'Nation, Reason and Religion' sought to draw a distinction between religious sensibility and religious bigotry. Belonging to a generation bred in the Nehruvian secular tradition, it seemed especially important to me not to continue making the mistake of regarding religion as the enemy of the nation.

The essays written closer to the sixtieth anniversary of Independence deal with the theory and history of different universalisms and colourful cosmopolitanisms as well as visions of India as a free and flexible federal union. They question assumptions about any necessary contradiction between cosmopolitanism and patriotism and argue against the tendency among religious majoritarians and secularists alike to confuse uniformity with unity. As we approach the seventieth anniversary of freedom, I have revisited Mahatma Gandhi's lonely struggle against partition as his erstwhile political lieutenants abandoned him.

From 2014 to 2017 I have had the rather unusual anthropological experience of being a participant-observer in the maelstroms of India's democratic politics as a member of the Lok Sabha representing the Jadavpur parliamentary constituency. The insights I gleaned as a historian among the politicians will have to be the subject of another book. However, I have included a few of the speeches I delivered in Parliament towards the end of this book. Speaking in the Lok Sabha often felt like teaching an MOOC, or a Massive Open Online Course, eliciting a wide variety of responses from the younger generation of listeners. These efforts to rescue nationalism from the chauvinists and religion from the religious bigots seemed to find some resonance even if it is not clear whether the plea for cultural intimacy among India's diverse communities will succeed in the current atmosphere of unreason and inhumanity. I can only hope that this book will contribute to a fresh understanding of different facets of nationalism on the occasion of the seventieth anniversary of India's Independence. History matters in contemporary debates on nationalism.

As I write these lines while flying between Trump's America and Modi's India, I am once more startled by the prescience in Tagore's 1917 book. Tagore had criticized the 'anti-Asiatic agitations' in America 'for depriving the aliens of their right to earn their honest living on these shores'. 'Either you shut your doors against the aliens or reduce them into slavery,' Tagore said in his rebuke. He had something even more perceptive and far-sighted to say about the tyranny of social restrictions and political *jumla* in India. 'The social habit of mind,' he wrote, 'which impels us to make the life of our fellow beings a burden to them where they differ from us even in such a thing as their choice of food is sure to persist in our political organization and result in creating engines of coercion to crush every rational difference which is the sign of life. And tyranny will only add to the inevitable lies and hypocrisy in our political life.'[8] Can we save the expression of rational difference that can nurture and nourish a healthy national life?

THE NATION AS MOTHER[1]

'Our history,' wrote the Swadeshi leader Bipin Chandra Pal, 'is the sacred biography of the Mother. Our philosophies are the revelations of the Mother's mind. Our arts—our poetry and our painting, our music and our drama, our architecture and our sculpture, all these are the outflow of the Mother's diverse emotional moods and experiences. Our religion is the organized expression of the soul of the Mother. The outsider knows her as India . . . It is, I know, exceedingly difficult, if it be not absolutely impossible, for the European or American to clearly understand or fully appreciate this strange idealization of our land, which has given birth to this cult of the Mother among us.'[2] A cornerstone of what Pal described as his 'constructive study of Indian thought and ideals', this narration of the nation as Mother was the literary and cultural patent of the Bengali political generation of 1905 as they strenuously sought to 'unsettle' the 'settled fact' of George Curzon's partition of Bengal.[3]

By the time of Mountbatten's more far-reaching partition of India a generation later, many political attitudes had changed and many roles reversed. In the spring of 1947 the erstwhile votaries of Indian unity started demanding the partition of Bengal and Punjab. In an editorial entitled 'Banga-bhanga Andolon' (The

Agitation to Divide Bengal) on 11 April 1947 the newsmagazine *Millat* (Nation) accused the Congress and the Hindu Mahasabha of performing the role of Parashuram as they 'together raised a sharpened pickaxe to slice "Mother" into two'. The Hindu Mahasabha's matricidal tendencies were more readily explicable. They had, according to *Millat*, been 'born mad' ('janma-batul' was the Bengali word used) and had always wanted to 'drive the Muslims to the shores of the Arabian Sea'. 'But Congress!' exclaimed *Millat* . . . 'For half a century they had talked big and had preached many high ideals . . . What had happened to them so suddenly that having taken off their mask they were dancing on the same platform with the Hindu Mahasabha?'[4]

THE PARASHURAM MYTH

The allusion to Parashuram refers to Puranic Hindu mythology. According to the Puranas, the rishi Jamadagni ordered his five sons, one by one, to murder their mother, Renuka. The four elder sons refused to commit such a heinous act. The fifth, Ram, obeyed without displaying any qualms. He lifted his *parashu* (or *kuthar*, axe, in simpler Bengali) and struck the fatal blow. Parashuram, as he came to be called, was widely recognized in the Puranas as the sixth avatar (incarnation) of Vishnu, the immediate predecessor of the more famous seventh avatar, Dasarath's son Ram, whose exploits were narrated in the epic Ramayana.[5]

ENGENDERING THE NATION

In a macabre twist to the narrative of the Indian nation, the apparently triumphal moment of independence coincided with a gory dismemberment, if not the death, of the Mother. This was particularly ironic since the awakening of a nation from slumber, if not its actual birth, was believed to have occurred when its children were blessed with a revelation—the magical vision of the Mother. As Aurobindo Ghose argued in 1907, it was only when the Mother had revealed herself that 'the patriotism that work[ed] miracles and save[d] a doomed nation [wa]s born'. He credited Bankim Chandra Chattopadhyay with having caught the first modern glimpse of this grand spectacle: 'It was thirty-two years ago that Bankim wrote his great song and few listened; but in a sudden moment of awakening from long delusions the people of Bengal looked round for the truth and in a fated moment somebody sang *Bande Mataram*. The mantra had been given . . .'[6]

Bankim's hymn to the Mother, originally written and printed in 1875 as a filler for a blank page in his journal *Bangadarshan* (Vision / Philosophy of Bengal), had a chequered and controversial career in the service of the nationalist movement. It was inserted into Bankim's novel *Anandamath* in 1882 and set to music and sung publicly for the first time by Rabindranath Tagore at the Calcutta session of the Indian National Congress in 1896. I quote the first verse of this remarkable song:

Bande mataram,
Sujalaang suphalaang, malayaja sheetalang,
Shasya shyamalaang mataram.
Shubra-jyotsna-pulakita-jamineeng,
Phullakusumita-drumadala-shobineeng,
Suhasineeng sumadhura bhasineeng,
Sukhadaang baradang mataram.
Saptakotikantha-kalakala-ninada-karale,
Dwisaptakotibhujaidhritakharakarabale,

Abala keno ma eto bale!
Bahubaladhaarineeng, namaami taarineeng,
Ripudalabaarineeng mataram.

I bow to you, Mother,
well watered, well fruited,
breeze cool, crop green,
the Mother!
Nights quivering with white moonlight,
draped in lovely flowering trees,
sweet of smile, honeyed speech,
giver of bliss and boons, the Mother!
Seven crore voices in your clamorous chant,
twice seven crore hands holding aloft mighty scimitars,
Who says, Mother, you are weak?
Repository of many strengths,
scourge of the enemy's army, the Mother![7]

The magic number of seven crore refers, of course, to Bengalis, and the Mother whom Bankim had in mind in 1875, even though there is no specific mention, is Bangamata or Mother Bengal. The name Bharatavarsha for the subcontinent as a whole was commonly used in the political discourse of Bengal, certainly since the Hindu Mela of 1867.[8] One of the earliest literary evocations of the concept of Bharatmata was Dwijendralal Roy's song:

Jedin sunil jaladhi hoite uthile janani Bharatabarsha,
Shedin bishwe she ki kalarab, she ki ma bhakti, she ki ma harsha.

The day you arose from the blue ocean, Mother Bharatavarsha,
The world erupted in such a joyful clamour, such devotion,
Mother, and so much laughter.

An early visual evocation came in 1905 with Abanindranath Tagore's painting *Bharatmata* (see p. 7). Visualized as a serene, saffron-clad ascetic woman, the Mother carried the boons of food, clothing, learning and spiritual salvation in her four hands. A conscious creation of an 'artistic' icon of the nation, Abanindranath tells us in a memoir that he had conceived his image as Bangamata and later, almost as an act of generosity towards the larger cause of Indian nationalism, decided to title it 'Bharatmata'.[9] I will directly address the contradictions between the linguistic region, Bengal, and the overarching nation, India, later in the essay, but for the moment it is necessary to probe a little further into the relationship between nation and gender.

The figure of gender has been central to a large array of modern and postmodern readings of the colonial encounter. Ashis Nandy, among others, has underscored the theme of male anxiety and fantasy in the projection of colonial knowledge and power and its attempted inversion, if not subversion, in Gandhian resistance.[10] Thoroughly 'Westernized' nationalists like Jawaharlal Nehru relied heavily on the metaphor of sexual aggression and rape in their critiques of the violence perpetrated by the colonial masters. Sara Suleri has objected that 'the continued equation between a colonized landscape and the female body represents an alteritist fallacy that causes considerable theoretical damage to both contemporary feminist and post-colonial discourses'. She points out that the 'colonial gaze' was not directed to 'the inscrutability of an Eastern bride' but rather to 'the greater sexual ambivalence of the effeminate groom'. '[N]o intelligent feminism,' she contends, 'should be prepared to serve as the landscape upon which the intimacy of homoerotic invitation and rejection can be enacted.'[11] Yet there was more to the casting of the nation in the image of a mother than is captured by the metaphors of heterosexual aggression and resistance and homoerotic invitation and rejection. The mother complex (I use the term 'complex' simply to refer to an engaging social–psychological phenomenon and not to mean any sort of disorder or neurosis) in Bengal and some other linguistic regions in India had fairly deep psychological and cultural roots.

It is tempting to interpret 'the concept of the Motherland-Deshmata', as Tanika Sarkar has done, as a 'cultural artefact'.[12] But to nationalist thinkers like Pal, the Mother, in what had come to be called Motherland by modern Western-educated Indians, was in origin 'not a mere idea or fancy, but a distinct personality. The woman who bore them and nursed them, and brought them up with her own life and substance was no more real a personality in their thought and idea than the land which bore and reared, and gave food and shelter to all their race.' While European expressions like fatherland were 'clearly metaphorical', the 'real concept Mother as applied to India' had 'no metaphor behind it'. The 'full truth and reality of this concept' could only be grasped, in Pal's view, 'in the light of the entire Nature Philosophy of the Hindus', especially the conception of the Earth as Prakriti.[13]

That the conception of the earth as mother was not peculiarly Indian is suggested by recent work on European environmental history which has posited a strong correlation between the earth and the nurturing mother before the historic rupture of the scientific revolution of the sixteenth and seventeenth centuries altered an organic view of the cosmos. Until that happened, the onslaughts on nature were restrained by the culture of a Nature-Mother equation for, the Parashurams of the world excepted, men did 'not readily slay a mother, dig into her entrails for gold, or mutilate her body . . .'[14] A relatively undisturbed 'cosmic balance' was, however, not the only bridge between the love of a mother and devotion to the motherland, but was importantly mediated by specific cultures and ideologies, and articulated by the vernacular languages of nationalism.

Did the element of 'reality', stressed by Pal, in the 'imagination' of the nation as mother lend a special quality to the 'profoundly self-sacrificing love'[15] inspired by this particular devotional movement? I will turn later in this essay to young Bengali revolutionaries who sacrificed their lives for the cause of the mother-nation. But it would be a grave error to treat the narrative of the nation as mother related by men like Pal as constituted outside the domain of ideology. Pal was not above resorting to analytical sleights of hand to locate a Prakriti-Ma or Nature-Mother equation within his particular project of cultural nationalism.[16] The ideological construction of the nation as mother was vectored on to a dynamic, discursive field previously unmarked by political values. The mobilizers and mobilized necessarily stood in different positions in relation to this construct.

In the cultural context of Bengal the nationalist cult of the Mother, not surprisingly, emphasized the female principle as Shakti or the source of strength. Consequently, a certain concordance came to be drawn between the Mother Goddess, whether in the form of Durga or Kali, and the mother country. Tanika Sarkar suggests that a contradictory image, that of the mother as an 'archetypical, hapless, female victim' was also present in the nationalist iconography. As an example she cites the *Bharatmata* painted by Abanindranath, whom she describes as 'pale, tearful, frail'.[17] This may not be a particularly good example. To me, at any rate, 'Bharatmata' looks rather radiant, calm and reassuring. But 'Srinkhalita Bharatmata', the Mother bound in chains, was a widely used emotive image in nationalist posters and the contrast between *ma ki chhilen* (the way mother had been) and *ma ki hoiyachhen* (what mother has become or been reduced to) was quite enough to fire nationalist ire. In addition to her glorious past and her sorry present, the utopia of *ma ki hoiben* (what mother will be) constituted a powerful temporal sequence that boosted nationalist morale.

The concept of the nation as mother could not of itself even begin to address many problematic aspects of the relationship between nation and gender, not least the question of the social emancipation of women. Even though the most commonly used Bengali term for the mother's children, *santan*, was not gender-specific, early ideologues of nationalism implicitly, if not explicitly, portrayed a son–mother relationship. *Matribhakti*, devotion to the mother, was clearly not the monopoly of sons, but the psychological and cultural nuances and complexities of the daughter–mother relationship appear to be conspicuously sparse in early nationalist discourse. A few women like Sarala Devi and Kamini Roy, of course, composed panegyrics to the motherland; a few others performed Swadeshi service of various kinds for the Mother. The feminization (and peasantization) of the ideal type of the Mother's nationalist devotees nevertheless involved the imputation of certain values by men and elites to women (and peasants).

Even in the literature that glorified the nation as mother, the ideals of womanhood were mythical characters such as Sati, Savitri, Sita, Lilavati, Khana and Arundhati who were often distinguished by high learning, wisdom or other accomplishments that were tempered by devotion to their husbands as well as a desire not to outshine them.[18] In one famous Swadeshi song the wandering rural composer and singer Charankabi Mukundadas exhorts the women of Bengal to throw away their silk and glass bangles. He asks them not to be deceived by the false glitter of imported goods and not to wear *kalanka* (shame) instead of *shankha* (the white *chank* bangle, a symbol of chastity). That they don't have gold bangles is hardly a cause for mourning, he tells them. The daughters of Bengal must see to it that the Mother's wealth is not drained away any further.

Another sort of problem could stem from the intolerable burden placed on women who were idealized as mothers. This point was made forcefully in Prabhat Mukhopadhyay's story and Satyajit Ray's film *Devi* (1960) in which the family patriarch persuades himself that his daughter-in-law is an incarnation of the Mother Goddess.[19] The loss of value of woman as a human being that this entailed was considerable. The tyranny of divinity could only be countered by an invocation to humanity. When Abanindranath painted *Bharatmata*, he had in mind his daughter's face. It was the coming together of human intimacy and divine inspiration that gave not just the picture but the idea of the nation as mother its overpowering appeal.[20]

NATIONALIST THOUGHT AND COLONIAL KNOWLEDGE

How far was the narrative of nation as mother trapped within the 'essentializing' project of colonial knowledge as power and reduced to the status of a 'derivative discourse'? Making a distinction between the 'problematic' and the 'thematic' aspects of nationalist thought, its claims and its justificatory structures, Partha Chatterjee in his seminal book *Nationalist Thought and the Colonial World* has suggested that it constituted a 'different' but 'dominated' or derivative discourse.[21] In his equally important book *The Nation and Its Fragments* which 'carries forward an argument begun in' *Nationalist Thought* Chatterjee draws a sharp dichotomy between the inner, spiritual and outer, material domains. Arguing that anti-colonial nationalism 'creates its own domain of sovereignty' in the former, he asserts that the history of nationalism as a political movement by focusing on 'the material domain of the state' has 'no option but to choose its forms from the gallery of "models" offered by European and American nation-states: "difference" is not a viable criterion in the domain of the material'.[22]

Chatterjee also sets out in *Nationalist Thought* a 'theory of stages in the constitution of a nationalist discourse': the 'moment of departure' representing 'the encounter of a nationalist consciousness with the framework of knowledge created by post-Enlightenment rationalist thought'; the 'moment of manoeuvre' requiring the 'mobilization of the popular elements in the cause of an anti-colonial struggle' and 'distancing of those elements from the structure of the state'; and the 'moment of arrival' when nationalist thought becomes 'a discourse of order' and of 'the rational organization of power'.[23] Taking Bankim to be the exemplar of the 'moment of departure', Chatterjee asserts that he and, by implication, the moment, 'accepted entirely the fundamental methodological assumptions, the primary concepts and the general theoretical orientation of nineteenth century positivist sociology and utilitarian political economy'. So, in Bankim there was 'a reversal of the Orientalist problematic, but within the same general thematic'. 'Imprisoned within the rationalist framework of his theoretical discourse and powerless to reject its dominating implications', Bankim could merely 'dream' of 'a utopian political community in which the nation was the Mother, once resplendent in wealth and beauty, now in tatters. Relentlessly, she exhorts a small band of her sons, those of them who are brave and enlightened, to vanquish the enemy and win back her honour.'[24]

This sort of a formulation misses a nuance or two concerning the relationship between nationalist thought and colonial knowledge at the moment that the discourse of nation as mother was fashioned. First, the 'positivism' of nineteenth-century Europe which appealed to early Bengali nationalist thinkers was a more complex phenomenon than is acknowledged by Chatterjee. As Jasodhara Bagchi has shown, Comteist Positivism after 1848 showed a marked 'shift towards the Affective side (as contrasted with the Intellectual side) of human nature in his plan of social regeneration'. Women and the proletariat, the two 'underprivileged partners of the male patriciate', were accorded privileged positions 'in a harmonious scheme of social regeneration'. Such a scheme of 'order and progress' had its attractions for Bengal's nationalist patricians. The other 'specific feature about the Positivist programme, not adequately noticed so far, that recommended this model to the emerging Nationalist ethos' was 'its anti-imperialist stance', articulated by Comte's disciples like Richard Congreve.[25]

Second, the authors of the narrative of nation as mother attempted, not without some contortions, to draw as much (if not more) on rationalist traditions of precolonial India as on European post-Enlightenment reason. Pal, for instance, claimed as part of his ideological project to have taken the dialectic of Purusha and Prakriti, the principles of permanence and change, from the Sankhya system of philosophy. 'No rational interpretation of cosmic evolution is possible,' he wrote, 'except upon the hypothesis of these two fundamental principles ... The conception of Mother associated with our geographical habitat is filiated to this old, old, universal Hindu conception of Prakriti; but of Prakriti conceived especially as Shakti ...'[26]

In analysing nationalist thought it may be best to abandon any ahistorical quest for indigenous authenticity. Many current postcolonial readings of nationalist thought run the risk of being captivated within the stark binary dichotomies of colonial knowledge that they wish to critique.[27] The nineteenth-century colonial encounter was a messy historical process, which inevitably imparted a measure of imbrication to the domains of nationalist thought and colonial knowledge whether in terms of their content or form. Only the most prosaic critic would listen to Swadeshi songs set to tunes influenced by European music and sung to the accompaniment of the organ and relegate them to the status of 'dominated discourse'. Dwijendralal Roy's highly popular 'Banga amar, janani amar, dhatri amar, amar desh' (Bengal mine, Mother mine, my protector, my country) experimented with straight notes borrowed from European melodies and introduced the concept of the chorus lines hitherto unused in Indian music.[28] Atul Prasad Sen set his famous 'Utho go Bharatlakshmi' (Arise, Bharatlakshmi) to a tune he had heard on a gondola in Venice. Nationalist thought, even at the moment of departure, may well have found idioms of articulation that overlapped with European forms and yet at the same time opposed both the problematic and the thematic of colonial knowledge. An overemphasis on the nation and the novel has prevented the exploration of this possibility through the careful sifting of the poetry (and drama) of nationhood.[29]

NATION AND CLASS

The charge of elitism hurled at nationalist thought at the moment of departure has more force to it than the charge that it was completely subordinated to the colonial sociology of knowledge. Before the 'popular mobilization' resorted to at the moment of manoeuvre with its 'many contradictory possibilities', the nationalist ideal, Chatterjee argues, implied an 'elitist programme'.³⁰ But, as Tanika Sarkar has noted, 'food and cloth, the two basic necessities, were the two strongest metaphors' of nationalism even in its early phase.³¹ This provided a potential link between the elite and subaltern arenas of politics. To my mind, the materiality of nationalist ideology called as much for a 'declassing' of the privileged as a straightforward invitation to subordinated and marginalized groups to take equal part in nationalist rituals.

The evocation of nation as mother encompassed an inculcation of the ethic of *mota chal* and *mota kapar* (coarse, simple rice and thick, homely cloth). One of the best-known Swadeshi couplets by Rajanikanta Sen went:

Ma-er deya mota kapar, mathay tule ne re bhai,
Deen-dukhini ma je toder, tar beshi ar sadhya nai.

The Mother has given us this simple cloth, wear it with pride,
Poor and distressed is your Mother, and can afford no more.

The connection between a *mota khabo, mota porbo* (we will eat 'mota' and wear 'mota') attitude and devotion to the nation as mother was made more explicit in another of his songs 'Amra nehat gorib, amra nehat choto' which may be roughly rendered in English as follows:

We may be poor, we may be small,
But we are a nation of seven crores; brothers, wake up
Defend your homes, protect your shops,
Don't let the grain from our barns be looted abroad.
We will eat our own coarse grain and wear the rough, homespun cloth,
What do we care for lavender and imported trinkets?

Foreigners drain away our Mother's milk,
Will we simply stand and watch?
Don't lose this opportunity, brothers,
Come and congregate at the feet of the Mother.
Giving away from our own homes and begging from foreigners,
We will not buy the fragile glass, it breaks so easily,
We will rather be poor and live our simple lives,
No one can then rob us of our self-respect.
Don't lose this opportunity, brothers,
Come and congregate at the feet of the Mother.

Hardly a bugle call for class-based politics, the narrative of nation as mother nevertheless left a small opening for the poor and obscure to enter the story and perhaps even alter its denouement.

NATION AND RELIGIOUS COMMUNITY

Much more problematic was the question of whether the concept of nation as mother left any space whatsoever for the accommodation and expression of the religious diversity of the Bengali and Indian nations. Certainly on this issue the narrative started off on the wrong foot. The final verse of Bankim's song 'Bande Mataram' could not resist a conflation of the mother country with the Mother Goddess.

Twang hi durga dashapraharana-dhaarinee,
Kamalaa kamala-dala-biharinee,
Banee bidyadayinee, namaami twaam.

You are Durga bearing ten weapons of war,
Kamala at play in the lotuses

Goddess of learning, giver of knowledge,
I bow to you.

The equation of nation with goddess understandably left many Muslims cold. What compounded the problem further was the appearance of the song in Bankim's novel *Anandamath* that was dripping with anti-Muslim prejudice. A peculiar apologia that has been offered ever since, suggesting that Bankim meant British when he said Muslim, simply added insult to injury.

The narrative of the nation as mother that unfolded during the late nineteenth century and throughout the course of the twentieth century became much more complex and even flowed into divergent streams. Bengali Muslims were familiar with and understood the concept of the nation as mother even if they did not fully share the Bengali Hindus' mother complex. Perhaps the most powerful evocations of the nation as mother were made by the Bengali Muslim revolutionary poet Kazi Nazrul Islam. In one of his most popular nationalist songs he exhorts the leader, imagined as the captain of a ship in peril, to face up to the challenge of saving his nation or religious community and to say unambiguously that those who were drowning were all Mother's children.[32] Much later the Bengali Muslim nationalists who led the movement of independence for Bangladesh drew upon the entire corpus of early-twentieth-century nationalist literature, goddesses and all. In addition to Tagore's ode to Mother Bengal 'Amar sonar Bangla, ami tomay bhalobashi' (My golden Bengal, I love you) which became the national anthem, another Tagore song, very popular in 1971, explicitly drew the goddess imagery:

Aji Bangladesher hridoy hote kakhan aponi,
Tumi ei aparup rupe bahir hole janani.

Dan hate tor kharga jwale, ban hat kare shankaharan
Dui nayane sneher hashi, lalat netra agunbaran.

From the heart of Bangladesh spontaneously
You have emerged with such breathtaking beauty, Mother.
In your right hand flashes the scimitar, your left hand dispels fear
Your two eyes radiate a loving smile, the third eye on your forehead is a fiery glow.

Quite apart from the Bengali Muslim creative imagination contributing to the narrative of the nation as mother, many of the creative writers, nationalist ideologues and political revolutionaries of the early twentieth century did not agree with Bankim's attitude towards Muslims or his fictionalized version of the history of Muslim rule. Swami Vivekananda, who had a powerful influence on Bengali youth at the turn of the century, preached the equal truth of all religions, held on the whole a positive assessment of Islam and looked forward to a millennium when the Sudra and other downtrodden social groups would rise to power. The views of Aurobindo, who did more than anyone else to propagate the political cult of the mother-nation, are even more instructive. 'The vast mass of Mussulmans in the country,' he wrote, were and are Indians by race, only a very small admixture of Pathan, Turkish and Mogul blood took place, and even the foreign kings and nobles became almost immediately wholly Indian in mind, life and interest.' As for the Mughal empire, it was, according to Aurobindo, 'a great and magnificent construction and an immense amount of political genius and talent was employed in its creation and maintenance. It was as splendid, powerful and beneficent and, it may be added, in spite of Aurangzeb's fanatical zeal, infinitely more liberal and tolerant in religion than any medieval or contemporary European kingdom or empire and India under its rule stood high in military and political strength, economic opulence and the brilliance of its art and culture.'[33]

A very motley crowd of nationalists holding a variety of attitudes to other religious communities went to prison and detention camps during the first half of the twentieth century. It is hard, if not impossible, to draw up a balance sheet of bigotry and broad-mindedness. But among the revolutionaries who went to the gallows with 'Bande Mataram' on their lips there was clearly no need and no sense of another religious community as the 'other' to substantiate their own affective bond with the mother-nation. What evidence there is points to a substantial measure of generous eclecticism in the mental make-up of these revolutionaries. Dinesh Gupta, one of the three young men who stormed Writers' Buildings in Calcutta in December 1930, wrote to his sister-in-law days before he was hanged: 'If one believes in any of the world's religions, one has to believe in the indestructibility of the soul. That is, one has to accept that the body's death does not signify the end of everything. We are Hindus, we know something of what the Hindu religion has to say about this. Islam also says when human beings die, "khuda's fereshta", God's angel, comes for his/her "rukbaz" and calling upon the soul of the human being says, *"Ay rub nikal is kalib se chal khuda ka jannat me"*—meaning leave this body to be with God. So it can be understood that everything does not end when human beings die, Islam has faith in this. Christianity says, "Very quickly there will be an end of the here, consider what will become of the next world" . . . If I have faith in any one of these three religions, I have to believe that I cannot die. I am immortal. No one has the power to kill me.' What follows in Dinesh's letter is a blistering attack on social ills and injustices perpetrated in the name of religion: 'In a country where a fifty-year old man can marry a ten-year old girl in the name of religion, where is religion in such a country. I would set fire to the face of religion in such a country. Where touching another human being is polluting, one should drown the religion of such a country in the Ganga and be done with it . . . For a trivial cow or a bit of music played on drums we are murdering each other's brothers. For doing that will "bhagaban" open the doors of "baikuntha" for us, or will "khuda" give us a place in "behesht".'[34] Having had his say on religion and having assured his mother that she was from now on the mother of all India, Dinesh Gupta calmly accepted 'the garland' of the hangman's noose.

By the time the 'Bande Mataram' controversy exploded with full force at the all-India political level in 1937, there were at least three contexts in which the matter had to be seen. The most immediate context was the element of triumphalism inherent in the singing of 'Bande Mataram' in the legislatures 'thereby demonstrating Congress victory'. Since the Gandhian Congress was infected with Hindu communalism at the regional level in many provinces, this was bound to outrage many Muslims. The original context, referred to by Nehru, was provided by Bankim's unfortunate novel. Nehru took the trouble to procure an English translation of the book and did not need much time to figure out that the background was 'likely to irritate the Muslims'. Stretched out between the original and immediate contexts was the process of sanctification of a problematic cultural icon through sacrifice, in the case of the revolutionaries, supreme sacrifice. The question, therefore, was whether the song should be performed as a national anthem at Congress gatherings. At the suggestion of Subhas Chandra Bose it was decided to seek the advice of Tagore in an attempt to resolve this question at the meeting of the All India Congress Committee in Calcutta in October 1937.[35]

Tagore wrote privately to Bose that the song containing adoration of Durga was wholly inappropriate for a national organization that was the meeting place for different religious communities. He wrote, 'Bengali Hindus have become restless at this debate, but the matter is not confined to the Hindus. Where there are strong feelings on both sides, what is needed is impartial judgement. In our national quest we need peace, unity, good sense—we don't need endless rivalry because of one side's obstinate refusal to yield.' In a measured press statement the poet explained that he had found the feelings of devotion and tenderness as well as evocation of the beauty of Bharatmata in the first verse of the song appealing. But he had had no difficulty in detaching this verse from the whole song as well as the book in which it had appeared. He had never entertained any love for the whole song. Once 'Bande Mataram' was transformed into a national slogan many noble friends had made unforgettable and huge sacrifices for it. At the same time the song as a whole and the history associated with it hurt Muslim feelings. Tagore argued that the first part of the song stood on its own and had an inspirational quality which was not offensive to any religious community.[36] The Congress accepted Tagore's advice and resolved that henceforth only the first part of the song would be sung in national meetings. Bengal's two luminaries, Tagore and Bose, were showered with abuse by a sizeable section of Bengali Hindu literary and political circles. But in the year of his birth centenary, 1938, Bankim's equation of the mother-nation with Durga was banished from the platform of India's premier nationalist party. Bose did close his presidential speech with the slogan 'Bande Mataram', but he refused to entertain any controversy sought to be raised by some Hindu politicians over the decision to abridge the song.[37]

The problem posed by the narrative of nation as mother in its connection with the history of relations between religious communities was that it was sought to be directed, if not hijacked, in different directions. It could be sanctified by those prepared to die in the cause of the mother-nation and defiled by those ready to kill in the name of religion. The trouble was that as the narrative reached its denouement it was the living rather than the dead who had any chance of capturing political power.

NATION AND LINGUISTIC REGION

In a dramatic overstatement of the case for nationalist thought being ensnared by the cunning of reason and positivist knowledge, Chatterjee has written in *Nationalist Thought*: 'The "subject" is a scientific consciousness, distanced from the "object" which is the Indian, the Bengali, the Hindu (it does not matter which, because all of them are defined in terms of the contraposition between the Eastern and the Western).' On this view, nationalist thought, certainly at its moment of departure and to a lesser extent at the later stages too, makes 'no attempt' to 'define the boundaries of the Indian nation *from within*'.[38] In *The Nation and Its Fragments* Chatterjee devotes a mere three pages to a strand in nationalist thought that 'raises doubts about the singularity of a history of India'. He accepts that '[t]here is a great disjuncture here between the history of India and the history of Bengal' and speculates that 'there were many such alternative histories for the different regions of India'. Yet in a startling intellectual abdication to the votaries of a singular nationalism who managed to capture state power Chatterjee pleads that 'we do not yet have the wherewithal to write these other [suppressed] histories'.[39]

Far from being completely tied up in knots by Orientalist discourse, nationalist thought retained a certain awareness of multiple social identities and the freedom of manoeuvre to stress one over another in politics. Yet the language and idiom of nationalism operated in the late nineteenth and early twentieth centuries with the greatest potency at the level of the linguistic community and region. The predominant vision of the mother-nation in this period was the image of Mother Bengal. There could be gifts made to Mother India and a keen awareness of the dangers for the nationalist cause of evoking a Hindu Mother. But the conception of the mother-nation was in inspiration and exposition that of Mother Bengal. The all-India nationalist movement sought to harness the energy of this phenomenon by seeking to make measured concessions to linguistically based provincial organizations in 1920 and came to fear its strength in the course of efforts to enforce central discipline on the way to grasping centralized state power. In the end, the potential threat posed to central authority by linguistic nations played a role in the Congress's compromise on partition along lines of ostensibly religiously based communalism.

We have seen how the mother in Bankim's 'Bande Mataram' and Abanindranath's *Bharatmata* was originally conceived as Mother Bengal and then ungrudgingly offered in the service of a wider Indian nation. Aurobindo in an essay entitled 'Desh o Jatiyata' (The Country and Nationhood), written in 1920, candidly acknowledged that during the heyday of the Swadeshi movement they had seen the vision of Bangamata. Aurobindo believed that this was an undivided vision and over-optimistically predicted that unity and progress of 'Bangadesh' were inevitable.

But, he wrote, 'Bharatmata's undivided image has not yet been revealed . . . the Bharatmata that we ritually worshipped in the Congress was artificially constructed ("kalpita" was the Bengali word used), she was the companion and favourite mistress of the British, not our mother . . . The day we have that undivided vision of the image of the mother . . . the independence, unity and progress of India will be facilitated.' But he kept warning that the vision had to be one that was not divided by religion. He concluded, ' . . . if we hope to have a vision of the mother by invoking the Hindus' mother or establishing Hindu nationalism, having made a cardinal error we would be deprived of the full expression of our nationhood.'[40]

The interchangeable use of Mother Bengal and Mother India in poetic imagination makes it difficult to clinch the argument about the relative strength of the idea of the mother-nation at the level of the linguistic region. But the emotive appeal of the linguistically defined mother-nation is compelling. Consider a letter written by Pradyot Bhattacharya, a young man who had assassinated one of Midnapore's British district magistrates in 1932. A day before he was hanged he wrote: 'Mother, you cannot ask me for any justification for what I have done. Perhaps you do not know that you have created us for your own purpose. But I am letting you know that for thousands of years we were being quietly created in your minds, the minds of Bengal's mothers. Today we are slowly revealing ourselves. And I have always known that I am Bengali and you are Bengal, the same element, could never think of us separately . . . Through the ages you have endured insult, humiliation and oppression . . . the undercurrent of revolt against these that was flowing deep within you, I am that accumulated revolt . . . If that revolution achieves self-expression today, why should you shed tears . . . Mother, can your

Pradyot ever die? Look around today, lakhs and lakhs of Pradyots are smiling at you. I'll continue to live, Mother, imperishable, immortal. Bande Mataram.'[41] It is hard not to be persuaded that this young life was being sacrificed at the altar of Mother Bengal.

A few years later, in 1939, Tagore and Bose came together for the foundation-laying ceremony of a house to be called 'Mahajati Sadan' which they hoped would be home to an enlightened and dignified idea of a 'great nation'. As part of his speech on the occasion, Tagore recited a prayer he had composed in the Swadeshi era:

> The Bengalis' faith, the Bengalis' hope,
> The Bengalis' work, the Bengalis' language,
> Bless them with truth, O Lord.
> The Bengalis' heart, the Bengalis' mind,
> All the brothers and sisters in Bengali homes,
> May they be one, O Lord.

After a short pause he said: 'And let this word be added: may Bengal's arm lend strength to India's arm, may Bengal's message make India's message come true.'[42]

NATION AND STATE

Literary and cultural representations of the nation are often disfigured by hard historical and political realities. In 1947 the leadership of the Indian National Congress accepted the transfer of power from British hands at the apex of a unitary and centralized structure of the Indian state. Bengal paid a hefty price to enable the Congress to inherit the strong centre of the British Raj. The official ideology of the Indian state came to rest on a monolithic concept of sovereignty borrowed from modern Europe, denying the multiple identities and several-layered sovereignties that had been its complex legacy from its precolonial past.[43]

Chatterjee has provided an insightful analysis of nationalist thought at what he has called its 'moment of arrival' when its discourse is conducted not only in 'a single, consistent, unambiguous voice' but also 'succeeds in glossing over all earlier contradictions, divergences and differences'. Yet a flaw creeps into his method in seeking to 'give to nationalist thought its ideological unity by relating it to a form of the post-colonial state'.[44] This sort of reasoning backwards denudes nationalist thought of 'all earlier contradictions, divergences and differences' and can have the unintended effect of playing into the hands of the postcolonial state's ideological project which it promises to question and critique. A postcolonial state, unitary in form, could only accommodate the one strand of singular nationalism. Although Chatterjee is not unaware of its dangers, he still resorts to a kind of teleology that leaves not enough theoretical space for the recovery of contested visions of nationhood and alternative ideological frameworks for the postcolonial state. It assumes and asserts a conflation of nation and state where it can be argued that none existed, at least not until very late in the colonial era.

Here it is relevant to absorb the nuances of Edward Said's thesis that *'at its best,* nationalist resistance to imperialism was always critical of itself'. While recognizing the insights provided by Chatterjee's critique of nationalism, Said points out he 'does not emphasize enough . . . that the culture's contribution to statism is often the result of *a* separatist, even chauvinist and authoritarian conception of nationalism. *There is also,* however, a consistent intellectual trend within the nationalist consensus that is vitally critical, that refuses the short-term blandishments of separatist and triumphalist slogans in favour of the larger, more generous human realities of community . . . ' So 'we must also focus on the intellectual and cultural argument within the nationalist resistance that once independence was gained new and imaginative reconceptions of society and culture were required in order to avoid the old orthodoxies and injustices'.[45]

If not all nationalist thinkers were having megalomaniacal dreams of the bourgeois acquisition of power in a centralized nation-state, how did they view the relationship between nation and state? While the affective bond of Bengali nationalists at the 'moment of departure' was stronger with the nation conceived as Mother Bengal, they did ponder and think about political arrangements covering all India. But the kind of Indian unity they aspired to and the type of state structure and ideology they believed to be appropriate on a subcontinental scale may have been in many instances quite different from the centralized monolith that was declared to be sacrosanct in 1947. The structural and ideological underpinnings of the 'India, that is Bharat' of the Indian Constitution of 1950 were a far cry from theories of the state articulated by generations of nationalist thinkers. A multiplicity of visions of Indian unity and the nature of the state lent nationalist thought an important dimension of ideological disunity and discontinuity.

Most nationalists since the late nineteenth century claimed, of course, that an at least inchoate sense of Indian nationhood and Indian states wielding authority on a subcontinental scale had existed prior to the imposition of British rule and administrative unification. India or Bharat, they asserted, signified much more than geographic location. Pal wrote, ' . . . while the stranger called her India, or the Land of the Indus, thereby emphasizing only her strange physical features, her own children, from of old,

..ve known and loved her by another name . . . That name is Bharatavarsha. To clearly understand and grasp the nature and reality of the fundamental unity in which all our divergent and even apparently conflicting usages and customs, cults and cultures, our racialities and provincialities, have almost from the very beginning of our history been rationally reconciled, you must try to realize the deep significance of this old and native name of the land which the foreigner has so long called and known as India.' Even though Pal left many points of ambiguity, he did not proceed to make an argument about Hindu religious or Aryan racial unity. In fact, he argued strongly against political and administrative centralization. What he did do was read cultural meaning and a 'federal' idea into Bharatavarsha which was 'not a physical name like India or the Transvaal, nor even a tribal and ethnic name like England or Aryavarta, but a distinct and unmistakable historic name like Rome'. Pal recognized that Bharata (a Vedic personage) and Romulus were, 'strictly speaking', 'more legendary than perhaps historical' but felt that 'the profound significance of the name which they gave to these two great countries of the ancient world' was 'by no means affected by their legendary or even mythical character'. Bharata had been described in ancient texts as *rajchakravarti*. Pal took some pains to explain that the 'literal meaning of the term is not emperor, but only a king "established at the centre of a circle of kings". King Bharata was a great prince of this order.' His position was 'not that of the administrative head of any large and centralised government, but only that of the recognized and respected centre' which was the 'general character' of all great princes in ancient times. Under Muslim rule, according to Pal, Indian unity, 'always more or less of a federal type', became 'still more pronouncedly so'.[46]

Aurobindo's analysis of the ideal type of the Dharmarajya described in the epics suggested that it was 'not an autocratic despotism but a universal monarchy supported by a free assembly of the city and provinces and of all the classes'. The ancient ideal recognized that 'unification . . . ought not to be secured at the expense of the free life of the regional peoples or of the communal liberties and not therefore by a centralised monarchy or a rigidly Unitarian imperial State'. Aurobindo suggested that 'a new life' that 'seemed about to rise in the regional peoples' in the eighteenth century was 'cut short by the intrusion of the European nations'. The 'lifeless attempt' to 'reproduce with a servile fidelity the ideals and forms of the West' was 'no true indication of the political mind and genius of the Indian people'.[47] Whatever else Pal and Aurobindo may have been doing, they were not borrowing wholesale, as Chatterjee asserts they must have been condemned to doing, from modular forms offered by European and American nation-states.[48] If there was a measure of such borrowing in nationalist thought at the 'moment of departure' in the material domain of the state, there seems to have been a powerful critique as well of Western ideals and forms. Tagore's writings on nationalism and modernity disdainfully rejected European forms of the nation-state while accepting universalist ideals of humanism. Steering a creative path between an unthinking eulogy of European 'enlightenment' and an undiscriminating assault on the 'modern', the more imaginative strands of anti-colonial thought fashioned a cultural and political space where there was no necessary contradiction between nationality and human community. Chatterjee's analytical binarism sharply separating the inner, spiritual from the outer, material domain leads to an ahistorical exaggeration of the 'sovereignty' of anti-colonial nationalism in the former and its deterministic subservience in the latter.

A thoroughgoing nationalist critique of the entire Western concept of civil society was, of course, available in Gandhian thought at the so-called 'moment of manoeuvre'.[49] The problem with Gandhi was that he did not offer any theory of the state. His was a relentless nihilism, a celebration of extreme anarchy and the pursuit of decentralization to the point of atomization. In 1908 Gandhi had written in *Hind Swaraj*: 'India's salvation consists in unlearning what she has learnt during the past fifty years or so. The railways, telegraphs, hospitals, lawyers, doctors and such like have all to go, and the so-called upper class have to learn to live consciously and religiously and deliberately the simple life of a peasant.'[50] By 1945 Gandhi had made many political compromises with the 'modernists' but only slightly modified his ideological stance: '... I still stand by the system of Government envisaged in *Hind Swaraj* ... I am convinced that if India is to attain true freedom and through India the world also, then sooner or later the fact must be recognized that people have to live in villages, not in towns, in huts, not in palaces ... I do not want to draw a large-scale picture in detail. It is possible to envisage railways, post and telegraph offices etc. For me it is material to obtain the real article and the rest will fit into the picture afterwards.'[51] There is much that is valuable in the critique of modernity in the anti-modern Gandhi which postmodern culture critics can and have drawn on. Yet Gandhi's unwillingness 'to draw a large-scale picture in detail' has made him especially appealing to a particular brand of postmodernism which uncritically exults over the fragment. There were other nationalist models of the state, such as C.R. Das's draft Constitution, which offered, by contrast, something of a blueprint of a decentred democracy where there was room for a dialectic between fission and fusion, centrifugal and centripetal tendencies.⁵²

The conception of a state of union reflecting and presiding over the balance and harmony of free regional peoples and religious communities was a major theme running through Bengali nationalist thought. As Tagore put it, 'Where there is genuine difference, it is only by expressing and restraining that difference in its proper place that it is possible to fashion unity. Unity cannot be achieved by issuing legal fiats that everybody is one.'⁵³ When Tagore and Bose came together in 1939 to give expression to their idea of a 'mahajati' (great nation), the poet said: 'The shakti (strength) of the Bengali nation that we have resolved to establish today is not that rashtrashakti (state power) which instils fear and doubt in friends and foes alike.'⁵⁴ While Bose's belief in 'samyavada' (socialism) occasionally led him to praise the virtues of a strong state in implementing a radical social and economic programme, he seemed more willing than Nehru to build that state on the foundations of regional autonomy and an equitable sharing of power among religious communities. The irony of the twentieth-century intellectual and political history of Bengal is that the powerful strand in nationalist thought that had stressed a federal unity and cross-communal understanding was defeated at the critical moment of the postcolonial transition. The insistence of a large section of paranoid and pulverized Bengali Hindu educated classes on the partition of Bengal facilitated the Congress high command's acquisition of centralized state power. Those who stood for the unity of Bengal till the very end could only lament the denial of an opportunity 'to work from the bottom and bring into being an Indian Union of our free choice' once the British attempt 'to impose an Indian Union from the top had failed'.⁵⁵

Most of the 'brave and enlightened sons' must have died, literally and metaphorically, in the service of the Mother. This had left the field wide open for the Congressmen and Mahasabhaites with their matricidal tendencies. At the end of the day the partitioner's axe had been wielded by the mother's own sons.

RAM, PARASHURAM AND MOTHER INDIA

Although Jamadagni's son Ram and Dasarath's son were the sixth and seventh avatars of Vishnu respectively, they had overlapped for a while in cosmic time. Parashuram had been banished eventually after several murderous sprees for the ultimately unpardonable crime of murdering his mother. But, according to the Ramayana, he found his way back and confronted Ram as he returned to Ayodhya after marrying Sita. Ram had just won in a contest by performing a marvellous feat with the Haradhanu, Shiva's bow. Putting forward another formidable bow, the Vaishnavdhanu, Parashuram challenged Ram to break it or use it if he could. Ram did so with ease, upon which powerless, impotent and inert, Parashuram retired to Mahendraparbat, the Himalayas, and Ram for the moment enjoyed his patrimony. Not an unfair outcome (only to be expected of a good storyteller like Valmiki), since Parashuram was guilty of matricide and Ram could not as yet be accused of misogyny. Much later in the story—on their return to Ayodhya from their lengthy forest exile—Sita, who had already walked through fire unscathed once, was asked by her noble husband to go through the test a second time to satisfy the inhabitants of the kingdom of Ayodhya. Having had enough, Sita asked Mother Earth to save her from the humiliation. Mother Earth opened up and took Sita back into her womb. As the Parashurams of the 1990s hurled their pickaxes in Ayodhya and the votaries of *Ramrajya* and Shiva's soldiers demanded shuddhi or extermination, one could not but muse over *Millat's* 1947 warning that the Congress and the Hindu Mahasabha, beset by Curzon's ghost, had raised a sharpened parashu to 'slice "Mother" into two'.

NATION, REASON AND RELIGION[*]
India's Independence in International Perspective[1]

'A prize I got for good work at school,' Jawaharlal Nehru writes in his autobiography, 'was one of G.M. Trevelyan's Garibaldi books. This fascinated me, and soon I obtained the other two volumes of the series and studied the whole Garibaldi story in them carefully. Visions of similar deeds in India came before me, of a gallant fight for freedom, and in my mind India and Italy got strangely mixed together.' To the young Nehru, Harrow seemed a rather small and restricted place for these ideas. So it was that at the beginning of October 1907, inspired by the first of Trevelyan's Garibaldi trilogy, he arrived at Trinity College, Cambridge, where he felt elated at being an undergraduate with a great deal of freedom.[2] When freedom came to India at the famous midnight hour of 14–15 August 1947, Trevelyan, then Master of Trinity College, 'rejoiced'. He had remained, his biographer David Cannadine tells us, 'equivocal and uncertain about the British Empire, which he always thought a far more

---

[*] The G.M. Trevelyan Lecture, University of Cambridge, 26 November 1997.

formidable instrument of aggression and domination than any of Italy's colonizing endeavours, which seemed small-scale by comparison'.³

Nehru's Cambridge years, which coincided almost exactly with the Garibaldi phase of Trevelyan's life in history, represented the climactic moment of triumphant liberalism in the domestic politics of Britain. In Europe these were the last days of liberal nationalism before Italy launched on its imperialist expedition in 1911 and the nation-states of the Continent as a whole moved recklessly towards the precipice of total war. The high tide of liberalism did not, however, reach the shores of Britain's colonies where this was a period of political denial and repression. India was 'showing fight' for the first time since the revolt of 1857 and 'was seething with unrest and trouble'. News reached Indian students in Cambridge of Swadeshi and boycott, of the activities and imprisonment of Tilak and Aurobindo Ghose. 'Almost without exception,' Nehru recalled, 'we were Tilakites or Extremists, as the new party was called in India.' Yet looking back from the 1930s he also believed that in social terms 'the Indian national renewal in 1907 was definitely reactionary'. 'Inevitably,' Nehru commented gloomily, 'a new nationalism in India, as elsewhere in the East, was a religious nationalism.' After graduating from Cambridge, he visited Ireland in the summer of 1910 where he was 'attracted' by 'the early beginnings of Sinn Fein'.⁴ What he neglected to note in Britain and Ireland was that a religious tinge to nationalism was not a monopoly of the East. At the end of the day the nationalist leaderships in both India and Ireland, quite as much as their departing colonial masters, failed to negotiate a satisfactory solution to the problem of religious difference. If there was cause to rejoice at the end of the Raj in India, the celebrations were certainly marred by a tragic partition ostensibly along religious lines which took an unacceptable toll in human life and suffering.

CHURCH AND STATE IN EUROPE AND INDIA

The political failure at the moment of formal decolonization has been matched by a certain intellectual failure in the post-colonial period to unravel the complex weave of nation, reason and religion in historical analyses. Decades of secular, rationalist discomfort with assessing the role of religion in modern political philosophy and practice have given way in more recent years to cultural critiques of modernity and one of its key signs—nationalism—which tend to valorize an ahistorical notion of indigenous religion while denouncing the cunning of universal reason. In an essay entitled 'Radical Histories and the Question of Enlightenment Rationalism' Dipesh Chakrabarty has berated secular and Marxist historians for their lack of imagination in addressing the question of religiously informed identities in modern South Asia. '[S]cientific rationalism,' he contends, 'or the spirit of scientific enquiry, was introduced into colonial India from the very beginning as an antidote to (Indian) religion, particularly Hinduism . . .' The opposition between reason and emotion, characteristic of our colonial hyper-rationalism, is seen to have generally afflicted the attempt by historians to understand the place of the religious in Indian public and political life.[5] That may well be so, but is there any reason to believe, if it is permissible to use such a turn of the phrase, that hyper-rationalism was characteristic of modernity under colonial conditions?

One of the key empirical premises of Benedict Anderson's theory in *Imagined Communities* is that 'in Western Europe the eighteenth century mark[ed] not only the dawn of the age of nationalism but the dusk of religious modes of thought'.[6] 'It is a common error,' Trevelyan had observed in his *English Social History*, 'to regard the eighteenth century in England as irreligious.' Religion continued to be in his view 'an imposing fabric' of British history in the nineteenth century until the Darwinian revolution made its full impact.[7] The views of the early Gladstone and Trevelyan's great-uncle Thomas Babington Macaulay probably covered the full spectrum of opinion among the British ruling classes in the mid-nineteenth century on the place of religion in public life. Gladstone had argued a powerful case in his book *The State in Its Relations with the Church* published in 1839 that propagation of religious truth should be one of the principal aims of paternal government. He had no doubt that the religion of the sovereign ought to be the only one to be propagated and allegiance to that religion must be an absolute requirement for holding political office. Yet he was opposed to religious persecution of unbelievers among the subjects as something unbecoming of government's paternalistic function. Macaulay launched a searing attack on Gladstone's advocacy of political and civil disability on grounds of religious belief which he saw as a sure recipe for undermining efficient governance. He was also unconvinced by the Gladstonian logic of stopping short of persecution since a father's duty was to crack the whip on wayward children.

Whatever their differences on political theory, it was the positions that Gladstone and Macaulay took on the practice of governance in India that provide insights into religion as a characteristic of colonial modernity. 'In British India,' Gladstone had written, 'a small number of persons advanced to a higher grade of civilization, exercise the powers of government over an immensely greater number of less cultivated persons, not by coercion, but under free stipulation of the governed.' In a situation so plainly peculiar a theory of paternal principles could not have unrestricted play and the rights of government were based 'upon an express and known treaty, matter of positive agreement, not of natural ordinance'. The former law member of William Bentinck's council pointed out that the treaty known only to Gladstone was in truth a 'nonentity'. 'It is by coercion, it is by the sword,' Macaulay thundered, 'and not by free stipulation with the governed, that England rules India; nor is England bound by any contract whatever not to deal with Bengal as she deals with Ireland.' If there was a single state in the whole world where Gladstone's theory of paternal government should have been applicable, it was according to Macaulay the British Empire in India:

> Surely, if it be the duty of government to use its power and its revenue in order to bring seven millions of Irish Catholics over to the Protestant Church, it is *a fortiori* the duty of the government to use its power and its revenue in order to make seventy millions of idolaters Christians. If it be a sin to suffer John Howard or William Penn to hold any office in England, because they are not in communion with the Established Church, it must be a crying sin indeed to admit to high situations men who bow down, in temples covered with emblems of vice, to the hideous images of sensual or malevolent gods. But no. Orthodoxy, it seems, is more shocked by the priests of Rome than by the priests of Kalee [Kali].

Macaulay's concise view with respect to the alliance of Church and State was that the latter could pursue religious education as a secondary end of government if it did not interfere with the primary end of maintaining public order. 'No man in his senses would dream of applying Mr Gladstone's theory to India,' Macaulay wrote, 'because, if so applied, it would inevitably destroy our empire, and, with our empire, the best chance of spreading Christianity among the natives.' Gladstone must have sensed this and so had engaged in a bit of '[i]naccurate history' as 'an admirable corrective of unreasonable theory'.[8]

It was at least a partial application of Gladstonian theory that created the history which in turn transformed the 'treaty' of Gladstone's imagination into reality. The defence of Indian faiths, both Hinduism and Islam, against perceived threats from evangelical religion, not Enlightenment reason, played a significant part in the revolt of 1857 which almost made Macaulay's nightmare come true. After a cataclysmic war, in which incidentally as many as ten Trevelyans lost their lives, the colonial power solemnly announced in the form of the Queen's Proclamation of 1858 that none of her subjects would be 'molested or disquieted by reason of their religion, faith or observances'. This formal separation of religion and politics in the colonial stance was, however, breached almost immediately as the British took the momentous decision to deploy religious enumeration to define 'majority' and 'minority' communities. In order to gain the political attention of the colonial state, Indian publicists of the late nineteenth century needed to dip their pens in the ink of religious community. Far from being a mirror of the abstractions of European rationalism, colonial modernity was a complex and concrete phenomenon; its reasons of state were deeply enmeshed with the communities of religion.

RATIONAL REFORM, RELIGIOUS REVIVAL AND INTIMATIONS OF AN ANTI-COLONIAL MODERNITY

'Somehow, from the very beginning,' writes Partha Chatterjee, 'we have made a shrewd guess that given the close complicity between modern knowledges and modern regimes of power, we would forever remain consumers of universal modernity; never would we be taken seriously as its producers. It is for this reason that we have tried, for over a hundred years, to take our eyes away from this chimera of universal modernity and clear up a space where we might become the creators of our own modernity.'[9] As an example of the rejection of uncritical imitation of English modernity he quotes the following passage from Rajnarayan Basu's 1873 tract *She Kal aar E Kal* (Those Days and These Days):

> Two Bengali gentlemen were once dining at Wilson's hotel. One of them was especially addicted to beef. He asked the waiter, 'Do you have veal?' The waiter replied, 'I'm afraid not, sir.' The gentleman asked again, 'Do you have beef steak?' The waiter replied, 'Not that either, sir.' The gentleman asked again, 'Do you have ox tongue?' The waiter replied, 'Not that either, sir.' The gentleman asked again, 'Do you have calf's foot jelly?' The waiter replied, 'Not that either, sir.' The gentleman said, 'Don't you have anything from a cow?' Hearing this, the second gentleman, who was not so partial to beef, said with some irritation, 'Well, if you have nothing else from a cow, why not get him some dung?'[10]

Chatterjee goes on to argue that while 'Western modernity' in the voice of Immanuel Kant looked for the definition of modernity 'in the difference posed by the present . . . as the site of one's escape from the past', it is precisely the present 'from which the colonized intellectual in search of a national modernity had to escape to find solace in an imagined past'.[11] What remains underplayed in this argument is that Basu's ruminations on modernity were contested by his contemporaries, not least by his close friend and frequent correspondent, the poet Michael Madhusudan Datta. The category 'we' contained a wide range of internal variation which made certain that 'our' modernity was never a monolith. While Indian intellectuals often had an awareness that modern rational knowledge from its very inception was deeply implicated in modern regimes of power, that never negated the possibility of selective appropriation and effective resistance within these fields of power. To put it another way, I would contend that colonized intellectuals sought alternative routes of escape from the oppressive present, not all of which lay through creating a *mayajal* or web of illusions about *our* past and denouncing *their* modernity.

What is needed here is a dynamic and historicized conception of religion that might enable us to consider how the place of the 'religious' in Indian public and political life changed in the course of India's colonial history. There is a certain static quality to Dipesh Chakrabarty's invocation of age-old Indian religion set under siege by the modern forces of scientific rationalism. Chatterjee concedes that the 'idea that "Indian nationalism" is synonymous with "Hindu nationalism" is not the vestige of some pre-modern religious conception but an entirely modern, rationalist and historicist idea'.[12] But he explains away the apparent contradiction between this rationalist idea and the religiously inspired emotional attachment to the nation by resorting to an unsatisfactory dichotomy between the material and spiritual domains that he reads into anti-colonial nationalism.[13] In facing up to the fundamental dilemma of having to simultaneously resist colonial power and appropriate elements from modern European knowledge, colonized intellectuals of the late nineteenth and early twentieth centuries harnessed reason and religion in multifarious ways to the cause of the nation.

Religious sensibility could in the late nineteenth century be perfectly compatible with a rational frame of mind, just as social reform calling upon practical reason almost invariably sought divine sanction of some kind. Speaking at the Eleventh Social Conference in Amraoti in 1897 Mahadev Govind Ranade scored a debating point against his 'revivalist' critics:

> When my revivalist friend presses his argument upon me, he has to seek recourse in some subterfuge which really furnishes no reply to the question—what shall we revive? Shall we revive the old habits of our people when the most sacred of our caste indulged in all the abominations as we now understand them of animal food and drink which exhausted every section of our country's Zoology and Botany? The men and the Gods of those old days ate and drank forbidden things to excess in a way no revivalist will now venture to recommend.[14]

What Chatterjee presents as Basu's critique of English modernity appears in Ranade as a critique of ancient Indian tradition. Even more fascinating is Ranade's exposition of reason in the service of reform. In 'Our Modernity' Chatterjee offers us this reading of Kant's essay on Aufklarung:

> According to Kant, to be enlightened is to become mature, reach adulthood, to stop being dependent on the authority of others, to become free and assume responsibility for one's own

actions. When man is not enlightened, he does not employ his own powers of reasoning but rather accepts the guardianship of others and does as he is told.[15]

What lay at 'the root of our helplessness', Ranade declared, was 'the sense that we are always intended to remain children, to be subject to outside control, and never to rise to the dignity of self-control by making our conscience and our reason the supreme, if not the sole, guide to our conduct. . . . We are children, no doubt, but the children of God, and not of man, and the voice of God is the only voice [to] which we are bound to listen. . . . With too many of us, a thing is true or false, righteous or sinful, simply because somebody in the past has said that it is so. . . . Now the new idea which should take up the place of this helplessness and dependence is not the idea of a rebellious overthrow of all authority, but that of freedom responsible to the voice of God in us.'[16] Seven years later in a 1904 article entitled 'Reform or Revival' Lala Lajpat Rai sought to argue that, while the reformers wanted reform on 'rational' lines, the revivalists wanted reform on 'national' lines. Attempting to turn Ranade's argument on its head, Lajpat Rai wrote:

> Cannot a revivalist, arguing in the same strain, ask the reformers into what they wish to reform us? . . . Whether they want to reform us into Sunday drinkers of brandy and promiscuous eaters of beef? In short, whether they want to revolutionise our society by an outlandish imitation of European customs and manners and an undiminished adoption of European vice?[17]

By this time Ranade was dead and he could not reply that there need be no necessary contradiction between the rational and the national.

Yet it must be emphasized that the first radical intellectual challenge to moderate nationalism had been remarkably discriminating, judicious and balanced in its attitude to European modernity. As Aurobindo put it in his sixth essay 'New Lamps for Old' published on 4 December 1893:

> We are to have what the West can give us, because what the West can give us is just the thing and the only thing that will rescue us from our present appalling condition of intellectual and moral decay, but we are not to take it haphazard and in a lump; rather we shall find it expedient to select the very best that is thought and known in Europe, and to import even that with the changes and reservations which our diverse conditions may be found to dictate. Otherwise instead of a simple ameliorating influence, we shall have chaos annexed to chaos, the vices and calamities of the West superimposed on the vices and calamities of the East.[18]

Aurobindo called the Congress un-national in 1893 not because of its imitation of the West or its inability to attract Muslims in sufficient numbers, but because it did not reach out to the working classes. 'The proletariat [sic] among us is sunk in ignorance and overwhelmed with distress. But with that distressed and ignorant proletariat [sic],—now that the middle class is proved deficient in sincerity, power and judgment,—with that proletariat [sic] resides . . . our sole assurance of hope, our sole chance in the future.' He even saw some hope in the communitarian conflicts over Hindi–Urdu and cow slaughter in the early 1890s. 'A few more taxes, a few more rash interferences of Government, a few more stages of starvation, and the turbulence that is now religious will become social. I am speaking to that class . . . called the thinking portion of the Indian community: Well, let these thinking gentlemen carry their thoughtful intellects a hundred years back. Let them recollect what causes led from the religious madness of St. Bartholomew to the social madness of the Reign of Terror.'[19]

Did the version of Indian nationalism authored by Tilak and Aurobindo get marooned in the world of religious madness that failed to make the grade to social madness? On the key questions of relations between the overarching Indian nation on the one hand and religious communities and linguistic regions on the other, anti-colonial thought and politics of the Swadeshi era left contradictory legacies. The anti-colonialism of both Hindus and Muslims was influenced in this period by their religious sensibilities. But since the colonial state's scheme of enumeration had transformed one into the 'majority' and the other into the 'minority' community, it became easier for Hindu religious symbolisms and communitarian interests to be subsumed within the emerging discourse on the Indian nation. If the Irish nation in 1905 was, as D.P. Moran insisted, 'de facto a Catholic nation',[20] the writings and speeches of most Swadeshi nationalists certainly left the impression that the Indian nation was permeated by a Hindu ethos. The granting of 'communal' electorates in 1909 compounded the problem in India even further. As Maulana Mohamed Ali complained to his Congress colleagues in 1912, the educated Hindu 'communal patriot' had turned Hinduism into an effective symbol of mass mobilization and Indian 'nationality', but 'refuse[d] to give quarter to the Muslim unless the latter quietly shuffles off his individuality and becomes completely Hinduized'.[21]

If religiously based notions of majority and minority were already beginning to pose problems for a unified Indian nationalism, as yet there appeared to be little contradiction between Bengali or Tamil linguistic communities or 'nations' on the one hand and a broader, diffuse Indian 'nation' on the other. Few, if any, of the nationalist ideologues were thinking at this stage of the acquisition of power in a centralized nation-state. India's two most famous poet-philosophers—Rabindranath Tagore and Muhammad Iqbal—whose Bengali and Urdu poetry celebrated patriotic sentiment, were both during the first two decades of the twentieth century impassioned critics of the Western model of the territorial nation-state.[22]

GANDHI'S REASON AND HINDU–MUSLIM UNITY

It required Gandhi's genius to fuse the love for a territorial homeland with the extraterritorial loyalty of religion in the mass nationalist movement of 1920. Without detracting from his distinctive qualities, the Mahatma's reason needs to be rescued by historians from the mystical haze created by latter-day cultural critics flying the banner of indigenous authenticity. It is sometimes too easily supposed, as Chatterjee does, that Gandhi's thought did not accept 'the conceptual frameworks or the modes of reasoning and inference adopted by the nationalists of his day' and 'emphatically reject[ed] their rationalism, scientism and historicism'. Although Chatterjee provides some brilliant insights into Gandhi's critique of the Western concept of civil society in *Hind Swaraj*, his extended discussion of Gandhi contains not one reference to Muslims or Islam.[23] Yet the classic 'moment of manoeuvre' in the history of Indian nationalism, if ever there was one, came with Gandhi's espousal of the cause of the Khilafat which not only paved the way for his rise to power but enabled him to achieve a quite spectacular success in popular mobilization cutting across lines of religious community.

Urged by C.F. Andrews to publicly clarify his position on the Khilafat, Gandhi wrote in *Young India* on 21 July 1920:

> I should clear the ground by stating that I reject any religious doctrine that does not appeal to reason and is in conflict with morality. I tolerate unreasonable religious sentiment when it is not immoral. I hold the Khilafat claim to be both just and reasonable and therefore it derives greater force because it has behind it the religious sentiment of the Musulman world.[24]

Gandhi could 'conceive the possibility of a blind and fanatical religious sentiment existing in opposition to pure justice'. Under those circumstances he would 'resist the former and fight for the latter'.[25] But since the Indian Muslims had an issue that was first of all reasonable and just, and in addition to that supported by scriptural authority, 'then for the Hindus not to support them to the utmost would be a cowardly breach of brotherhood and they would forfeit all claim to consideration from their Mahomedan countrymen'.[26]

The crux of Gandhi's case was Lloyd George's 'broken pledge',[27] the pledge to respect the immunity of the holy places in Arabia and Mesopotamia and of Jeddah and not to deprive Turkey of its capital or of its lands in Asia Minor and Thrace. In the event, Smyrna and Thrace had been taken away 'dishonestly', mandates had been established in Syria and Mesopotamia 'unscrupulously' and a British nominee had been set up in the Hejaz 'under the protection of British guns'. Gandhi believed 'the spirit of Islam' to be 'essentially republican in the truest sense of the term' which would not stand in the way of Arab and

Armenian independence from Turkey if the Arabs and Armenians so wished. On this point he endorsed Mohamed Ali's call for a mixed, independent commission of Indian Muslims, Hindus and Europeans 'to investigate the real wish of the Armenians and the Arabs and then to come to a *modus vivendi* whereby the claims of the nationality and those of Islam may be adjusted and satisfied'.[28] The 'most thorny part of the question', Gandhi recognized, was Palestine. Promises had been made by the British to the Zionists. But Palestine was 'not a stake in the war', and so he maintained that by 'no canon of ethics or war' could Palestine be given to the Jews 'as a result of the war'.[29] The Khilafat question was to Gandhi 'an imperial question of the first magnitude' which, he wanted Hindus to realize, overshadowed the Montagu–Chelmsford 'Reforms and everything else'.[30] If the Muslim claim were unjust apart from the scriptures, there may have been cause for hesitation, but an intrinsically just claim backed by scriptural authority was irresistible.

Gandhi could not have been more forthright in acknowledging the extraterritorial nature of the Muslim sentiment:

> Let Hindus not be frightened by Pan-Islamism. It is not—it need not be—anti-Indian or anti-Hindu. Mussalmans must wish well to every Mussalman state, and even assist any such state, if it is undeservedly in peril. And Hindus, if they are true friends of Mussalmans, cannot but share the latter's feelings. We must, therefore, co-operate with our Mussalman brethren in their attempt to save the Turkish empire in Europe from extinction.[31]

Closer to home, Gandhi supported the proposal of 'Brother Shaukat Ali' that there should be three national cries—'Allah-hu-Akbar',

'Bande Mataram' or 'Bharat Mata ki Jai' and 'Hindu–Mussalman ki Jai'. Gandhi called upon all Hindus and Muslims to join in the first cry 'in reverence and prayerfulness' since Hindus 'may not fight shy of Arabic words, when their meaning is not only totally inoffensive but even ennobling'. He preferred 'Bande Mataram' to 'Bharat Mata ki Jai', as 'it would be a graceful recognition of the intellectual and emotional superiority of Bengal'. And since India was nothing without 'the union of the Hindu and the Muslim heart', 'Hindu–Mussalman ki Jai' was a cry never to be forgotten.[32]

Gandhi appeared to have devised the perfect formula for harnessing the emotive power of nationalism in the linguistic regions and forging Hindu–Muslim unity based on a respectful attitude towards the fact of religiously informed cultural difference in an anti-colonial movement on an all-India scale. Gandhi was not using religious means for political ends; nation and religion were precious ends in themselves, religion perhaps even more so than nation. For both Maulana Mohamed Ali and him, he asserted, the Khilafat was 'the central fact'—with the Maulana because it was 'his religion' and 'with me because, in laying down my life for the Khilafat, I ensure the safety of the cow, that is my religion, from the Mussalman knife'. 'Both hold Swaraj equally dear,' he added, 'because only by Swaraj is the safety of our respective faiths possible.'[33] The entire movement of non-cooperation was in his view 'a struggle between religion and irreligion' because the motive behind every crime perpetrated by a Europe, nominally Christian but beset by Satan, was 'not religious or spiritual, but grossly material' while the Hindus and Muslims had 'religion and honour as their motive'.[34]

There were at least two points of weakness in the Mahatma's grand scheme of Hindu–Muslim unity in his non-violent holy war. First, as in his staunch defence of the caste system, Gandhi clung dogmatically to social closure along lines of religious community when it came to inter-dining and intermarriage. Likening eating to the other privately performed sanitary processes of life, he refused to dine even in the company of the Ali brothers. And he gave the meaning of Hindu–Muslim brotherhood an inimitable Gandhian twist in his opposition to intermarriage. 'If brothers and sisters can live on the friendliest footing without ever thinking of marrying each other,' he wrote, 'I can see no difficulty in my daughter regarding every Mahomedan [a] brother and *vice versa*.'[35] Gandhi changed his views later in life and attended only inter-caste and intercommunity marriages, but his attitude had caused hurt if not offence, despite his claim that the Ali brothers 'scrupulously respect[ed his] bigotry, if [his] self-denial may be so named'.[36] The second weakness stemmed from his determination not to countenance the possibility of any legitimate class dimension in Muslim subaltern resistance to Hindu economic power. When the Mappila rebellion broke out in the summer of 1921, he saw it as fanaticism pure and simple for which 'cultured Mussalmans' were sorry.[37] The response to the 'Moplah madness' was cited by him as proof of Hindu–Muslim solidarity. 'As members of a family,' he assured himself, 'we shall sometimes fight, but we shall always have leaders who will compose our differences and keep us under check.' Besides, 'in the face of possibilities of such madness in future', he asked, what was 'the alternative to Hindu–Muslim unity? A perpetuation of slavery?'[38] Even when in December 1921 Rufus Isaacs Reading had 'flung Ireland' in his face, Gandhi was unfazed. '[I]t is not the blood that the Irishmen have taken,' he contended, 'which has given them what appears to be their liberty. But it is the gallons of blood that they have willingly given themselves.' So Indians had to learn 'the art of spilling their own blood without spilling that of their opponents'.[39]

For Gandhi's closest comrade Mohamed Ali it was the British call to Muslims to spill the blood of their own which, as Ayesha Jalal has shown, constituted an intolerable infringement of religious freedom.[40] On the charge of making seditious speeches at the Khilafat Conference in Karachi on 9 July 1921, Mohamed Ali and six others were put on trial. Staged in a colonial law court, the defendants' case of necessity took the form of an interrogation of power in which the memory of past British promises and present British perfidy loomed large. Mohamed Ali took two long days to address the jury. He did not hope to sway them in order to be found not guilty. His greatest success was in trying the patience of the British judge, all of whose attempts to rule his lengthy treatises on religious law to be irrelevant proved utterly futile. The judge exercised his power to sentence Mohamed Ali to two years' rigorous imprisonment, but the defendant had successfully communicated his argument to his audience of Islamic universalists and Indian anti-colonialists and, in the process, made the colonial masters squirm. Mohamed Ali reminded the court of the promise in the Queen's Proclamation of 1858, a promise reaffirmed by two subsequent British sovereigns: 'The Sepoys' Mutiny after which the Queen's Proclamation was issued had originated with greased cartridges in which cow's and swine's grease was believed to be mixed.' But Islamic law, the learned Maulana insisted, permitted a Muslim to eat pork if faced with starvation but laid down an absolute injunction against killing another Muslim. 'And yet a Government which is so tender as to ask soldiers before enlistment whether they object to vaccination or re-vaccination,' he concluded, 'would compel a Muslim to do something worse than apostatize or eat pork. If there is any value in the boast of toleration and in the Proclamations of three sovereigns, then we have performed a religious and legal duty in calling upon Muslim soldiers in these circumstances to withdraw from the army, and are neither sinners nor criminals.'[41]

UNITARY NATIONALISM AND HINDU–MUSLIM DISUNITY

Mohamed Ali emerged from prison as president of the Indian National Congress. Nehru was present at the annual session of the Congress in Coconada (Kakinada) in December 1923 where the Maulana, 'as was his wont', 'delivered an enormously long presidential address'. But Nehru thought it was 'an interesting one', largely because it showed the historic Muslim deputation demanding separate electorates to have been 'a command performance . . . engineered by the Government itself'. Nehru considered Mohamed Ali to be 'most irrationally religious' but a 'bond of affection' tied together the Congress president and the young man he appointed secretary of the All India Congress Committee. One frequent subject of argument between the two was 'the Almighty'. The Maulana liked to refer to God in Congress resolutions by way of thanksgiving and when Nehru protested he was shouted at for his irreligion. But Mohamed Ali forgave his younger colleague, believing him to be 'fundamentally religious' in spite of his 'superficial behaviour'. 'Perhaps,' Nehru mused, 'it depends on what is meant by religion and religious.'[42]

Mohamed Ali's stirring call for 'a federation of faiths' notwithstanding, the Coconada Congress failed to ratify C.R. Das's Bengal Pact for an equitable power-sharing arrangement between Hindus and Muslims. As Das's political disciple Subhas Chandra Bose noted ruefully, it was 'rejected on the alleged ground that it showed partiality for the Moslems and violated the principles of Nationalism'. It was adopted by a large ty at the Bengal Provincial Conference at Sirajganj in May 1924 overcoming the opposition of 'some reactionary Hindus'.⁴³ But at the all-India level the Punjab line articulated by Lala Lajpat Rai had won out over the Bengal line advocated by Das. When Das died in 1925, Bose, who deplored the absence of 'cultural intimacy' between India's two great religious communities, wrote from Mandalay prison:

> I do not think that among the Hindu leaders of India, Islam had a greater friend than in the Deshbandhu . . . Hinduism was extremely dear to his heart; he could even lay down his life for his religion, but at the same time he was absolutely free from dogmatism of any kind. That explains how it was possible for him to love Islam.⁴⁴

The mid-1920s, most contemporary observers and historians agree, were a period of Hindu–Muslim strife. Nehru titles the chapter in his autobiography dealing with this phase of riots 'Communalism Rampant' in which he concludes: 'Surely religion and the spirit of religion have much to answer for. What killjoys they have been.'⁴⁵ This Nehruvian misdiagnosis of the cause of Hindu–Muslim disunity was to have large implications for the history of Indian anti-colonial nationalism in the last two decades of the British Raj. As the discourse of mainstream Indian nationalism turned more strident in its insistence on singularity, a sense of unease among those condemned to 'minority' status at the all-India level led them to call for safeguards and eventually to couch their own demands in the language of nationalism. What infuriated Mohammed Ali Jinnah in early 1938 was Nehru's statement reported in the press: 'I have examined this so-called communal question through the telescope, and if there is nothing, what can you see?'⁴⁶ Paradoxically, it was precisely this myopic vision of non-communal nationalism towards the Muslim question which enabled the politics of religiously based Hindu identity to occupy comfortable spaces within the regional outfits of the Indian National Congress. The 'moral conception of Gandhian politics', it has been suggested, was in this period incompatible with 'the realities of power within a bourgeois constitutional order'. But Gandhi had not only 'acceded to the political compulsions of bourgeois politics', as Chatterjee sees it,[47] but had succumbed from the mid-1920s to the political compulsions of Hindu majoritarianism in the United Provinces and Hindu minoritarianism in the Punjab. By the time Gandhi rediscovered the imperative of Hindu–Muslim accommodation in the mid-1940s he had already ceded too much political ground to the forces of unitary nationalism and Hindu majoritarianism which were bound in a tense but symbiotic relationship.

The colonial rules of representation in the formal arenas of politics based on religious enumeration were undoubtedly tailor-made for communitarian rivalry. But there was also a significant shift in nationalist ideology on the issue of religious difference which made certain that the Muslim masses were never enthused in the same way by the civil disobedience and Quit India movements of the 1930s and 1940s as they had been in the years of non-cooperation and Khilafat. At the height of the 1942 movement Leonard Woolf wrote in his preface to Mulk Raj Anand's *Letters on India*:

> The nationalism of the Irish—largely due to British imperialism—has started an insoluble Ulster problem in which religion and nationalism have intertwined to produce incalculable harm. You and the Congress Party are beginning to treat the Muslims and Mr Jinnah as Mr de Valera treated

Ulster. You may succeed in deluding Tom Brown on this point, but do you really wish to turn Mr Jinnah into an Indian Lord Craigavon? For that is what you will certainly do.[48]

The transformation of the would-be Charles Parnell of Indian politics to an unlikely James Craig—such was the measure of success of inclusionary nationalism of the Congress variety.

BLOOD BROTHERS IN A WAR OF LIBERATION

Yet during the Second World War there was a movement, led by another Cambridge man and avid admirer of Garibaldi, which sought to forge unity in anti-colonial politics based on respect for and accommodation of religious difference. In his speech as Congress president in 1938 Bose had warned against accepting colonial constitutional devices designed to divide and deflect the anti-colonial movement, but felt that 'the policy of divide and rule' was 'by no means an unmixed blessing for the ruling power'. He could see Britain getting 'caught in the meshes of her own political dualism' resulting from divisive policies, whether in India, Palestine, Egypt, Iraq or Ireland.[49] After war broke out in 1939 he likened the Congress proposal of 'a Constituent Assembly under the aegis of an Imperialist Government' to the Irish Convention of Lloyd George. In 1940 as Britain suffered reverses in the 'war between rival imperialisms' and the Muslim League passed its Lahore resolution, Bose noted that the problem of 'fighting British imperialism' was likely to give way to the more pressing problem of 'internal unity and consolidation', which, in order to succeed, would have to include unity between the Congress and the Muslim League on a joint Hindu–Muslim demand for a provisional national government.[50]

Between 1943 and 1945 Bose made a very deliberate effort to build unity among India's religious communities in the movement he led in South East Asia. Interestingly, the man who became the seniormost field commander in Bose's Indian National Army (INA) had early in his career been the victim of exactly the sort of bias that stoked 'communal' animosity. In 1931 Mohammed Zaman Kiani had faced a choice—either to go to the Olympic hockey trials being held in Calcutta or to appear in the examination for admission into the new Military Academy at Dehra Dun. He passed the examination but the medical officer ruled him out from being admitted to the first term of the academy. The medical officer was a Hindu and the next man to be selected was a Sikh. This enraged all the Muslims of the battalion who believed the 'whole thing had been manoeuvred with a communal bias'. Fortunately Zaman was later selected and joined the academy in its second term that started after six months. 'Little did I then realize,' writes Kiani in his memoirs, 'that in time to come, in a revolutionary movement . . . I would be one of the strongest advocates of inter-communal unity and harmony for the purpose of fighting against the foreign rule of our country.'[51] In 1943 Kiani was the top Muslim officer flanking Bose at a 'national demonstration' and fundraiser at the Chettiar temple in Singapore. Bose had refused to set foot in the temple unless his colleagues belonging to all castes and communities could come with him.[52]

'When we came to the temple,' Bose's closest political aide Abid Hasan, a Hyderabadi Muslim, has written, 'I found it filled to capacity with the uniforms of the I.N.A. officers and men and the black caps of the South Indian Muslims glaringly evident.'[53] When Hasan, a civilian, volunteered to go to the war front, he found himself in an army which had altered all the rules of Britain's Indian Army as these had applied to religious and linguistic communities, caste and gender. And yes, they dined together before they went into battle. 'No one had asked us,' he writes, 'to cease to be a Tamilian or Dogra, Punjabi Muslim or Bengali Brahmin, a Sikh or an Adivasi. We were all that and perhaps fiercely more so than before, but these matters became personal affairs.' When their Netaji came to see the retreating men from Imphal at Mandalay, the 'Sikhs oiled their beards, the Punjabi Muslims, Dogras and Rajputs twirled their moustaches and we the indiscriminates put on as good a face as we could manage'.[54]

Faced with military defeat, there could be two sources of solace—one was rational analogy with the Irish example, the other was religious faith drawn from India's own history. 'It is a strange phenomenon in history,' Bose said in a speech on 21 May 1945, 'that while the British could easily crush the Irish rebellion of 1916 at a time when they were engaged in a life and death struggle, they had to acknowledge defeat at the hands of the same Irish revolutionaries after they (the British) emerged victorious from the World War.'[55] But he had already observed in his reply of 2 November 1943 to a message of felicitations from De Valera upon the proclamation of a provisional government in Singapore that British imperialism had 'brought about the partition of Ireland in the past and if British Imperialism were to survive this War, a similar fate would be in store for India'.[56]

In an attempt to forestall such a fate the INA's march to Delhi had commenced with a ceremonial parade on 26 September 1943 at the tomb of the last Mughal emperor Bahadur Shah Zafar in Burma. At the ceremony Bose handed over a *nazar* of two and a half lakh rupees to the Burmese government 'as a very small token of . . . love and admiration for Burma'.[57] Accepting the gift the Burmese leader Ba Maw said: 'We Burmans also attach a great deal of importance to certain sacred spots, to certain victory-bearing earth as in Shwebo.'⁵⁸ Once the march to Delhi had been halted at Imphal, the defeated warriors and their leader gathered once more at Bahadur Shah's tomb on 11 July 1944. On that sombre occasion Bose closed his speech with a couplet composed by Bahadur Shah after the collapse of the 1857 revolt:

> *Ghazion me bu rahegi jab talak iman ki*
> *Takht London tak chalegi, tegh Hindustan ki.*

> So long as *ghazis* are imbued with the spirit of faith
> The sword of Hindustan will reach London's throne.⁵⁹

FROM THE UNION OF HEARTS TO THE AMPUTATION OF LIMBS

Whether due to a British error in rational decision-making or in answer to the prayers offered at Bahadur Shah's tomb, India's anti-imperialists were given a last opportunity to reach an honourable settlement of the problem of religious difference when three Punjabi officers of the INA—a Hindu, a Muslim and a Sikh—were put on public trial at the Red Fort for waging war against the King-Emperor. The venue was the same as on the occasion of the historic trial of Bahadur Shah, so was the sentence—deportation for life. But on this occasion the sentence could not be carried out and the three were released almost immediately by Commander-in-Chief Claude Auchinleck under intense public pressure.⁶⁰ Yet the union of hearts in the winter of 1945–46 could not prevent the amputation of limbs in the summer of 1947. The all-important question as to why at the end of the day the Punjab pushed the subcontinent towards partition rather than union has been addressed more fully by Ayesha Jalal.⁶¹ What needs emphasizing in conclusion today is that division was not a foregone conclusion until the moment of the actual wielding of the partitioner's axe. The principle of *Ausgleich* was alive in the Cabinet Mission's proposal of a three-tiered federal structure for India in 1946 as it had been in the ideas for a Council of Ireland in 1920 and perhaps even as late as the James Craig–Michael Collins pact of March 1922, and also in the plans for a binational state in Palestine in 1948.[62] What made partition—a decision born of short-term expediency—into such a long-term feature of the political landscapes of both India and Ireland was that in order to ensure rule by religiously defined majorities the provinces of Punjab and Bengal and the province of Ulster had to be divided by totting up numbers in districts and counties.

The spirit of religion had little to do with these temporal sins. Throughout the entire course of the history of Indian anticolonialism, religion as faith within the limits of morality, if not the limits of reason, had rarely impeded the cause of national unity and may in fact have assisted its realization at key moments of struggle. The variegated symbols of religion as culture had enthused nationalists of many hues and colours but had seldom embittered relations between religious communities until they were flaunted to boast the power of majoritarian triumphalism. The conceits of unitary nationalism may well have caused a deeper sense of alienation among those defined as minorities than the attachments to diverse religions. The territorial claims of a minority-turned-nation heaped further confusion on the furious contest over sovereignty in the dying days of the Raj. Having failed to share sovereignty in the manner of their precolonial forebears, late-colonial nationalist worshippers of the centralized state ended up dividing the land. Surely godless nationalism linked to the colonial categories of religious majorities and minorities has much to answer for. What a killer it has been!

I can do no better than close with a few lines of a poem that the 'great sentinel' Tagore, a zealous guardian of reason against unreason, printed in his little book on nationalism in 1917. It was an English rendering of a Bengali poem he had composed on the last day of the nineteenth century:

> The last sun of the century sets amidst the blood-
> red clouds of the West and the whirlwind of
> hatred.
> The naked passion of self-love of Nations, in its
> drunken delirium of greed, is dancing to the
> clash of steel and the howling verses of
> vengeance . . . .
> Keep watch, India . . . .
> Let your crown be of humility, your freedom the
> freedom of the soul.
> Build God's throne daily upon the ample bare-
> ness of your poverty
> And know that what is huge is not great and pride
> is not everlasting.[63]

INSTRUMENTS AND IDIOMS OF COLONIAL AND NATIONAL DEVELOPMENT
India's Historical Experience in Comparative Perspective

An elephant with its feet unchained was the chosen motif on the government's publicity handouts advertising its new 'liberalization' policies in 1991 as India seemed poised to make a U-turn from the course it had set since the end of colonial rule in the quest for 'national development'.[1] Unimpressed by the image of a plodding elephant, a popular and influential Western mouthpiece championing robust economic growth likened the Indian economy to a tiger caged and proclaimed that '[t]his tiger, set free, can be as healthy and vigorous as any in Asia'.[2] Whatever the preferred metaphor from the animal kingdom, many Indian commentators and outside observers were wondering aloud whether India had not in the process of freeing itself from British chains unwittingly tied up its development potential in a tangled web of self-imposed constraints.

India at any rate did not seem to offer a developing 'third world' model to the ex-communist 'second world' that was about to taste the mixed treats of first world–directed development efforts. As Vaclav Klaus, the freest of Eastern Europe's free-marketeer politicians, exclaimed, 'I have read everything about Indian planning from Mahalanobis onwards. It's wrong, all wrong.'[3] This must have sounded a trifle ironic to those who knew something of the history of development. In the halcyon days of development planning in the 1950s and early 1960s, Nehruvian India had 'appeared to theorists of reformed capitalism as an answer to the challenge posed by the model of growth presented by Mao's China'.[4] Now India was being asked to unlearn its long-cherished dogmas of development and be tutored in the lessons of stabilization and structural adjustment by those international paragons of virtuous economic discipline based in Washington.

India's failings in its developmental efforts are many and the disenchantments and disillusionments among its own populace deep and widespread. All but the most churlish would acknowledge that there have been some successes to report as well. What is truly remarkable about the current convergence of criticisms of India's post-Independence development efforts is that the volleys have come from diverse and occasionally conflicting sources and premises. The critics range from 'neoclassical' and liberal advocates of the 'free market' to 'postmodern' votaries of the 'fragment' and 'anti-development'. In order to make a measured assessment of India's development experience in the midst of this cacophony, there is no alternative but to return to the drawing board of history. It is only by recovering the intellectual and political origins and aims of development and reappraising the strategies and trajectories pursued towards the set goals that it may be possible to ferret out not only the successes from failures but also the legitimate from flawed criticisms. 'Any evaluative judgment,' as Amartya Sen stresses, 'has to be . . . comparative.'[5] The recourse to history immediately opens the way to one comparative dimension—that over time. The other comparative dimension—that with other countries—often has been at least partially blocked by a weighty Orientalist intellectual tradition of essentializing India and its history as plain peculiar. The development paradigm, whatever its other limitations may be, is not on the whole wedded to ahistorical attributes of cultural uniqueness and consequently not hostile to careful and meaningful cross-country and cross-regional comparisons.

Before delving into history in the comparative vein, it may be useful to clarify the senses in which the terms 'instruments' and 'idioms' are used in this essay. Each term is used in at least two senses. Scholars and practitioners in the field of development economics generally take instruments to refer to 'means-enhancing'[6] variables, such as savings rates and investment, foreign exchange reserves, food stocks and so on. This is the first sense in which the term 'instruments' is used in the appropriate contexts of economic analysis. Any attempts to probe the relationship between development knowledge and the social sciences must, however, also deploy a broader definition of instruments that refers to state institutions and policies. This is of the essence since development efforts have been generally conducted over the past half-century under the aegis of centralized, late colonial and postcolonial states. Any rethinking about development must include ideas about restructuring the modern nation-state. The term 'idioms' in the first place encapsulates the goals, such as removal of poverty and improvement in the quality of life, that assigned the idea of development its normative privilege. Yet in order to avoid the methodological pitfalls usually associated with a sharp separation between means and ends, 'idioms' will also refer to the singular concepts of nationhood and particular state forms that came to be favoured by the dominant ideology of development as better suited to its purpose. Idioms in this connotation could well serve as political instruments.

HISTORICAL ORIGINS OF THE CONCEPTS OF COLONIAL AND NATIONAL DEVELOPMENT

Two years before the passage of the landmark British Colonial Development and Welfare Act of 1940, the Indian National Congress had set up a National Planning Committee to draw up blueprints for the economic and social reconstruction of India once independence was won. By contrast with Africa, the institutional expression of the concept of 'national development' predated that of 'colonial development' in India. An economic critique of colonial rule was articulated, of course, in both continents long before colonialism under siege turned to development as an ideology of self-justification. At the turn of the century in India leaders of the Indian National Congress like Dadabhai Naoroji and Romesh C. Dutt wrote powerful critiques of the high land revenue demand and the drain of wealth funnelled through India's export surplus, which they held squarely responsible for poverty and famines in India.[7] In 1908 Mohandas Gandhi in *Hind Swaraj* offered his own particular reading of the early tomes of economic nationalism: 'When I read Mr Dutt's economic history of India, I wept; and as I think of it again my heart sickens. It is machinery that has impoverished India.'[8] While Gandhi condemned modern industrialism as evil, other nationalist critics denounced colonial fiscal and financial policy for stunting India's potential for industrialization, which was a necessary condition if not the panacea for eradicating poverty. Whatever the differences in nationalist positions, Indian nationalism 'began as a critique of policy' and 'became a critique of British power by its being denied a voice in government'.⁹

The precise relationship between colonial and national development marked both by contradictions and imbrications can be clarified and elucidated only by bringing into play the analytical distinctions between instruments and idioms. David Ludden has recently assigned joint authorship and copyright to 'colonial capitalism' and 'bourgeois nationalism' in the creation of 'an institutional complex—a development regime . . . as a vital force in the cultural and material life of India'.¹⁰ This regime with its built-in trend towards more centralized and ramified state power has fairly deep historical roots going back at least to the mid-nineteenth century. 'By 1900,' Ludden writes, 'institutional foundations of the state information apparatus and the surrounding constellation of public debate and expertise *that sustain India's development regime today* were in place.'¹¹ Such an observation has a measure of accuracy with reference to the inheritance of instruments of development in the form of institutions of state. Yet, as Ludden acknowledges but does not sufficiently emphasize, the trend in India's development regime towards instrumental centralization and expansion of state power was not inevitable or inexorable and had to overcome significant opposition and resistance.

The idiom of national development, on the other hand, might be construed to be the only distinguishing feature of the façade of a postcolonial state that was erected on the authoritarian, institutional foundations of the colonial state.¹² The 'transfer of power' in India in 1947 involved the transfer of the colonial military, police, bureaucracy and judiciary from the British to the hands of the leadership of the Indian National Congress. As Chatterjee aptly notes, 'Even today one is forced to witness such unlovely ironies as regiments of the Indian Army displaying the trophies of colonial conquest and counter-insurgency in their barrack-rooms or the Presidential Guards celebrating their birth two hundred years ago under the governor-generalship of Lord Cornwallis!' In such a scenario, the postcolonial state found its 'distinctive content' only in the idiom of national development. Planning for development enabled the postcolonial state to 'claim its legitimacy' as an embodiment of 'the will of the nation'. It was in its 'legitimizing role' that the idiom of planning for national development 'was to become an instrument of politics'.[13]

As a general proposition, it is doubtless true that 'goals themselves are very often fixed because certain instruments have to be used' and 'instruments in politics can become goals in themselves'.[14] But in the specific historical context of India, the mischief of invoking legitimizing idioms to privilege preferred instruments was committed, I will argue, at the conjunctural moment of the postcolonial transition. Recent attempts at unravelling Indian nationalist thought, whether construed as 'a derivative discourse'[15] or as 'a cultural product of nineteenth-century capitalism, on the same plane with bourgeois nationalisms in the West', have tended towards a teleology that confuses the outcome of 1947 with a long-term, essentially unilinear, trend inherent in the ideology of the political economy of nationhood.[16] Caveats about 'noninevitability' and 'possibilities' notwithstanding, these teleological views leave little theoretical space for the recovery of historically contested visions of nationhood, alternative ideological frameworks for the postcolonial state and real debates about the instruments and idioms of national development.

These debates deserve a closer analysis, especially since the lines of division did not always reflect the dichotomies of modernity versus tradition, reason versus unreason, science versus superstition, or most simplistically, Nehru versus Gandhi that many latter-day commentators have read into them. Analyses based on these dichotomous schemes often enable particular critiques of India's development experience to parade as general critiques of science, reason and development. A consideration of the debates over national planning during the final decade of the British Raj in India may help throw light on the complex relationship of universal values to the particular history of Indian development.

At the third general meeting of the Indian Science News Association on 21 August 1938, Meghnad Saha, a renowned scientist, asked Bose, the president of the Indian National Congress, a loaded question:

> May I enquire whether the India of the future is going to revive the philosophy of village life, of the bullock-cart—thereby perpetuating servitude, or is she going to be a modern industrialized nation which, having developed all her natural resources, will solve the problems of poverty, ignorance and defence and will take an honoured place in the comity of nations and begin a new cycle of civilization?

The Congress president said in reply:

> I must say that all Congressmen do not hold the same view on this question. Nevertheless, I may say without any exaggeration that the rising generation are in favour of industrialization and for several reasons.

The reasons cited were fourfold. Industrialization was necessary for (1) 'solving the problem of unemployment', (2) 'national reconstruction' based on 'Socialism', (3) ability 'to compete with foreign industries', and (4) 'improving the standard of living of the people at large'. What was needed in the cause of national development was 'far-reaching cooperation between science and politics'.[17]

At his presidential address at Haripura in February 1938, Bose had outlined 'the long-period programme for a Free India'. The 'first problem to tackle', according to him, was the 'increasing population'. As regards 'reconstruction' the 'principal problem' would be 'how to eradicate poverty from our country'. That would 'require a radical reform of our land system, including the abolition of landlordism'. 'Agricultural indebtedness' would 'have to be liquidated and provision made for cheap credit for the rural population'. But to 'solve the economic problem' agricultural improvement would 'not be enough' and an ambitious plan of state-directed industrial development would be necessary. 'However much we may dislike modern industrialism and condemn the evils which follow in its train,' Bose declared, 'we cannot go back to the pre-industrial era, even if we desire to do so.' The state in independent India would 'on the advice of a planning commission' have 'to adopt a comprehensive scheme for gradually socializing our entire agricultural and industrial system in the spheres of both production and appropriation'.[18]

In October 1938 Bose announced the formation of the National Planning Committee of which he made Jawaharlal Nehru the chair.[19] Many leading Indian minds, including Rabindranath Tagore, who was keenly aware of the evils of the modern nation-state, responded with alacrity to the idea of rational and scientific planning for Indian industry and seemed enthused by a 'modernist' vision of India's economic and social reconstruction.[20] This vision was at variance with Gandhi's evocation of self-governing and self-sufficient village communities.

The sole Gandhian purist on the National Planning Committee, J.C. Kumarappa, almost succeeded in putting the spanner in the works by questioning the committee's authority to plan for industrialization since the national priority ought to be the containment if not the abolition of modern industrialism. Nehru promised safeguards for 'cottage industries' but could scarcely conceal his exasperation with such 'unscientific' obduracy. On the whole, however, Nehru enjoyed his work on the National Planning Committee, finding it 'soothing and gratifying' and 'a pleasant contrast to the squabbles and conflicts of politics'.[21]

Planning, Chatterjee has argued, by being constituted as a domain outside politics, served as an instrument to politically resolve the debate on the need for industrialization in India. There can be little disagreement about the political instrumentality of the planning exercise before and, more pronouncedly, after Independence. But that was not all that there was to it. What Chatterjee's critical formulation on development planning misses is that the 'modernist' rational idiom of national development was no more and no less visionary as well as no more and no less politically instrumental than the Gandhian utopia. It is worth noting that some of the biggest Indian industrialists of the inter-war era were financial backers of the Gandhian Congress and harboured a sense of deep unease about the agenda of socialist visionaries who were among Gandhi's critics. The Gandhian notion of self-regulating, harmonious village communities and the associated concept of elite trusteeship of common property were designed to politically resolve potentially explosive class and caste conflicts within Indian agrarian society. It requires an analytical sleight of hand to counterpose anti-modernist vision to modernist politics.

Another false dichotomy has crept into the scholarly literature on nationalism and development around the issue of authenticity. Gandhian nationalism, it has been argued by Ashis Nandy and Chatterjee in slightly different ways, represented a truly 'indigenous', and thereby authentic, form of resistance to the modern West.[22] This ahistorical view underplays the extent to which the Gandhian vision of village republics, for example, borrowed from mid-nineteenth-century Western misperceptions of India's past portrayed in the writings of Henry Maine and others.[23] The unfolding of the colonial encounter as a messy historical process means that the search for wholly 'untainted' anti-colonial nationalist thought can only end in futility and carry the unfortunate implication of erasing significant strands of resistance that fail to meet the ahistorical litmus test of purity.

This is not to deny that Gandhian thought provided a powerful critique not only of modern industrial civilization but of 'fundamental aspects of civil society'.[24] But it would be an error to invest all non-subscribers to Gandhi's anti-modernist idiom with having megalomaniacal dreams of the bourgeois acquisition of power at the apex of a centralized nation-state. To focus on Gandhi's localism and Nehru's centralism is to miss out on the multifarious ways in which nationalist thought construed the relationship between nation and state as well as the role of the state in development. Beyond evoking the utopia of Ramrajya, where the patriarchal ruler was the embodiment of the collective will of his subjects in a way that rendered representative institutions unnecessary, Gandhi did not elaborate on a theory of the state. His was a relentless nihilism, a celebration of extreme—

albeit enlightened—anarchy and a pursuit of decentralization to the point of atomization. It was Gandhi's unwillingness 'to draw a large-scale picture in detail' that explains his current appeal to a particular brand of postmodernism that exults over the 'fragment'. Many socialists within India's anti-colonial movement, by contrast, favoured a strong centralized state which could in theory serve as a better instrument to carry out a radical economic and social programme. But even within this camp there were variations. Some seemed more willing than others to build the socialist state on the basis of regional autonomy and an equitable sharing of power among different religious communities. In any case, the bureaucratic and authoritarian colonial state was not the kind of centralized state socialist ideologues had in mind. Science and reason, according to this idiom, would be the servants, not the masters, of the efforts at development. The aim was to reverse the process of rural poverty and urban decay that was seen to have set in under colonial rule. There were other models, such as C.R. Das's draft Swarajist 'Constitution' of 1923, which offered something of a blueprint of decentred democracy and planning for economic generation from the local communities upwards. According to this remarkable model, the 'ordinary work' of a 'Central government' in free India 'should be mainly advisory'. It called for 'a maximum of local autonomy, carried on mainly with advice and coordination from, and only a minimum of control by, higher centres'.[25]

The ideology of official nationalism adopted at the moment of the acquisition of centralized state power cannot be permitted to obfuscate the important dimension of ideological disunity and discontinuity in anti-colonial nationalism and development planning. What got marginalized in 1947 were conceptions of a state of union forged from below that reflected and presided over the balance and harmony of free regional peoples and religious communities.[26] The victory of singular nationalism conflated with a centralized postcolonial state also marked the primacy of instruments over the idioms of national development. It was a paradigm shift in the idea of development brought about by the capture of centralized state power by the machine politicians among the nationalist elite.

NATIONAL DEVELOPMENT AND THE POSTCOLONIAL STATE

The project of planning for national development in the postcolonial phase privileged instruments over idioms, means over goals, in at least two distinct ways. First, the exercise of planning concentrated on questions of means enhancement, such as ways to increase the rate of savings. Consequently, means came to be confused with goals; and the accumulation of capital rather than betterment of the quality of life often turned out to be the end-all of development efforts. Second and more important, an insufficiently decolonized, centralized state structure seized upon national development as a primary source of its own self-justification. Instead of the state being used as an instrument of development, development became an instrument of the state's legitimacy. Even though India opted for a political system of representative parliamentary democracy, elections based on universal adult franchise were incapable of bridging the gap between a democratic political process and a postcolonial state imbued with a strong element of bureaucratic authoritarianism.

Even in the specific domain of planning, postcolonial India lost sight of the vision of eradicating poverty, morbidity and illiteracy that had inspired the debates on national development in the colonial era. This was not a case of Nehruvian modernism triumphing over Gandhian traditionalism. Some of the fiercest critics of the Nehruvian state were those modernist socialists who deplored the nationalist leadership's eagerness to inherit the colonial mantle. For example, the scientist Meghnad Saha, who had been a stalwart of the National Planning Committee during 1938–40, had warned on the eve of Independence that planning had become a 'catchword'. The Bombay Plan of 1944 had been hatched by 'a syndicate of capitalists', the Department of Planning and Development established later that year was the handiwork of 'foreign bureaucrats' and in the case of the Bengal Government Plan of 1945 'the Civil Service provided the philosophy and the direction'.[27] In other words, the official version of development had arisen after and in reaction to the popular, national efforts. Capitalists and colonialists were stealing the idea mooted initially by socialists within the nationalist movement. In the early 1950s, Saha, as a scientist-cum-socialist politician, kept up a steady tirade against the sellouts by Nehru's government in the Indian Parliament. He argued in 1953 that if India's First Five Year Plan were 'not altered root and branch, it will perpetuate our "Colonial Status" in the economic field, and greatly jeopardize our hard-won "Political Freedom"'.[28]

The early exercise in development planning in postcolonial India drew much more from the colonial Department of Planning and Development set up in 1944 than the work of the National Planning Committee during 1938–40. The First Five Year Plan of 1950–55 was little more than a collection of public projects that had been under consideration during the last years of the British Raj.[29] The Second and Third Five Year Plans drawn up under the direction of the famous statistician P.C. Mahalanobis represented something of a break with the past in its emphasis on capital goods–led import-substituting industrialization. A departure from both the 'textiles first' and 'export-led' strategies adopted by other industrializing countries, these plans nevertheless relied heavily on influential means-enhancing models of development. The Second Five Year Plan of 1955, 'the single most significant document on Indian planning', was 'a variant of the Lewis model'.[30] Arthur Lewis's celebrated comment that development economics was about transforming a country which saved 5 per cent of its income to one which saved 20 per cent remains a classic statement on development as means enhancement. The Indian variation from the pristine Lewis model related to the role given to a development bureaucracy and not just capitalist industrialists in powering growth in the 'modern' sector of the economy.

The Third Five Year Plan built in many important ways on the second, but also placed a special emphasis on agriculture and 'distributional considerations'. The opening chapter of the plan document, partly written by Nehru himself, talked about reducing income disparities by 'raising the level of the minimum [income]'. But, as even a staunch defender of Indian planning had to concede, 'there was no clearly laid out strategy which could be expected to raise the "minimum level"—at least, not one that could match the industrialization targets articulated with great eloquence in the first two plans'.[31] The shift of emphasis from growth to distribution and the new concern with income did not, in any case, entail a sensitivity to entitlements and capabilities of people which, Amartya Sen has forcefully argued, have a much more direct bearing on the means-using goals of development.[32]

The acknowledged successes of India's first three plans—a dramatic improvement in the savings rate, the establishment of a heavy industrial base, the upgrading of the skill base and the breakout from the agricultural stagnation of the first half of the twentieth century—were major achievements of means enhancement towards which the development effort had been geared. The 'crisis of Indian planning' in the mid-1960s is generally put down by its apologists to 'external shocks' in the form of war-induced increase in defence expenditure and monsoon failures, and by its critics to either 'urban bias' or 'neglect of foreign trade'. While quirks in the weather pattern may well have compounded India's food situation and the unwarranted export pessimism of the early 1960s may well have been something of a missed opportunity in India's development trajectory, the real problem was that the planners had forgotten the idioms of national development.

In the late 1960s and early 1970s there was a partial recovery of these idioms in the 'populist' political and economic programme of Indira Gandhi with its emphasis on poverty eradication and rural employment. This particular paradigm shift was triggered by a realization of the limits of the Nehruvian form of oligarchical democracy whose project of 'national development' had not cared to address the means-using needs of the poor. In the 1967 elections, the party bosses had failed to deliver their vote banks as before. Indira Gandhi's populist initiative to 'abolish poverty' was designed to widen and deepen the party's social base of support. But this attempt to make the Centre the fount of redistributive justice for those at the bottom of the agrarian hierarchy was not matched by political empowerment at the base and became vulnerable to challenges mounted by middling agrarian groups and rich farmer lobbies in several states. Agrarian development was turned into a fiercely contested site where the Centre's populist championing of the rural poor was countered by an agrarian populism anxious to gloss over class differentiation in the countryside.[33]

Yet even Indira Gandhi's brand of populism remained high on rhetoric and low on performance and did not really grasp the issue of capabilities and entitlements of the poor. The Fifth and Sixth Five Year Plans of 1974 and 1980 respectively—marking a 'shift in emphasis away from the earlier concept of a "traverse", with its so-called heavy-industry bias, to a strategy centring around "food" and "fuels"'—did not represent a departure from the obsession with means enhancement.[34] Improvements achieved in instrumental variables like savings, foreign exchange reserves, and food stocks in the mid-1970s were consequently not reflected in indicators of the quality of life. As Kaushik Basu points out, 'These . . . are all instruments. We must realize that food stocks with the Government is not something which the people eat, the savings rate is not something you wear and one cannot sleep under the roof of foreign exchange.'[35] By the early 1980s the Centre's populist fervour had already waned. Clarion calls for 'a sharper focus on employment and poverty alleviation' in the *Approach to the Seventh Five Year Plan* of 1985 were immediately and resoundingly contradicted by the minuscule allocations for employment generation and poverty eradication and a real decline in plan outlay in the very first budget of the plan period.[36]

In assessing the lessons and non-lessons of the Indian development experience, Amartya Sen makes a clear distinction between what is instrumental and what is intrinsic: 'The importance of savings and investment is instrumental rather than intrinsic, and any enhancement of instrumental variables may be washed out, in the tally of final accounting, by a deterioration of the impact of that instrumental variable on things that are intrinsically valuable.'[37] What post-1947 India lacked, by contrast for example with post-1949 China, was direct and massive public action to improve living conditions. It was this apathy to questions concerning means use which explained the fifteen-year difference in average life expectancy in the two countries by the late 1980s. India's democratic political process, characterized by a relatively free press and political opposition, enabled it to avoid catastrophes like the Chinese famine of 1958–61. This 'elimination of famine' was 'achieved despite India's food availability per head being no higher than that in sub-Saharan Africa'.[38] Yet the Indian development effort has launched no major onslaught on chronic malnutrition and morbidity. If India had China's lower mortality rates, 'there would have been 3.8 million fewer deaths in India around the mid-1980s'. Looked at another way, 'every eight years or so more people in addition die in India—in comparison with Chinese mortality rates—than the total number that died in the gigantic Chinese famine'.[39]

Instead of focusing on these means-using failures, the bulk of self-serving, right-wing criticism of the history of Indian development, seeking to justify the recent 'liberalization' policies, has concentrated even more than before on issues of means enhancement.[40] The development debate in India has witnessed clear lines of disagreement within the rounded circle of such issues as import substitution versus export promotion, industrialization versus agricultural dynamism, and, of course, state direction versus market incentives. Some have recently pointed out, for example, that the fast-growing and high-performing economies of South East and North East Asia have relied less on the magic wand of the market and more on the whip of strategic state intervention. While such debates are not altogether irrelevant, Amartya Sen has made a compelling case that 'the main shortcoming of Indian planning' has been 'to wit, not aiming at the ultimate objectives of planning'.[41]

The question remains, however, whether the Indian state as currently constituted has the will or the capacity to aim clearly and unambiguously at the original goals of national development. This leads us to consider the broader definition of instruments referring to state institutions and policy. Pranab Bardhan has argued that the heterogeneity of dominant proprietary classes in India—industrial capitalists, rich farmers and professionals—has led to 'the proliferation of subsidies and grants to placate all of them, with the consequent reduction in available surplus for public capital formation'. The scramble among the heterogeneous proprietary classes for a share of the spoils turned India's public economy into 'an elaborate network of patronage and subsidies'. The 'relative autonomy' of the Indian state from any single dominant class is qualitatively different from the 'embedded autonomy' of some of the East Asian states which makes for more efficacious public responses to market conditions. One of the 'symptoms' of India's spoils system and subsidy 'raj', according to Bardhan, has been the rapid decline of 'a semi-insulated technocratic institution' like the Planning Commission. A 'lack of political insulation from conflicting interests' increasingly kept the Indian state confined to regulatory functions rather than 'more active developmental functions'.[42]

Bardhan's analysis is insightful in so far as it explains certain macroeconomic inefficiencies arising out of the demand overload in India's political processes. Yet I would argue that the very 'political insulation' of the planning apparatus, nestling within a state structure inherited almost intact from the colonial era, may explain the imperviousness of the centralist Indian state to the means-using development needs of subordinated social groups. In other words, an insufficiently decolonized and inadequately democratized state structure can hardly be expected to perform means-using miracles for India's poor. But should the critique of the postcolonial state as an instrument be so extended as to produce an all-encompassing rejection of the idioms of development?

IS DEVELOPMENT HISTORY?

The 'neo-liberal', 'market-oriented' critics of India's development experience have seized upon the more obvious bureaucratic logjams in the path of economic development to justify the search for a 'liberalized' economic regime. It is not difficult to argue that in the quest for the label 'made in India' the Indian strategy of import-substituting industrialization paid a high price in spiralling costs and plummeting quality. The overall record in the agrarian sector, which witnessed scuttled land reforms and a pale green revolution, was not much more impressive. But the crux of the problem, as we have seen, may well have been the failure of Indian development planners to focus on means use and concentrate unambiguously and determinedly on the intrinsic values of development.

The free marketeers' attack on the state has found an unlikely convergence with the anti-modern traditionalist and postmodern fragmentalist onslaughts on centralized state monoliths. The criticisms have gone far beyond doubting the efficacy of modern nation-states in playing their developmental role to call into question two reasons of state—science and development.[43] In so far as development planning was an exercise in instrumental rationality, the failures of development have been seen to have constituted sufficient, legitimate grounds for denunciations of the cunning of reason. I would accept that the centralizing modern state has often resorted to employing reductionist mega-science to buttress itself, to homogenizing development to legitimize itself and to anaesthetizing rationality to transcend the 'irrational' arena of politics. It is also undoubtedly true, as David Ludden has stated, that 'the national state has like its colonial predecessor turned its guns against those who oppose the trajectory of its development regime'.[44] Nandy goes a step further to claim that 'a part of the growing resistance to the ideas of development and modern science in India derives from the contradiction that has arisen between them and the democratic process'.[45] For all this, it is not entirely clear why science, reason and development should be culpable for the crimes of the modern state. Such a sweeping rejection of 'modernity' flows from a failure to take a nuanced and differentiated approach towards, and instead attach a singular label to, complex historical phenomena.

'Development regimes,' writes Ludden, 'hire historians to make themselves look good.'[46] These are the historians who not only concentrate on, but celebrate, the genealogy of the nation-state. But history, if not historians, can also turn out to be the most formidable enemy of development regimes. As Ludden acknowledges:

> Precolonial political culture produced multiple, overlapping levels and arenas of authority more than centralized states. Even the Mughal state was more patrimonial than bureaucratic, and its centralization was more ideological than operative. From medieval to late precolonial times, centralization was episodic. Precolonial traditions hardly sustain India's 'stateness' and may better explain its opposition.[47]

A similar argument could be made about anti-colonial political culture if we are careful to avoid the conflation of nation and state until its actual historical occurrence at the moment of the postcolonial transition and resist the temptation to give nationalist thought its unity by reading back from the telos of 1947.

The challenge in this connection is to recover from anti-colonial thought alternative models of state structures and ideologies that might be better suited to the achievement of democratic development. If the particular postcolonial historical form of India's 'stateness' is wholly inappropriate to aiming for means-using developmental imperatives, 'statelessness' might be equally antithetical to democratic aspirations. This is why the project of decentring the discourse of development has to do more than resurrect 'indigenous' forms of anti-modernism with a deeply ingrained aversion to the state. Bardhan has recently underlined the trace of patronizing elitism running through much of what he has termed the 'anarcho-communitarian critique' of the state and development.[48] Undiscriminating denunciations of an ill-defined 'modernity' and uncritical eulogies of 'tradition', 'community' and, most recently, 'the fragment', achieve little more than an inversion of the old and worn tradition–modernity dichotomy. The problem of reconfiguring the relationship between nationalism, democracy and development needs to be relocated in the very different context of the dialectic between domination and resistance, privilege and deprivation at the global, national and local levels.[49]

The call for a thorough decolonization of both the idea of development and institutions of state may sound like a tall order in the current conditions of drift in civil society and crisis of the centralized state. Yet the atmosphere of uncertainty and flux affords opportunities for a fresh round of rethinking and restructuring fifty years after the decisions of expediency which characterized formal, political decolonization. A major reorientation of the terms of public debate already seems under way to recapture the values that had informed the early initiatives of national development. There is a growing recognition that the development debate in India should be taken 'well beyond liberalization' and the spotlight redirected towards 'expanding social opportunities'.[50] The economic reforms pursued by the Congress government from June 1991 to May 1996 addressed only the first of a two-part problem facing Indian economic development. This was largely because a significant paradigm shift in 1991 was triggered by a particular balance-of-payments crisis and not by an overall reassessment of the country's economic trajectory. So, the reformers concentrated on redressing the negative effects of over-intervention by the state in certain sectors and removing the more stifling bureaucratic controls on industry. They moved tardily, if at all, to rectify state negligence of critical social sectors, notably, health and education. The political costs of pursuing a lopsided reform process appear to be enabling the long-forgotten intrinsic values of development to re-enter the discourse, but the failed institutions of state have yet to be imaginatively refashioned. On the one hand, the privileged but besieged defenders of the centralized monolith have resorted to the dangerous course of a bigoted religious majoritarianism. On the other, the populism of the 1996 United Front government in New Delhi, of which several regional parties are members, displayed deep taints of localism and agrarianism while proclaiming solidarity with the aspirations of the poor and disadvantaged majority. Actual allocations did not match the resurgence of pro-poor rhetoric. The successful realization of the idioms of equitable development requires the appropriate instruments, both economic and political. Simple-minded decentralization will provide little help in that direction and mindless anti-statism may well prove counterproductive. Anti-colonial thought, if not the actual denouement of nationalist politics, was never so impoverished as to be contained within the stark dichotomies of centralism and localism, Nehru and Gandhi. Indeed, most thoughtful anti-colonial activists would have been surprised if they were told that a substantial measure of autonomy for regions and communities could not be combined with a radical, redistributive impulse from a negotiated centre. Any number of 'Constitutions' of the Indian Union—from the hare-brained to the highly sophisticated—had vied in the realm of ideas with the one that was adapted in 1950 from the colonial Government of India Act of 1935. If the dismantling of the structures and ideologies of the postcolonial state is long overdue, it needs to be reconstituted on the basis of careful consideration of proposals, old and new, for a state of union presiding over a multilayered, democratic political system and functioning on terms forged by its various constituent units.

If the postmodern quest for decentred democracy is not to fall into the embrace of a conservative, economic elitism and unbridled capitalism in its attempt to escape the clutches of the anti-democratic modern state, it must be able to come forward with alternative democratic models of state. The history of development had been marred in its early stages by the tainted history of the politics of decolonization, characterized by the inheritance of state structures rather than the rebuilding of new ones from the very foundations. Any attempt to historicize development underscores the imperative to fashion the instruments to realize the idioms which remain as salient as ever to democratic aspirations in the postcolonial world.

THE SPIRIT AND FORM OF AN ETHICAL POLITY
A Meditation on Aurobindo's Thought[1]

'Long after this controversy is hushed in silence,' Chittaranjan Das had said of Aurobindo Ghose during the Alipore bomb trial in 1909, 'long after this turmoil, this agitation ceases, long after he is dead and gone, he will be looked upon as the poet of patriotism, as the prophet of nationalism and the lover of humanity. Long after he is dead and gone, his words will be echoed and re-echoed, not only in India, but across distant seas and lands. Therefore, I say that the man in his position is not only standing before the bar of this court but before the bar of the High Court of History.'[2] The future Deshbandhu's forensic skills contributed in no uncertain measure to Aurobindo's acquittal by Judge C.P. Beachcroft who, by a strange coincidence, had read Classics with the accused at King's College, Cambridge. Aurobindo had beaten Beachcroft to second place in an examination in Greek, but the broad-minded judge did not hold that against the prisoner. Das persuaded the court that a letter allegedly written to Aurobindo by his younger brother Barindra Kumar Ghose— presented by the prosecution as clinching evidence of a terrorist conspiracy—was nothing but a forgery, 'as clumsy as those Piggott had got up to incriminate Parnell after the murder of Lord Cavendish in Phoenix Park'.³ Sifting through Aurobindo's letters and essays, his counsel showed him to be motivated by the 'lofty ideal of freedom' in the pursuit of which he had preached the doctrine of 'not bombs, but suffering'.⁴

Acquitted by a British judge presiding over the trial at the sessions court, one would have thought that Aurobindo would hardly be in need of an argument to exonerate him before the High Court of History. He is certainly revered in popular memory as one of the iconic leaders of the great Swadeshi movement that swept Bengal a hundred years ago, between 1905 and 1908. Yet half a century of indoctrination in the dulling ideology of statist secularism has led to profound misunderstandings of Aurobindo's political thought and an utter inability to comprehend its ethical moorings. Latter-day Bengali scholars of great distinction, even more so than his British prosecutor Eardley Norton, have provided sterile, literalist interpretations of Aurobindo's nationalism. The misappropriation of Aurobindo by the Hindu right has been facilitated by the secularists' abandonment of the domain of religion to the religious bigots. To a secularist historian like Sumit Sarkar the invocation to *sanatan dharma* by Aurobindo is deeply troubling and makes him implicitly, if not explicitly, the harbinger of communalism in the pejorative sense the term came to acquire some two decades after Aurobindo had retired from active political life.⁵ To an anti-secularist scholar like Ashis Nandy the 'nationalist passions' of Aurobindo located in 'a theory of transcendence' are mistakenly deemed to be too narrowly conceived compared to the broader humanism of the more universalist, civilizational discourses ascribed to Tagore and Gandhi.⁶ The specific failures in fathoming the depths of

Aurobindo's thought are related to more general infirmities that have afflicted the history of political and economic ideas in colonial India. Both Marxist and non-Marxist preoccupations with interest to the exclusion of sentiment have led, as Andrew Sartori puts it, to a 'vacuum of ideological content', while the tendency to view nationalist thought as derivative of European discourses has resulted in a 'vacuum of native subjectivity'.[7] Indian intellectual history needs to be rescued from this impoverished state.

Modern Indian nationalism, far from being exclusively derived from European discourses, drew significantly on rich legacies of precolonial patriotism and kept it alive through a constant process of creative innovation. Indians in the late nineteenth century were also intensely curious about social and political experiments elsewhere in the world. In order to imagine one's own nation, as C.A. Bayly has contended, it was important to figure out how other nations were being imagined.[8] In the late nineteenth and early twentieth centuries the Indian nation was very much in the process of its own making with a variety of individuals, linguistic groups and religious communities seeking to contribute to imagining it into being. There were territorial as well as universalist aspects of this nation in formation, even though it is only the former that has been emphasized by theorists of the nation as an 'imagined community'.[9] These theorists tracked the global dispersal, replication and piracy of the nation-state form from the West to the East, leaving out of account the multiple meanings of nationhood and alternative frameworks of states that were imagined in the colonized world of Asia and Africa. Indian anti-colonialism was nourished by many regional patriotisms, competing versions of nationalism and extra-territorial affinities of religiously informed universalisms. It is a travesty to reduce the engagement in colonial India with ideas circulating in contemporary Europe to the trope of piracy. The Indian intellectual deserves to be put on par with the European thinker and, as Kris Manjapra argues, ought to be viewed 'as engaging and revising through *phronesis*' the full range of Indian, European and in-between ideational traditions which he or she encountered.[10] The varieties of liberalism in the nineteenth century and the multiple voices of Marxist internationalism of the post–World War I era are beginning to be studied in this new light. The Swadeshi conjuncture of the early twentieth century deserves the same sophisticated treatment in order to elucidate the meaning of nationalism and its connection to religious universalism as a problem of ethics.

This essay engages in that exercise of elucidation by interpreting a few of the key texts by Aurobindo on the relationship between ethics and politics. This interpretation owes a debt to an insight gleaned from Ranajit Guha's delicate reading of Netaji Subhas Chandra Bose's autobiography, *An Indian Pilgrim*. In putting moral sentiments back into the study of nationalism, Guha notices 'a movement of individuation that ran parallel' to the mass campaigns of the nationalist era and suggests that the mass aspect was nourished by 'the energies of such individuation'. The young Bose found in Vivekananda's maxim *Aatmano mokshaartham jagaddhitaya [ca]* the central principle to which he could devote his whole being. 'For your own salvation and for the service of humanity—that was to be life's goal,' he wrote, adding that the service of humanity 'included, of course, the service of one's country'. The triad of *seva* (service), *shraddha* (respect) and *tyag* (sacrifice) would form the ethical bedrock of this existential dimension of nationalism.[11]

Aurobindo's biographer, Srinivasa Iyengar, regards some of his early poetical works including *Urvasie, Love and Death* and *Perseus the Deliverer* as indicative of an engagement with 'the problem of service and sacrifice and of right aspiration and conduct'.[12] Even though the young Aurobindo had tried to light new lamps for old through his powerful political journalism in the 1890s and nursed a desire to enter the fray of anti-colonial politics since 1902, the die had not yet been cast. The trials of becoming a nationalist had not yet been fully negotiated. The moment of individual commitment in Aurobindo's case coincided with the affront to the Bengali nation in the form of George Curzon's partition.[13] In an intense letter to his wife in August 1905 he described himself to be seized of three great convictions—first, that all his worldly possessions belonged truly to God; second, that he wished to encounter God face-to-face; and third, that he viewed his country as the Mother whom he was determined to free from a demon's grasp through the application of his *brahmatej* (divine power). The world might consider these mad ideas, but he assured his wife that a madman upon the fulfilment of his mission was usually acknowledged as a great man.[14]

Aurobindo's brahmatej in the cause of the Mother was mostly on display in the editorials of *Bande Mataram*, the paper he jointly edited from July 1906 with the other intellectual giant of the Swadeshi era (1905–08), Bipin Chandra Pal. The most important series of articles from Aurobindo's pen to appear in this paper were the ones on the doctrine of passive resistance published between 9 April and 23 April 1907. He could see that organized national resistance to alien rule could take three possible forms. First, there could be passive resistance of the sort orchestrated by Charles Parnell in Ireland. Second, resistance might take the shape of 'an untiring and implacable campaign of assassination and a confused welter of riots, strikes and agrarian risings' that had been witnessed in Russia. The third path for an oppressed nation was the time-honoured one of 'armed revolt, which instead of bringing existing conditions to an end by making their continuance impossible sweeps them bodily out of existence'. A subject nation had to make its choice by taking account of 'the circumstances of its servitude' and Indian circumstances indicated passive resistance to be the correct path. While anticipating many elements of Mahatma Gandhi's methods, Aurobindo argued from a different ethical standpoint. He was certainly not prepared to regard other methods as 'in all circumstances criminal and unjustified'. 'It is the common habit of established Governments and especially those which are themselves oppressors,' he wrote, 'to brand all violent methods in subject peoples and communities as criminal and wicked.' The refusal to listen to 'the cant of the oppressor' attempting to lay 'a moral as well as a legal ban on any attempt to answer violence by violence' had the approval of 'the general conscience of humanity'. Passive resistance could turn into a battle in which the morality of war ruled supreme. In those situations to 'shrink from bloodshed and violence' deserved 'as severe a rebuke as Sri Krishna addressed to Arjuna'.[15]

In spelling out the limits of passive resistance Aurobindo—for all his adoration of the Mother—made a few unfortunate, gendered remarks that were not unusual for the times, but nevertheless have a jarring quality. He was not in favour of 'dwarfing national manhood' in the face of coercion as that would be a sin against 'the divinity in our motherland'. Passive resistance had to be 'masculine, bold and ardent in its spirit' and capable of switching over to active resistance. He did not want to develop 'a nation of women' who, in his essentialized view, knew 'only how to suffer and not how to strike'. Passive resistance was an exercise in 'peaceful and self-contained *Brahmatej*'. But, as 'even the greatest Rishis of old could not, when the Rakshasas were fierce and determined, keep up the sacrifice without calling in the bow of the Kshatriya', that weapon had be kept 'ready for use, though in the background'.[16]

In what way was the quality of patriotism in the Swadeshi conjuncture different from the 'liberal' conjuncture that is often seen to have preceded it? It would be a mistake to imagine a complete break since ideas about a religion of humanity and the theme of Mazzinian suffering supplied connecting threads. But the Swadeshi era did offer a compelling and intellectually sophisticated critique of the abstract nature of late-nineteenth-century liberal nationalism. In 1905 Pal wrote of the new patriotism in India, different from the period when Pym, Hampden, Mazzini, Garibaldi, Kossuth and Washington were 'the models of young India'. The old patriotism 'panted for the realities of Europe and America only under an Indian name'. 'We loved the abstraction we called India,' Pal wrote, 'but, yes, we hated the thing that it actually was.' But the new patriotism was based on 'a love, as Rabindranath put it . . . for the muddy weed-entangled village lanes, the moss-covered stinking village ponds, and for the poor, the starved, the malaria-stricken peasant populations of the country, a love for its languages, its literatures, its philosophies, its religions; a love for its culture and civilization'.[17]

One finds an echo of this sentiment in Aurobindo's essay 'The Morality of Boycott' written for *Bande Mataram* but not actually published in it. He wrote lyrically of love of one's country and 'the joy of seeing one's blood flow for country and freedom':

> The feeling of almost physical delight in the touch of the mother-soil, of the winds that blow from Indian seas, of the rivers that stream from Indian hills, in the hearing of Indian speech, music, poetry, in the familiar sights, sounds, habits,

dress, manners of our Indian life, this is the physical root of that love. The pride in our past, the pain of our present, the passion for the future are its trunk and branches. Self-sacrifice and self-forgetfulness, great service, high endurance for the country are its fruit. And the sap which keeps it alive is the realization of the Motherhood of God in the country, the vision of the Mother, the knowledge of the Mother, the perpetual contemplation, adoration and service of the Mother.

A deep affective bond with the motherland was then to replace the abstract nationalism of the preceding decades. But just as there were several strands within 'liberal' thought,[18] so too Swadeshi patriotism had a number of variants. Aurobindo's essay justifying the morality of boycott was written partly in response to 'a poet of sweetness and love' who had deprecated boycott as 'an act of hate'. While wishing to discharge minds of hate, Aurobindo at this stage was prepared to see even hatred if it came 'as a stimulus, as a means of awakening'. As for violence, it was not reprehensible from the point of view of political morality. It had been 'eschewed' 'because it carried the battle on to a ground where we are comparatively weak, from a ground where we are strong'. In different circumstances Indians might have followed the precedent set by the American War of Independence and, had they done so, 'historians and moralists would have applauded, not censured'. 'The sword of the warrior,' Aurobindo concluded, 'is as necessary to the fulfilment of justice and righteousness as the holiness of the saint.'[19]

Until the end of 1907 Aurobindo's exhortations to the youth were balanced in his articles by the application of a razor-sharp intellect. Charged with sedition, he stepped down as principal of the Bengal National College with a parting advice to his students to serve the motherland: 'Work that she may prosper; suffer that she may rejoice.'[20] While the sedition case was going on, Aurobindo wrote three important articles in *Bande Mataram* titled 'The Foundations of Sovereignty', 'Sankharitola's Apologia' and 'The Unities of Sankharitola' that were masterpieces of political polemic. Already in his pieces on passive resistance he had identified the need for a central authority to guide the movement. He now answered those who contended that the diversity of races in India doomed the prospect of national unity. 'One might just as well say,' he wrote, 'that different chemical elements cannot combine into a single substance as that different races cannot combine into a single nation.'[21] His more nuanced studies on Indian unity belong, however, to a much later phase of his writing career.

In 1908 Aurobindo's rhetoric was elevated to an altogether different spiritual plane. In January of that year he spent a few days practising yoga under the direction of Bishnu Bhaskar Lele in Baroda. When he rose to speak before the Bombay National Union on 19 January 1908, 'he seemed to the audience as one in the grip of a trance'.[22] Bengal had once judged all things through 'the imperfect instrumentality of the intellect', but the work of 'unaided intellect' was now done. 'What is Nationalism?' he asked. 'Nationalism,' the answer came, 'is not a mere political programme. Nationalism is a religion that has come from God . . . Nationalism is immortal . . . God cannot be killed, God cannot be sent to jail.' The country could not be saved merely by boycott, national education, or Swadeshi. In place of the pure intellect, the need of the hour was faith of which another name was selflessness. 'This movement of nationalism,' Aurobindo clarified, 'is not guided by any self-interest, not at the heart of it . . . We are trying to live not for our own interests, but to work and die for others.' The third name for faith and selflessness was courage which came not from being 'a Nationalist in the European sense, meaning in a purely materialistic sense', but from a realization that 'the three hundred millions of people in this country are God in the nation'.[23]

Aurobindo carried this message of the spirit from Bombay to Bengal, from Baruipur to Kishoreganj. He spoke of faith and the dispelling of illusion through suffering, but he was no traditionalist, which is why he is probably so misunderstood today by neo-traditionalists like Nandy. Speaking to the Palli Samiti of Kishoreganj, he accepted the virtues of village upliftment, but was not ensnared by the mirage of self-sufficient village communities. 'The village must not in our new national life be isolated as well as self-sufficient,' he advised, 'but must feel itself bound up with the life of its neighbouring units, living with them in a common group for common purposes.' The unity that he urged was not of opinion or speech or intellectual conviction. 'Unity is of the heart,' he was convinced, 'and springs from love.'[24]

Aurobindo's spiritual fervour deepened further during his nearly year-long stay in Alipore jail during the bomb case trial of late 1908 and early 1909. There he read the Gita and saw visions of Sri Krishna as his protector and guide. He gave a vivid description of his experiences in jail in his famous Uttarpara speech delivered immediately after his release from detention. It is a speech hugely misunderstood by historians, thoroughly imbued with the secular ideology of the postcolonial Indian state. 'I spoke once before with this force in me,' Aurobindo declared near the conclusion of this speech, 'and I said then that this movement is not a political movement and that nationalism is not politics but a religion, a creed, a faith. I say it again today, but I put it in another way. I say no longer that nationalism is a creed, a religion, faith; I say that it is the *Sanatana Dharma* which for us is nationalism.'[25] Sumit Sarkar cites these lines disapprovingly in his book on the Swadeshi movement indicating an inversion from the cultivation of religion as 'a means to the end of mass contact and stimulation of morale' to religion as 'an end in itself'. The implication here is that the instrumental use of religion for the purpose of mass nationalism can perhaps be condoned from the secular standpoint, but the protection of religion as a goal of the campaign for swaraj—an end sought by anti-colonial leaders from Aurobindo to Gandhi— could not. Dipesh Chakrabarty has been right in pointing to 'the remarkable failure of intellect' and, one might add, imagination, in Sarkar's book in particular, but in works by secularist historians in general, in dealing with the question of religion in public life.[26] Sarkar sees the Uttarpara speech as the product of a moment of 'strain and frustration' without caring to delve into what Aurobindo might have meant by sanatan dharma.

The speeches Pal and Aurobindo gave in Uttarpara after their release from Buxar jail and Alipore jail respectively in 1909 were certainly different in tenor from Surendranath Banerjea's Uttarpara speech on Mazzini in 1876. Both spoke of their realization in jail 'of God within us all'. 'I was brought up in England amongst foreign ideas,' Aurobindo recalled, 'and an atmosphere entirely foreign.' He had believed religion to be a delusion and when he first approached God he had 'hardly had a living faith in Him'. But now he understood not only intellectually but realized what it was to 'do work for Him without demand for fruit'. The sanatan dharma that Aurobindo invoked in his Uttarpara speech was no narrow or bigoted creed, but as large as 'life itself'. It was the dharma that had been cherished in India for 'the salvation of humanity'. India was rising again not 'as other countries do, for self or when she is strong, to trample on the weak'; she was rising 'to shed the eternal light entrusted to her over the world'. 'India has always existed for humanity and not for herself,' Aurobindo contended at Uttarpara, 'and it is for humanity and not for herself that she must be great.'[27] The inversion of the humanistic aspiration in Hinduism and Islam alike to a parody called communalism is the signal achievement of our secularist historians, not of Aurobindo.

The relationship between the nationalism of the age and an eternal humanistic religion was articulated with even greater vigour in Aurobindo's new journal *Karmayogin* in 1909. The ideal of the *karmayogin* was clearly stated to be 'building up India for the sake of humanity'. Yet each nation had its character distinct from 'the common nature of humanity'. India in the nineteenth century had been 'imitative, self-forgetful, artificial'. In that situation the resistance of even 'the conservative element in Hinduism, *tamasik* [dark], inert, ignorant, uncreative though it was', prevented an even more thorough disintegration and gave some respite for the 'national self to emerge and find itself'. Nationalism so far had been 'a revolt against the tendency to shape ourselves into the mould of Europe'. But it was also necessary to guard 'against any tendency to cling to every detail that has been Indian' for that had 'not been the spirit of Hinduism in the past' and ought not to be in the future. In an essay titled 'The Doctrine of Sacrifice' Aurobindo warned that the 'national ego may easily mean nothing more than collective selfishness'. The only remedy for that tempting evil was to 'regard the nation as a necessary unit but no more in a common humanity'. Nationalism at its first stage makes stringent demands on the individual. But at the second stage 'it should abate its demands . . . and should preserve itself in a Cosmopolitanism somewhat as the individual preserves itself in the family, the family in the class, the class in the nation, not destroying itself needlessly but recognizing a larger interest'.[28] Aurobindo spoke not only of the sacrifice of the individual, but also the greatness of the individual. As his biographer puts it, 'if all and sundry begin talking about "inner voices" and proclaiming themselves to be agents of the Divine, ordinary life would grow quickly untenable'.[29] In Aurobindo's view only that individual who had mastered the discipline of yoga could interpret and implement the divine will. 'The greatness of individuals,' he concluded, 'is the greatness of the eternal Energy within.'[30] 'All great movements,' he believed, 'wait for their Godsent leader.' In the open letter he wrote as a farewell to his countrymen in 1910 he restated once more the ideal Bengal had aspired to in the first decade of the twentieth century. 'Our ideal of patriotism proceeds on the basis of love and brotherhood,' he wrote in what he thought might be his last will and political testament, 'and it looks beyond the unity of the nation and envisages the ultimate unity of mankind. But it is a unity of brothers, equals and freemen that we seek, not the unity of master and serf, of devourer and devoured.'[31]

'And so,' Sarkar writes somewhat derisively, 'the revolutionary leader becomes the yogi of Pondicherry.'[32] Aurobindo may have retired from active participation in politics, but his days as a thinker on the problem of ethics and politics were far from over. In that respect the best was perhaps yet to come. On his forty-third birthday in 1914 Aurobindo launched a new journal called *Arya*, a philosophical review, which did not cease publication until 1921. The tainted history of European racism and totalitarianism has cast a cloud over the meaning of this term. In Aurobindo's connotation the word had nothing to do with race. 'Intrinsically,' Aurobindo explained, 'in its most fundamental sense, Arya means an effort or an uprising and overcoming.'[33] Much like the term jihad, therefore, also much maligned in the contemporary world, *arya* signified an aspiration to and endeavour towards self-perfection, and the surmounting of forces within and without that stood in the way of human advance. For seven long years, Aurobindo wrote prolifically in the pages of *Arya* on philosophy, literature, art, culture, religion and politics. In a short sequence titled 'The Renaissance in India' he offered a clarification of his opinion on the place of religion in the public life of India. He noted that there was no real synonym for the word religion in Sanskrit. He ventured to suggest that the ethical malady in India was caused not by too much religion, but too little of it, in the most generous sense of the term. 'The right remedy is,' he recommended, 'not to belittle still farther the age-long ideal of India, but to return to its old amplitude and give it a still wider scope, to make in very truth all the life of the nation a religion in this high spiritual sense.'[34]

The major sequence in *Arya* of the greatest relevance for students of cultural criticism, political thought and human values today is the one published under the title 'The Defence of Indian Culture' between 1918 and 1921. One of its components, called *The Significance of Indian Art*, a scintillating essay on the aesthetic side of Indian civilization, anticipates Edward Said's critique of Orientalism by some sixty years.[35] More pertinent to our immediate concerns is another component, *The Spirit and Form of Indian Polity*, from which the title of this essay takes its inspiration. In it Aurobindo resoundingly rejected the charge that India had 'always shown an incompetence for any free or sound political organisation'. A 'summary reading of Indian history' that the country was 'socially marked by the despotism of the Brahmin theocracy' and 'politically by an absolute monarchy of the oriental' had been 'destroyed by a more careful and enlightened scholarship'. Aurobindo considered the attempt by some Indian scholars to read back modern parliamentary democracy into India's past to be 'an ill-judged endeavour'. He recognized 'a strong democratic element', but 'these features were of India's own kind'. While Aurobindo's treatise rehearses in some detail the history of Indian ethics of good governance, the normative lesson to be derived from it was clearly meant for the future. It was perhaps for a future India that Aurobindo modestly expressed a hope 'to found the status and action of the collective being of man on the realisation of the deeper spiritual truth'.[36]

Aurobindo's discourse began with a consideration of republican freedom in India's ancient past which turned out to be deeper and more resilient than in either Greece or Rome. Even after the drift in India as elsewhere from republican towards monarchical forms, Indian monarchy was not 'a personal despotism or an absolutist autocracy'. The power of the Indian king was balanced by a council as well as metropolitan and general assemblies which were 'lesser co-partners with him in the exercise of sovereignty and administrative legislation and control'. The social hierarchy was not replicated in the political hierarchy and 'all the four orders had their part in the common political rights of the citizen'. In theory women in ancient India were 'not denied civic rights', even though in practice, Aurobindo conceded, 'this equality was rendered nugatory for all but a few by their social subordination to the male'. 'A greater sovereign than the king was the Dharma', which Aurobindo defined as 'the religious, ethical, social, political, juridic and customary law organically governing the life of the people'. Secular authority was denied 'any right of autocratic interference' with this Dharma. The 'subjection of the sovereign power to the Dharma was not an ideal theory inoperative in practice'. In practical terms it exercised a restraint on the king's power of legislation. More important, the 'religious liberties of the commons were assured' against infringement by secular authority. Powerful sovereigns like Asoka might have attempted to increase royal influence in this domain. But even Asoka's edicts, Aurobindo felt, had 'a recommendatory rather than an imperative character'. A sovereign aspiring to promote change in the area of religious beliefs or institutions had to abide by 'the Indian principle of communal freedom' or make a reference to 'a consultative assembly for deliberation, as was done in the famous Buddhist councils'. Whatever the sovereign's personal predilections, 'he was bound to respect and support in his public office all the recognised religions of the people with a certain measure of impartiality'. 'Normally,' as a consequence, 'there was no place in the Indian political system for religious oppression and intolerance and a settled State policy of that kind was unthinkable.'[37] It is odd that a set of restraints and responsibilities enjoined on secular authority in an ethical Indian polity to respect religious freedom is today appropriated as one of the meanings of secularism alongside a contrary meaning of the separation of religion from politics.

There were further safeguards in the ancient Indian polity against any 'autocratic freak'. Notwithstanding the 'prestige attaching to the sovereign', obedience to the king was no longer binding 'if the king ceased to be the faithful executor of the Dharma'. In extreme cases of oppression 'the right or even the duty of insurrection and regicide' was acknowledged. 'Another more peaceful and more commonly exercised remedy,' Aurobindo noted, 'was a threat of secession or exodus.' He cited a case of such a threat against an unpopular king in south India as late as the seventeenth century. What then was 'the theory and principle' as well as 'the actual constitution of the Indian polity'? It was 'a complex of communal freedom and self-determination with a supreme coordinating authority, a sovereign person and body', but 'limited to its proper rights and functions'. The 'economic and political aspects of the communal life' were 'inextricably united' with 'the religious, the ethical, the higher cultural aim of social existence'. To take dharma out of politics would have been to erode its ethical foundations. By not taking apart the yoke of dharma, Indian civilization had, in Aurobindo's view, 'evolved an admirable political system', but 'escaped at the same time the excess of the mechanizing turn which is the defect of the modern European state'.[38]

The ancient Indian polity propounded an imperial idea of unity that was at sharp variance with 'a mechanical western rule' that had 'crushed out all the still existing communal or regional autonomies and substituted the dead unity of a machine'. Indian history did, of course, afford an instance of expansion or conquest that spread 'the Buddhistic idea' and its associated thought and culture to the lands abutting the eastern Indian Ocean. 'The ships that set out from both the eastern and western coast were not,' as Aurobindo correctly pointed out, 'fleets of invaders missioned to annex those outlying countries to an Indian empire.' But he slipped inadvertently into the language of cultural imperialism when he described this as a movement of 'exiles or adventurers carrying with them to yet uncultured peoples Indian religion, architecture, art, poetry, thought, life, manners'. But this slippage did not vitiate the main point that he wished to make about the imperial idea. 'The idea of empire and even of world-empire was not absent from the Indian mind,' Aurobindo argued, 'but its world was the Indian world and the object the founding of the imperial unity of its peoples.' It was this idea that animated efforts at unity through the ages of the Vedas, the epics, the Mauryas, the Guptas, the Mughals and the Marathas until came a final failure after which the British imposed 'a uniform subjection in place of the free unity of a free people'.[39]

Aurobindo then touched upon 'the secret of the difficulty in the problem of unifying ancient India'. It was that 'the easy method of a centralized empire could not truly succeed in India'. The rishis from the Vedic age onwards, therefore, spoke of 'the ideal of the Chakravarti, a uniting imperial rule, uniting without destroying the autonomy of India's many kingdoms and peoples, from sea to sea'. The dharma of a powerful king was to set up a suzerainty. Aurobindo found the 'full flowering' of this ideal in 'the great epics'. The Mahabharata narrates the legendary and quasi-historic pursuit of this ideal of empire which even 'the turbulent Shishupala' is represented as accepting by attending Yudhisthira's *dharmic* Rajasuya sacrifice. The Ramayana too presents 'an idealized picture of such a Dharmarajya, a settled universal empire'. It is, Aurobindo says, 'not an autocratic despotism but a universal monarchy supported by a free assembly of the city and provinces and of all the classes that is held up as the ideal'. The 'ideal of conquest' is 'not a destructive and predatory invasion', but 'a sacrificial progression' aiming at 'a strengthening adhesion to a suzerain power'. According to this ideal, unification 'ought not to be secured at the expense of the free life of the regional peoples or of the communal liberties and not therefore by a centralized monarchy or a rigidly unitarian imperial State'. The closest Western analogy that Aurobindo could find for this conception was 'a hegemony or a confederacy under an imperial head'.[40]

Aurobindo doubted whether this ideal was ever executed in practice with full success even though he regarded the empire created and recreated by the Mauryas, the Sungas, the Kanwas, the Andhras and the Guptas as 'among the greatest constructed and maintained by the genius of the earth's great peoples'. It contradicted 'the hasty verdict' that denied India's ancient civilization 'a strong practical genius or high political virtue'. With the benefit of more recent historical evidence Aurobindo might have found that the actually existing empire in ancient India was not that far removed from the ideal as was commonly supposed in the early twentieth century. The Muslim conquest, in Aurobindo's temporal scheme, occurred at a moment when India 'needed a breathing space to rejuvenate itself by transference from the Sanskrit to the popular tongues and the newly forming regional peoples'. The early Muslim sovereigns generally respected this process of vernacularization so that, in Aurobindo's terms, 'the Mussulman domination ceased very rapidly to be a foreign rule'. 'The vast mass of the Mussulmans in the country were and are Indians by race,' he wrote, 'and even the foreign kings and nobles became almost immediately wholly Indian in mind, life and interest.' Aurobindo had no doubt that 'the British is the first really continuous foreign rule that has dominated India'.[41]

The Muslim conquest did not, therefore, introduce the difficulty of 'subjection to a foreign rule', but it did pose a challenge of 'the struggle between two civilizations'. Aurobindo could see that there were 'two conceivable solutions' to this problem: one, 'the rise of a greater spiritual principle' and two, 'a political patriotism surmounting the religious struggle'. Akbar tried the first from the Muslim side, but his religion was too intellectual to receive 'the assent from the strongly religious mind of the two communities'. Nanak tried it from the other side, but his religion, 'universal in principle, became a sect in practice'. Akbar also fostered a common political patriotism, but, in Aurobindo's estimation, 'the living assent of the people was needed' in the creation of 'a united imperial India' beyond the administrative talent of nobles from both religious communities. The Mughal empire was, in Aurobindo's very positive assessment:

> A great and magnificent construction and an immense amount of political genius and talent was employed in its creation and maintenance. It was as splendid, powerful and beneficent and, it may be added, in spite of Aurangzeb's fanatical zeal, infinitely more liberal and tolerant in religion than any medieval or contemporary European kingdom or empire and India under its rule stood high in military and political strength, economic opulence and the brilliance of its art and culture.

But it eventually disintegrated because, in Aurobindo's view, 'a military and administrative centralized empire could not effect India's living political unity'. Here the sage from Pondicherry was overestimating the Mughal tendency towards military–administrative centralization, the best new research having suggested that the Mughal emperor sought no more than an overarching suzerainty that was India's imperial ideal. But he was closer to the mark in presaging at least in part the revisionist historiography of the eighteenth century when he wrote that 'although a new life seemed about to rise in the regional peoples, the chance was cut short by the intrusion of the European nations'.[42]

Aurobindo noted two final creative attempts by 'the Indian political mind' in the late seventeenth and eighteenth centuries. He interpreted the Maratha revival crafted by Ramdas and Shivaji as 'an attempt to restore what could still be understood or remembered of the ancient form and spirit'. But the Peshwas succeeded in setting up nothing more than 'a military and political confederacy'. Their imperial ambition floundered because it was 'inspired by a regional patriotism that failed to enlarge itself beyond its own limits'. The second attempt by the Sikh Khalsa, despite its originality, 'achieved intensity but no power of expansion'. After that came 'a temporary end to all political initiative and creation'. 'The lifeless attempt of the last generation,' Aurobindo concluded, 'to imitate and reproduce with a servile fidelity the ideals and forms of the West has been no true indication of the political mind and genius of the Indian people.'[43]

By the time Aurobindo completed his arya on Indian political ethics in 1921, a godsent leader had arrived on the scene to take charge of a new phase of Indian mass nationalism. Aurobindo's doctrine of sacrifice contributed to the recruitment of a young firebrand to Mahatma Gandhi's movement. 'The illustrious example of Arabindo Ghose looms large before my vision,' Bose wrote to his elder brother Sarat as he prepared to resign from the Indian Civil Service in 1921. 'I feel that I am ready to make the sacrifice which that example demands of me.' Bose comments in his autobiography that 'it was widely believed about this time' that Aurobindo 'would soon return to active political life'.[44] But Aurobindo's political work was done and the baton had been handed over. The year 1921, not 1910, marks the close of Aurobindo's career in inspiring the spirit and fashioning the form of an ethical polity. He had done his bit as a great individual in contributing to the dynamics that, in Ranajit Guha's words, 'made dignity and self-respect the very condition of Indian nationalism'.[45] But he had done more. He had shown that in the domain of creating a state Indian nationalism was not condemned to pirating from the gallery of models crafted by the West.[46] The imitative fidelity of the Nehruvian moment of arrival has been 'no true indication of the political mind and genius of the Indian people'. The alternatives that lost out in that battle for power at the helm of a centralized state were represented not just by Gandhi or even Tagore, but a broad spectrum of moral personalities who had adopted nationalism as the religion of the age.

Although Aurobindo believed that the night had descended on Indian political creativity under colonial rule, he could still see 'amid all the mist of confusion' the possibility of 'a new twilight, not of an evening, but a morning Yuga-sandhya'. As the world stands on the threshold of a new dawn in the realm of political thought, if not political practice, it may not be inappropriate to recall Aurobindo's words of hope: 'India of the ages is not dead nor has she spoken her last creative word; she lives and has still something to do for herself and the human peoples.'[47]

DIFFERENT UNIVERSALISMS, COLOURFUL COSMOPOLITANISMS
The Global Imagination of the Colonized

On 10 February 1937, Rabindranath Tagore composed his poem 'Africa' towards the end of his long and creative life in literature. Even more than the empathy for Africa's history of 'blood and tears', what marked the poem was a searing piece of sarcasm directed at the false universalist claims of an unnamed Europe. Even as the 'barbaric greed of the civilized' put on naked display their 'shameless inhumanity', church bells rang out in neighbourhoods across the ocean in the name of a benign God, children played in their mothers' laps and poets sang paeans to beauty.[1] The sanctimonious hypocrisy of the colonizer stood in stark opposition to the wretched abjection of the colonized.

In my book *A Hundred Horizons* I had claimed that Tagore was an eloquent proponent of a universalist aspiration, albeit a universalism with a difference.[2] This specific claim was part of a larger contention that modern history could be interpreted—not wholly or in full measure, but very substantially—as an interplay of multiple and competing universalisms. The colonized did not simply erect defensive walls around their notions of cultural difference. They were keen to be players in broad arenas of cosmopolitan thought zones and wished to contribute to the shaping of a global future. Their cosmopolitanism flowed not from the stratosphere of abstract reason, but from the fertile ground of local knowledge and learning in the vernacular.

Universalism, cosmopolitanism and internationalism are words and concepts jostling for interpretive space in new global, interregional and transnational histories. A different universalism in my connotation of the phrase shares significant common ground with the meaning of vernacular cosmopolitanism as evoked by Homi Bhabha or local cosmopolitanism as enunciated by Engseng Ho or rooted cosmopolitanism as described by Anthony Appiah while diverging in subtle points of emphasis.[3] Both notions of universalism with a difference and cosmopolitanism springing from vernacular roots are dramatically at odds with the dominant discourse and debates within the charmed circle of contemporary British and North American analytical philosophy. They are also located at some distance from the premises of French and North American intellectual currents that are deeply suspicious of all metanarratives and are prepared to only valorize the fragment.[4]

Champions of cosmopolitanism who see detached reason as its only source display a visceral distaste for patriotism, confusing it with the narrowest forms of particularism. Colourless cosmopolitanism is assigned a high moral ground; colourful patriotism is deemed to be seductive but devoid of any ethical content.[5] A figure like Tagore can be annexed to this version of cosmopolitanism only by denuding him of much of his poetry and music and all of his passion and moral philosophy. Tagore undoubtedly was a powerful critic of worshipping the Nation as God and was horrified by the crimes committed by modern nation-states. Yet he loved the land that had nurtured him and never abandoned a basic anti-colonial stance. He simply did not want Indian patriots to imitate European nationalists. It is not without reason that Mahatma Gandhi in his obituary comment on Tagore in 1941 lauded the poet as 'an ardent nationalist'.[6] The large ethical claims made by votaries of a brand of cosmopolitanism that is dogmatically opposed to patriotism need to be put to the test on the ground of the history of colonial empires. Cosmopolitanism would serve as a weak pillar of any theory of human justice if it ruled out as illegitimate most modes of anti-colonial resistance. Fortunately for the idea, that was not the dominant kind of cosmopolitanism that animated the colonized world in the age of global empire. There were various forms of patriotism perfectly compatible with a cosmopolitan attitude that transcended the lines of particular cultural differences.

Within the terms of the Anglophone philosophical debate the opposition to cosmopolitanism based on abstract universal reason is articulated by proponents of reason embedded in inherited traditions.[7] A useful enough corrective to the excesses of colourless cosmopolitanism, this intellectual position falters because of its insistence on the bounded and implicitly unchanging nature of inheritances from the past. It fails to bring to light the dynamic process of creating and recreating traditions as well as the flows between cultures and the fluidity of cultural boundaries. The history of colourful cosmopolitanism rather than the legacy of the deadweight of traditions might be a better antidote to the philosophical hubris of the votaries of colourless cosmopolitanism.[8]

What I have alluded to as the French-flavoured academic streams celebrating the fragment actually encompass a wide array of post-structuralist, postmodern, post-Orientalist and postcolonial philosophical and historiographical approaches.

Several of these had the salutary effect during the last two decades of the twentieth century of calling into question powerful Eurocentric and statist biases in thinking about modern history. Yet the time had come by the beginning of the twenty-first century to explore the ways in which the various fragments were connected to one another. In order to contest the universalist boasts of Europe, it seemed important on both conceptual and empirical grounds to recover the universalist aspirations emanating from the colonized world. For scholars of literature or textual traditions an evocation of cosmopolitanism in the sense of generous exchange beyond narrow particularisms, qualified by the linguistic and cultural specificity of the vernacular, may be a sufficiently deft semantic move. For modern historians, however, universalism animates a field of power that can hardly be abandoned; it can only be inflected by the countervailing energy of difference.

The argument about the colonized world as a fount of different universalisms can be made over the longue durée, but needs to be advanced rather more forcefully for the few decades spanning the late nineteenth and early twentieth centuries. The century spanning the 1860s to the 1960s has been described by an eminent historian of modern Europe as an age of territoriality.[9] This territorial principle was transplanted in the structure and form of states in Europe's colonies. But rival universalistic allegiances did not lose their hold on people's minds and may even have exercised a greater appeal than before for the colonized. If colonial empires globalized the nation-state form, anti-colonial nationalists mounted their challenge on a global scale. A universalist patriotism emerged at various venues across the colonized world that refused to recognize any false binary of the secular and the religious.

It is necessary to be somewhat precise about both the nature of the religious element in these universalisms and the relative importance of religiously tinged universalisms in the larger scheme of global history. There is a strand of current writing on international history that pays scant attention to the theme of religious inspiration underlying extraterritorial anti-colonial movements. A recent claim has been made, for example, of the supposed Wilsonian moment in international history towards the end of the First World War.[10] There is little question that individuals and parties in the colonized world made some strategic use of Wilsonian internationalism and the doctrine of national self-determination to advance patriotic causes. Not only did disillusionment set in very rapidly over the limited reach of Wilsonian benevolence, this Washington-centric view of global history hugely exaggerates its salience by comparison with rival nationalist and trans-nationalist conceptions. A view limited to internationalism of the secular assortment reveals Bolshevik internationalism to be the only competitor of the Wilsonian vision for anti-colonial hearts and minds. Lenin certainly had a far stronger appeal than Wilson. A truly un-blinkered perspective on the four decades stretching from the 1890s to the 1920s would undoubtedly bring into the frame of analysis an even more powerful current of Islamic universalism in the global history of anti-colonial resistance.[11]

Quite as important as the overall significance of religiously inspired universalism is the way in which religion as faith played itself out in the politics of multi-religious societies at home and abroad. The South African setting in the early twentieth century is a fascinating one in which to explore this issue a little further. Consider the passive resistance or *satyagraha* from late 1906 that began as a protest against the 'Asiatic registration' ordinance issued by the Transvaal government which would have required all 'Asiatics' in that territory to register and carry certificates bearing their fingerprints. Even though the proximate provocation for the movement was the registration ordinance, speeches against it harped on European designs on the Ottoman empire.

Religion as faith had always been part and parcel of Gandhi's political philosophy and a source of his political inspiration. For his followers too he was prepared to hold up religion and honour as motivating principles underlying his satyagraha. Gandhi typically invoked the blessings of Khuda-Ishvar, the hyphenated form of common terms for God among Hindus and Muslims, in support of the movement. His reading habits in jail reflected the political philosophy that underpinned unity among religious faiths in the movement. He read the Gita at dawn, the Koran at noon and used the Bible to give lessons to a fellow Christian convict. Eventually the great burning of some 2000 registration certificates by the Transvaal Indians took place on the grounds of the Hamidia mosque in Johannesburg on 16 August 1908. 'The whole assembly rose to their feet,' Gandhi wrote, 'and made the place resound with the echoes of their continuous cheers during the burning process.'[12]

Religious universalism was, however, not the only form of religion on offer in the late nineteenth century and, consequently, religion in politics could be a double-edged sword. Harnessing religion as faith and cultivating respect for religious differences, as Gandhi did, strengthened mass movements and lent them an intensity that they otherwise might not have had. But others might always appeal not to religion as faith but to religion as demarcator of separate, if not clashing, identities, something that tended to happen whenever mass movements went off the boil. Colonial schemes of enumeration of religious communities in

India and the privileging of the religious distinction in defining majorities and minorities for political representation triggered acrid communitarian discourses among seekers of the state's differential patronage. While no colonial society from Ireland to India and no British Indian province was immune from this communitarian plague, Punjab with its complex and competitive religious landscape was the worst affected in the late nineteenth century.[13] By April 1909 a Hindu religious figure Shankeranand had imported the politics of communitarian bigotry from the Punjab to Natal. By playing the Hindu communitarian card in the politics of the rising colonial-born elite, he undercut the unity that Gandhi and his colleagues had sought to nurture since the 1890s.

Just as the lofty ideals of the turn-of-the-century Hindu universalism of Vivekananda or Gandhi could fall prey to the lowly calculations of identity politics, much the same could be said about the history of the other great world religions in this period. The eastern Indian Ocean was witnessing at this time a powerful movement of Buddhist universalism that fed into the anti-colonial politics of countries like Burma. But Buddhism as an inspirational faith was not the same as Buddhism as the basis of identity politics, especially once it got entangled with colonial policy. One brief historical example ought to suffice in making this point. Bodhgaya in today's Bihar had a significant Chinese and Burmese scholarly presence in ancient times and was naturally a focal point of modern Buddhist universalism. Once the monument there came under the purview of George Curzon and the Archaeological Survey of India, a fracas broke out over the issue of a Hindu *mahant* being the caretaker of a Buddhist shrine. There had been nothing unusual about such an arrangement before. Even the famous Hindu pilgrimage destination Marutirtha Hinglaj in Balochistan had a Muslim woman as its patron and custodian at this time. But with more rigid and singular definitions of religious identity on the anvil, local cosmopolitanisms were soon set under siege. Some votaries of a modern Buddhist revival in India could not avoid the pitfall of seeking to invent an ancient 'pure' Buddhist past and denuding places like Nalanda, Bodhgaya and Paharpur of their multiple religious and historical strands.[14]

The path to a cosmopolitan anti-colonialism among expatriate patriots was forged only when they were able to combat religious prejudice without making religion the enemy of the nation. Gandhi's approach towards fashioning Indian unity through respect for cultural and religious difference and the fusion of nationalism and universalism was deployed with remarkable success in the Khilafat and non-cooperation movement of 1919–22. 'I am a good sailor,' Gandhi wrote in his autobiography, 'and do not get sea-sick.' The sailor who visited many shores knew how to reconcile love for the land and the sea, meld together territorial nationalism and religiously inspired extraterritorial universalism.[15]

The spirit of different universalism that appealed to anti-colonial nationalists may have been waterborne, but was never quite defined by an expanse of water except in a metaphorical sense. It is best in this context not to exaggerate the contradiction between oceans and continents that has crept into some of the scholarly literature today. The myth of continents has been subjected to a powerful indictment with some justice as a meta-geographical concept hopelessly tainted by the hubris of European imperialism.[16] The idea of Asia or of Africa, I might venture to add, was not a singular one and had almost as many variations as it had individual authors. More important, it was certainly at variance with the concrete expression of Asia invented by nineteenth-century

European geographers and cartographers as part of what has been debunked as the modern myth of continents. There were strands within Asian thought—worlds that merely inverted and did not undermine the Europe–Asia dichotomy, being content to invest the latter with a higher order of value and virtue. That forms a less interesting dimension of the modern tug of war between Europe and Asia. Far more fascinating was the imagination of Asia as an abstract entity transcending the imperial and national frontiers being etched by colonial powers on to the physical and mental maps of the colonized, and thereby serving as a prism to refract the light of universal humanity. If what I am arguing here about Asia on the theme of continental and oceanic universalisms has any valid analogy with Africa, there might not be as great a contradiction as is sometimes assumed between the so-called inward- and outward-looking orientations in the writing of African history.

The Swadeshi cultural milieu of early-twentieth-century India, despite its interest in rejuvenating indigenous traditions, was not wholly inward-looking; its protagonists were curious about innovations in different parts of the globe and felt comfortable within ever-widening concentric circles of Bengali patriotism, Indian nationalism and Asian universalism. Aspiring to reconcile a sense of nationality with a common humanity, they were not prepared to let colonial borders constrict their imaginations. The spirit of Asian universalism was brought to India by two turn-of-the-century ideologues—Okakura Kakuzo (1862–1913) and Sister Nivedita (1867–1911). Okakura had been deeply influenced in his early years by the Harvard scholar of Japanese art Ernest Francisco Fenollosa (1853–1908), whose collection of Japanese and Chinese paintings he later catalogued for the Boston Museum of Fine Arts. Okakura's blend of Japanese nationalism and Asian universalism was appealing as a potential model for Indian intellectuals and artists of the Swadeshi era. Okakura first came to India in 1902 on the eve of the publication of his book *The Ideals of the East*, for which Sister Nivedita, the Irish-born disciple of the Hindu sage Swami Vivekananda, wrote an introduction. Once Sister Nivedita introduced Okakura to the Tagore clan, a formidable cultural bridge was established between East and South Asia, and Japanese artists Taikan Yokoyama and Shunso Hishida soon followed Okakura's trail to Calcutta. By observing Taikan, Abanindranath Tagore learned the Japanese wash technique, of which his famous painting *Bharatmata* (*Mother India*, 1905) is a prominent example; the Japanese brush-and-ink style was more deeply imbibed by Abanindranath's brother, Gaganendranath Tagore. In Nandalal Bose's early masterpiece *Sati* (1907), a quintessentially Indian theme of selfless womanhood emerged in the colours and contours of the Japanese wash.

While the First World War raged in Europe and the Middle East, Rabindranath Tagore set off on a global oceanic voyage from Calcutta on 3 May 1916, aboard the Japanese ship *Tosamaru*. Travelling on this easterly route for the first time in his life, Tagore made his first stop in Burma. He stayed in Rangoon at the home of P.C. Sen, a leading Bengali lawyer, and was given a reception presided over by Abdul Karim Jamal, a prosperous Indian merchant. Other than the Shwedagon temple, Tagore did not find anything in the city that was distinctively Burmese. 'This city has not grown like a tree from the soil of the country,' he wrote, 'this city floats like foam on the tides of time ... Well, I have seen Rangoon, but it is mere visual acquaintance, there is no recognition of Burma in this seeing ... the city is an abstraction ...'[17]

From Burma the *Tosamaru* travelled further east towards Penang, Singapore and Hong Kong. The poet felt a sense of joy observing the strength and skill of Chinese labourers working at the port in Hong Kong and made an uncannily accurate prophecy about the future balance of power in the world. 'The nations which now own the world's resources,' Tagore argued, 'fear the rise of China, and wish to postpone the day of that rise.' On 29 May 1916, the *Tosamaru* reached the Japanese port of Kobe. Tagore's three-month sojourn in Japan represented the fulfilment not just of a personal quest, but also the search for an Asian universalism that had begun at the turn of the twentieth century.

Tagore's direct encounter with the power and scale of art in Japan during his 1916 visit to that country led him to urge Indian artists to look East in order to pioneer a fresh departure from the Swadeshi corpus of ideals. He asked his host, Taikan, to send one of his students to India, and Arai Kampo (1878–1945) travelled to Calcutta that year. His arrival triggered a fruitful collaboration with Nandalal: Arai taught Nandalal Japanese brush techniques while Nandalal explained the intricacies of the thirteenth-century eastern Indian sculptures of Konarak in Orissa to the Japanese visitor. Tagore was as impressed by Japanese visual arts as he was unimpressed by Japan's tendency to imitate the worst elements of European nationalistic imperialism. It was only after rebuking Japan on that count that Tagore undertook the long Pacific crossing to North America on 7 September 1916.

While he was in Japan Tagore had received an invitation to visit Vancouver. He flatly rejected it. Well aware of the *Komagatamaru* incident of 1914 when prospective Indian immigrants had been turned away from Vancouver harbour, Tagore refused to travel to Canada and Australia until these dominions withdrew their discriminatory immigration policies. Ironically, the ship that took Tagore across the Pacific was named *Canadamaru*. Tagore disembarked in Seattle. Journeying down the West Coast of the

USA he delivered powerful strictures against worshipping the new god called Nation in Seattle, San Francisco, Los Angeles and Pasadena. He then travelled from the West Coast to the East speaking out against nationalism during the presidential election season of 1916. Woodrow Wilson eked out a narrow victory campaigning on the slogan: 'He kept us out of war.' 'The Nation [with a capital N],' Tagore declared in his speech titled *The Cult of Nationalism* in Carnegie Hall, New York City, on 16 November 1916, 'with all its paraphernalia of power and prosperity, its flags and pious hymns, its blasphemous prayers in the churches, and the literary mock thunders of its patriotic bragging, cannot hide the fact that the Nation is the greatest evil for the Nation, that all its precautions are against it, and any new birth of its fellow in the world is always followed in its mind by the dread of a new peril.' He did not want Indian patriots to imitate the monstrous features of European nationalism and the territorially bounded model of the nation-state. Tagore's critique of nationalism was perfectly compatible with a basic anti-colonial stance and his patriotic poetry.

Yet Tagore's anti-Nation stance was a cause of some concern to anti-colonial nationalists at home. Although Tagore's book *Nationalism* was not published until later in 1917, reports of his speeches in the United States had appeared in the Calcutta journal *Modern Review*. In April 1917 at the Bengal Provincial Conference held in Calcutta Chittaranjan Das questioned and challenged the recently published opinion of the poet who had been 'the high-priest of the nation-idea at the inception of the Swadeshi Movement'. The 'whole of this anti-nation idea' appeared to Das to be 'insubstantial—based upon a vague and nebulous conception of universal humanity'. He refused to accept that the idea of nationalism was 'a foreign importation'. The 'spirit of nationalism', he contended, was founded upon a 'permanent and immutable relation which subsists between a particular people and the land which they inhabit'. Bengali nationalism was, therefore, moulded by the soil and atmosphere of Bengal. Das conceded that the First World War was 'the consequence of nationalism pushed to its excess'; yet 'the larger union among the peoples of Europe' in the future would also be founded on the principle of nationalism. 'And if at some dim and distant day, the Federation of Humanity is established in this world,' he continued, 'that will be because the different nations of this earth will each have reached the full development of its distinctive peculiarities; and it is my firm and deliberate belief that when things have reached that state, Kings and Kingdoms will be no more necessary for the good of the world than Nations and Nationalities.' As for the meeting ground between East and West, Das argued that 'true union' ought not to be confused with 'the complete merging of one in another'. 'Distinctiveness,' he asserted, 'can never be abolished.' However, he could see union bringing out in sharp relief 'the deeper harmony which underlies all outer differences between different nationalities'. That was the ground on which 'the universal brotherhood of man' could be forged, and the East and the West could be said to 'have met and not in vain'.[18]

If Swadeshi nationalism had forged connections with Asian universalism, the non-cooperation and Khilafat movements led by Mahatma Gandhi in the aftermath of the First World War were inextricably linked with the evocation of an Islamic universalism. 'Let Hindus not be frightened by Pan-Islamism,' Gandhi had written in *Young India*. 'It is not—it need not be—anti-Indian or anti-Hindu.'[19] In exhorting Hindus to extend support to Muslims on the Khilafat question, Gandhi saw no contradiction between a territorial conception of nationalism and an extraterritorial anti-colonial sentiment. The movement that united Hindus and Muslims was led in Bengal by none other than Das who tried to preserve this spirit of unity even after Gandhi called off non-cooperation through the Bengal Pact between the province's two religious communities. In his very last public speech delivered at the Bengal Provincial Conference in Faridpur on 2 May 1925, Das returned once more to the theme of nationalism and universalism. 'Nationalism,' he explained, 'is merely a process in self-realization, self-development and self-fulfilment. It is not an end in itself. The growth and development of nationalism is necessary so that humanity may realize itself, develop itself and fulfil itself; and I beseech you, when you discuss the terms of settlement, do not forget the larger claim of humanity in your pride of nationalism.'[20]

With the waning of the Khilafat movement and the abolition of the institution by Kemal Ataturk in 1924, Indian nationalists turned again towards the dream of an Asian universalism. In 1924 Tagore travelled once more by sea to Burma, China and Japan. The poet's entourage on his travels typically included a small but formidable team of intellectuals and artists. Mukul Dey was the artist who had accompanied Tagore to Japan in 1916; it would be the linguist Suniti Kumar Chattopadhyay's and painter Surendranath Kar's turn on a voyage to South East Asia in 1927; and the poet Amiya Kumar Chakravarty and writer Kedar Nath Chattopadhyay would go with the poet to Iran and Iraq in 1932. On the 1924 journey to East Asia, Tagore's two companions from Santiniketan were Nandalal and Kshitimohan Sen, an erudite scholar of Sanskrit and comparative religion. On this trip Tagore preached the virtues of close interaction among Asian cultures. Stung by the passage of the Immigration Act of

1924 (sometimes referred to as the Orientals Exclusion Act) in the United States, some of Tagore's admirers even established an Asiatic Association in Shanghai to foster solidarity among all Asians. As the group travelled, Nandalal was somewhat disappointed to see that painting and the other higher arts in China had 'become infected by the Western virus', as he termed it. He also noticed 'marvellous paintings' (even though the value of a work Tagore received as a gift from the titular emperor derived only from the 'seal impressed on it'). Nandalal also collected a few beautiful old rubbings and picked up 'prints, post cards, and books as also life stories of painters'. He himself did a number of sketches as picture postcards and documented the trip in photographs. In Japan Nandalal had the privilege of being hosted by Tagore's friend, the artist who had visited India, Taikan, and he was introduced to masterpieces of Japanese art.

While still respectful of the traditions of Indian art, Nandalal's work in the late 1920s and early 1930s reveals how far he had travelled from the predilections of the Swadeshi decade (1905–15). His artistic evolution is best exemplified in his experiments with the Madonna motif; these images were a radical break from the Bengal school's early forms of venerating country and goddess as mother. At an exhibition in 1926–27, he displayed a small tempera panel featuring a human mother and child flanked on either side by three animal mothers with their cubs.[21] The artistic equivalence of motherly love in the human and animal worlds was recognized by one important critic as a key innovation in the depiction of mother figures. Five years later Nandalal brilliantly portrayed a Bengali Madonna in his painting *Caitanya-Janani* (or *Birth of Caitanya*), celebrating the birth of the great fifteenth-century Indian exponent of bhakti, or personal devotion to God. A certain resemblance was discernible between the facial contours of the Bengali Madonna and the mother in the 1926–27 tempera panel.[22]

Even if Nandalal had moved artistically beyond the Swadeshi ideals of worshipping Bharatmata, patriotic sentiment still moved him. The civil disobedience movement stirred him sufficiently to create *Dandi March (Bapuji)*, a 1930 linocut depicting Mahatma Gandhi on his salt march. He made another linocut of Khan Abdul Ghaffar Khan, often known as the Frontier Gandhi, in 1936. However, his greatest contribution to the popular culture of mass nationalism was the several hundred Haripura posters. As many as eighty-six were by his own hand, and they embellished the public and private spaces of the annual session of the Indian National Congress at Haripura, Gujarat, in February 1938. 'Following the *pat[a]* style,' he later wrote, 'we did a large number of paintings and hung them everywhere—on the main entrance, inside the volunteers' camps, even in the rooms meant for Bapuji [Mahatma Gandhi] and Subhasbabu [Netaji Subhas Chandra Bose], the President.'[23] Many delegates at the Haripura session unfortunately had been afflicted with malaria. When Gandhi met Nandalal there, he smiled and asked, 'Still alive?'[24] Bose later visited Santiniketan in January 1939, where he met Tagore as well as Nandalal and his art students.

Developments in East Asia during the late 1930s had by this time brought a measure of disillusionment with the idea of Asia. Japan's invasion of China in 1937 had shown Asia to be as prone to nationalist wars as Europe. In its October 1937 issue the *Modern Review* carried a long essay by Bose titled 'Japan's Role in the Far East'. In some ways it offered a remarkably dispassionate, realist analysis of power relations in East Asia. Towards the end of the article, however, Bose did not hesitate to reveal where his sympathies lay. Japan, he conceded had 'done great things for herself and for Asia'. He recalled how Japan had been a beacon of inspiration for all of Asia at the dawn of the twentieth century. He welcomed Japan's stance against the Western imperial powers. But, he asked, could not Japan's aims be achieved 'without Imperialism, without dismembering the Chinese Republic, without humiliating another proud, cultured and ancient race?' 'No,' he replied, 'with all our admiration for Japan, where such admiration is due, our whole heart goes out to China in her hour of trial.' He then went on to draw some ethical lessons for India from the conflict in East Asia. 'Standing at the threshold of a new era,' he wrote, 'let India resolve to aspire after national self-fulfilment in every direction—but not at the expense of other nations and not through the bloody path of self-aggrandisement and imperialism.'[25]

The 1940s were a turbulent decade for Bengal, India, and indeed, the whole of Asia. Tagore passed away in August 1941, having lamented in the last year of his life the tendency of human civilization to kill itself with its own dagger. Nandalal did not paint the horrors of war, famine and Partition—that was left to his younger contemporaries, Somnath Hore and Jainul Abedin. There is, however, a deep sense of irony in his painting *Annapurna,* which was created in 1943, the year of the great Bengal famine in which three million people died. More than three decades earlier, Nandalal had painted a serene picture titled *Annapurna and Shiva.* In 1943, in a combination of tempera and wash, he created the haunting *Annapurna and Rudra* (later simply titled *Annapurna*). Annapurna, who is seated on a lotus, holds a bowl of rice in her hands. Before her stands Shiva, reduced to a skeleton, holding a begging bowl.[26] Nandalal's mood in the year of the great Bengal famine is captured in one of his letters: 'I have realized the following in a dream,' he wrote. 'Give up your attempts to find

God; go on creating what you like; you are an artist, paint picture after picture.'²⁷

Bose was by now in South East Asia organizing the Indian National Army with Japanese support. In late August and early September 1943 he tried to send rice from Burma to Bengal, which was being decimated by a terrible man-made famine. His offers to provide relief were nervously suppressed by the British in India. On 21 November 1943 he broadcast an appeal to Chungking from Shanghai. 'The Indian people,' he said, 'really sympathize with China and the Chinese people.' He reminded the Chungking government that as president of the Indian National Congress he had sent out the first medical mission to China as a token of sympathy for the Chinese people. He urged Chungking not to send troops to India 'to fight against us on the side of the British'. He tried to suggest that 1943 was not 1937 and that East Asia faced 'an entirely new situation'. He looked forward to the day 'not far off' when by means of 'an honourable peace' Japan would 'withdraw her troops' from China. An unrealistic hope given the recent history of Japanese atrocities in China, this wishful thinking about a rapprochement between China and Japan was evidence of a lingering faith in an Asian universalism being torn asunder by nationalist rivalries.²⁸

In the end Japanese art enabled the spirit of an Asian universalism to survive the depredations of Japanese nationalistic imperialism. After Indian independence was achieved in 1947, Nandalal began to quietly and confidently celebrate the Indian countryside in his art creatively drawing on the Japanese *sumie* style. While it may be true to say that towards the end of his life he returned to his forte as a linearist, it would be an injustice to Nandalal's genius to dub him an 'Oriental' artist by accepting uncritically Roger Fry's early-twentieth-century dichotomy between the 'linearism' of Eastern art and the 'plasticity' of Western art.[29] Nandalal, the master of lines, was equally adept at plasticity and tone. But more than that, Nandalal's artistic imagination aspired to what historians and cultural critics have variously called a different universalism or a vernacular cosmopolitanism.[30]

The idea of Asia and the spirit of Asian universalism were in important ways products of cosmopolitan thought zones created by passages across the Indian Ocean. In this sense, the continent and the ocean were not necessarily in an adversarial relationship but provided different contours of interregional arenas animated by flows of ideas and culture. Benoy Kumar Sarkar, writing in the *Modern Review* in the 1910s, stressed the role of both sea lanes and land routes in creating what he called an 'Asia-sense'.[31] By the 1920s most contributors to the same journal were enamoured of the oceanic connections that spread Indian cultural influences to South East Asia. I have sought to make a distinction between two strands of cultural imperialism and a more generous universalism that shaped early-twentieth-century discourses on this subject. When Indian eyes were cast across the waters of the Indian Ocean, there was often one glaring blind spot that made another continent look dark. Nelson Mandela forgave Gandhi's early prejudices against Africans as belonging to an era before he became a Mahatma. Yet, it is hard not to be aware at the same time of a long afterlife of deeply imbibed racial biases. Of course, Indians were a divided lot when it came to attitudes towards Africa in the early twentieth century and remained so throughout the anti-apartheid struggle of the latter half of the twentieth century. In 1928 during an especially sordid display of racism by an Indian over admissions to Fort Hare College, it was Tagore who redeemed Indian honour. He wrote:

> Such colour prejudice from an Indian, who has himself suffered from the racial prejudice of the European, is to me revolting in the extreme. It is neither in accord with Indian sentiment, or with Indian National Honour and Civilization. Our only right to be in South Africa at all is that the native Africans, to whom the soil belongs, wish us to be there.

During the modern age it has been a constant struggle not to allow universalist aspirations of the colonized to degenerate into universalist boasts and cosmopolitanism to be replaced by bigotry. The tussle goes on in new postcolonial settings. The outcome is yet uncertain, but the ethical choice before us seems clear enough.

UNITY OR PARTITION: MAHATMA GANDHI'S LAST STAND, 1945–48*

'My dear Sarat,' Mahatma Gandhi wrote from Haridwar on 21 June 1947, to Subhas Chandra Bose's elder brother, 'I have a moment to myself here. I use it for writing two or three overdue letters. This is one to acknowledge yours of the 14th inst. The way to work for unity I have pointed out when the geographical [sic] is broken. Hoping you are all well. Love, Bapu.'[1]

Louis Mountbatten's partition plan announced on 3 June had shattered Gandhi's lifelong dream of a united and independent India. He did not agree with the Congress Working Committee's decision to accept it. He had 'done his best to get people to stand by' the Cabinet Mission plan for a federal India, but 'had failed'. He confessed on 8 June that he had been 'taken to task' for supporting Sarat Bose's scheme for a united sovereign Bengal, while acknowledging that Sarat was 'undoubtedly his friend' and they were in correspondence with each other. His erstwhile lieutenants now considered him 'a back number'. He asserted on 11 June that he was 'as much of Pakistan, as of Hindustan'. Having stated his difference with Congress leaders, he nevertheless asked the All India Congress Committee (AICC)

---

* The B.R. Nanda Memorial Lecture, New Delhi, 19 December 2014.

at its meeting on 14 and 15 June to swallow the unpalatable decision to partition. The AICC did, by 153 votes to 29.[2]

Even at the moment of his biggest political defeat, the indefatigable Mahatma would neither cede the moral high ground nor stop showing the way to work for unity. Already on 6 June he had urged the Union of India and Pakistan to vie with each other in doing well. 'If Pakistan did better,' he said, 'then the whole of India would be Pakistan, in which there would be neither majority nor minority, and all would be equal.' On 12 June he wondered if 'the readjustment of the geography of India' meant two nations. He admitted that the territorial division made the challenge of unity difficult. Yet he urged the soon-to-be citizens of free India to 'rise to the occasion and by their character and bravery, incorruptibility and toleration prove to the Muslims of Pakistan that in the Union there is no discrimination whatsoever on the ground of religion, caste or colour and that the only test is merit which every industrious citizen of the Union will have ample opportunity to acquire'. The 'real unity of India' depended on whether the shrines of Islam and Muslim seats of learning were honoured equally with the others, and Hindustani, 'a compatible mixture of Hindi and Urdu', had a future.[3]

The Partition of 1947 was not a tragedy foretold. As the Second World War drew to a close in 1945, efforts were under way to share power equitably once the British quit India. Even though the Gandhi–Jinnah talks of September 1944 had failed to achieve a breakthrough, the leaders of the Congress and the Muslim League in the central legislative assembly—Bhulabhai Desai and Liaquat Ali Khan—produced a formula in early 1945 for their respective parties to have an equal number of seats—40 per cent each—in an interim government. The Simla conference of June 1945 foundered on Jinnah's insistence that the League should be allowed to nominate all the Muslim representatives. Gandhi drew an important distinction between religious communities and political parties. 'You will quite unconsciously, but equally surely,' he wrote to Archibald Wavell, 'defeat the purpose of the conference if parity between Caste-Hindus and Muslims is unalterable. Parity between the Congress and the League is understandable.'[4]

The Congress was at this stage demoralized, its leaders recently released from detention unsure about how to rekindle the freedom struggle that had been ruthlessly suppressed in 1942. At such a moment of uncertainty the Indian National Army (INA) appeared before the country and the Indian National Congress as a godsend. In September 1945 the AICC resolved that it would be 'a tragedy if these officers, men and women, were punished for the offence of having laboured, however mistakenly, for the freedom of India'.[5] The Congress formed a defence committee led by Bhulabhai Desai and Tej Bahadur Sapru and invited other parties to join it. Once the trial of Prem Kumar Sahgal, Gurbaksh Singh Dhillon and Shah Nawaz Khan began at the Red Fort in November 1945, political parties and religious communities united in a popular movement against the hubris of the British Raj. It was during the height of the Red Fort trial that Mahatma Gandhi forged a new intimate relationship with Bengal and began the process of acquiring his Bengali identity.

On his visit to Bengal in December 1945 Gandhi's first port of call was naturally Tagore's abode of peace. 'True monuments to the great,' he declared in Santiniketan, 'are not statues of marble or bronze or gold. The best monument is to adorn and enlarge their legacy.' In Calcutta he paid homage to his rebellious son Subhas in the bedroom of the Elgin Road home from where he had made his great escape in 1941. Gandhi was in Midnapore on 3 January 1946, when news came that the Red Fort three, who had been sentenced to deportation for life on 31 December 1945, had been released. These Hindu, Muslim and Sikh soldiers of freedom came from Punjab, but the INA had undermined the British separation of martial and non-martial races and had large numbers of Tamils in its ranks. Gandhi urged the INA soldiers he met in Madras to follow the lead of the Congress. On 10 February 1946, he decided to revive his journal, *Harijan*, after a gap of three and a half years. One of his first articles published on 12 February addressed the question of unity. 'Netaji's name,' Gandhi wrote, 'is one to conjure with. His patriotism is second to none. His bravery shines through all his actions. He aimed high but failed. But who has not failed? Ours is to aim high and to aim well . . . The lesson that Netaji and his army brings to us is one of self-sacrifice, unity—irrespective of class and community—and discipline.' He urged Indians to 'rigidly copy this trinity of virtues' and 'rigidly abjure all violence'.[6]

Netaji, Gandhi told the military men who came to visit him in Uruli Kanchan in March 1946, had 'rendered a signal service to India by giving the Indian soldier a new vision and a new ideal'. The Mahatma initially harboured a hope that Netaji would return to join him in the work for unity. On 30 March 1946, Gandhi explained in the *Harijan* his earlier 'feeling that Netaji could not leave us until his dreams of swaraj had been fulfilled'. 'To lend strength to this feeling,' he added, 'was the knowledge of Netaji's great ability to hoodwink his enemies and even the world for the sake of his cherished goal.' His 'instinct' had suggested to him 'Netaji was alive'. He now could no longer rely on 'such unsupported feeling' as there was 'strong evidence to counteract the feeling'. 'In the face of these proofs,' the Mahatma wrote, 'I appeal to everyone to forget what I have said and, believing in the evidence before them, to reconcile themselves to the fact that

Netaji has left us. All man's ingenuity is as nothing before the might of the one God. He alone is Truth and nothing else stands.'[7]

The ideal of unity that Netaji had instilled in his followers remained alive. On his return to Delhi in early April 1946 Gandhi visited INA prisoners in Kabul Lines and the Red Fort. He was told that they had never felt any distinction of creed or religion in the INA. 'But here we are faced with "Hindu tea" and "Muslim tea",' they complained. 'Why do you suffer it?' Gandhi asked. 'No, we don't,' they said. 'We mix "Hindu tea" and "Muslim tea" exactly half and half, and then serve. The same with food.' 'That is very good,' exclaimed Gandhi laughing.[8]

At the height of the non-cooperation and Khilafat movements in the early 1920s Gandhi had not dined together with even his closest political comrades, Shaukat and Mohamed Ali. Eating, he had said, was one of the privately performed sanitary practices of life and the Ali brothers were indulgent of his 'bigotry', if his 'self-denial could be so named'.[9] On the matter of inter-dining he had happily changed with the times. He was nostalgic about the euphoria of the common political struggle a quarter of a century ago. 'The Ali brothers and I used to go all over the country together like blood brothers,' he recalled on 6 April 1946. 'We spoke with one voice, and we delivered the message of Hindu–Muslim unity and *swaraj* to the masses.' The climax of the joint movement had been reached in Delhi where Swami Shradhanand addressed a gigantic gathering of Hindus and Muslims in the Jama Masjid. 'It was a glorious day in India's history,' Gandhi declared, 'the memory of which we shall always treasure.'[10] Gandhi knew that the Muslim masses, by and large, had not been enthused by his civil disobedience and Quit India movements of the early 1930s and 1942. The remembrance of the early 1920s' *satyagraha* and the example of the INA became recurring features of his discourses on unity.

The Mahatma was in Delhi to hold talks with the Cabinet Mission that had recently arrived in India. By the spring of 1946 the British had reckoned that their hold on India was no longer tenable. The issue now was not whether the British could be forced to quit but rather how power was to be distributed among communities and regions upon British withdrawal. Gandhi's relevance to the Congress as a leader of mass movements diminished as soon as it was clear that the colonial masters had read the writing on the wall and were making up their mind to depart. However, he had not yet been completely elbowed aside. He was present in Simla in early May during the tripartite talks among the British, the Congress and the League to try and reach a constitutional settlement. 'You have achieved a complete unity among the Hindus, Muslims, Parsis, Christians, Anglo-Indians and Sikhs in your ranks,' Gandhi told sixty senior INA officers who came to see him in Simla. That was 'no mean achievement' outside India and he urged them to keep that spirit of unity alive under Indian conditions.[11] Unity, however, eluded the Congress and League leaders who had gathered in Simla and the talks broke down on 12 May 1946.

The Cabinet Mission was then left with no option but to issue a statement on 16 May based on the lowest common denominator of the Congress and League positions, proposing a three-tiered federal constitutional structure based on three groups of provinces. Gandhi had suggested to Stafford Cripps on 8 May that grouping was 'really worse than Pakistan'.[12] After a careful perusal of the 16 May statement he rose above the usual nationalist suspicion of British perfidy to give a more measured opinion on 20 May. It was, according to him, 'the best document the British could have produced under the circumstances'. The possible infringement of provincial autonomy by the groups posed a potential problem.

For example, could the North West Frontier Province be bundled into group B dominated by Punjab or Assam into group C against their will? In Gandhi's interpretation, the provinces were free to join groups on terms attractive to them and were not being ordered to do so. His message to those worried by the grouping proposal and arbitrary assignment to groups was that there was 'not the slightest cause for perturbation'.[13]

Grouping of provinces in the Muslim-majority sections B and C was of the essence for the Muslim League which had given up the demand for a fully sovereign Pakistan on that assurance. Even though both the Congress and the League formally accepted the Cabinet Mission proposal in June, Jawaharlal Nehru's statement on 11 July, after taking over from Maulana Azad as Congress president, that grouping may not last unnerved the League. With Jinnah calling for 'direct action' to achieve the League's demand for Pakistan, Calcutta exploded in violence on 16 August 1946, and sporadic killings gripped Bombay in September. 'When will this orgy of madness end?' Gandhiji asked in anguish on his seventy-seventh birthday on 2 October 1946. 'Killings in Calcutta, and stabbings in Dacca, Agra, Ahmedabad and Bombay.' Tagore's song 'Jiban jakhan shukaye jay karunadharay esho' had never sounded more poignant—'When life is parched up, come with a shower of mercy'. Days later in an article titled 'Hindu Pani and Muslim Pani' Gandhi wrote:

> A stranger travelling in Indian trains may well have a painful shock, when he hears at railway stations for the first time in his life ridiculous sounds about *pani*, tea and the like, being either Hindu or Muslim.

Even as late as September 1946 Gandhi had believed that violence was lodged in 'the hearts of a handful of townspeople' and that as a villager he was 'one with the ocean of Indian humanity'.[14] The eruption of violence in the rural backwaters of Noakhali in the second week of October 1946 came as a rude shock, ensuring that the Bengal countryside became the venue of one of his most challenging experiments with truth.

Noakhali and neighbouring Tippera were Muslim-majority districts in the vortex of an economic crisis marked by sluggish jute prices and skyrocketing food prices. Credit relations between mostly Hindu moneylender-landlords and Muslim peasants were in a state of disrepair and Hindu traders were hated for their callous role in the famine of 1943. Demobilized ex-servicemen supplied an additional volatile element in a tense setting. Ghulam Sarwar, a former member of the legislative assembly who had lost to the Muslim League candidate in the recent provincial elections, led the attacks in quasi-military fashion against the vulnerable Hindu minority. Unlike earlier agrarian disturbances of the depression decade, there were murders, abductions of women, and forced conversions on a large scale.[15] It was 'the cry of the outraged womanhood' that had especially called Mahatma Gandhi to Noakhali. Even before he could reach Bengal, however, terrible violence was unleashed on the Muslim minority in Bihar. 'Is it nationalism,' Gandhi asked in indignation, 'to seek barbarously to crush the fourteen per cent of the Muslims in Bihar?'[16] He did not, however, interrupt his journey to Noakhali. The apostle of non-violence was destined to follow the trail of violence, putting out the embers after the fires had done their destruction and supplying a healing touch to those who had been singed by its flames.

On his arrival in east Bengal Gandhi fondly remembered his first visit to this region in the company of the Ali brothers during the non-cooperation movement. This time he had come 'not as a Congressman, but as a servant of God'. He told the beleaguered Hindu minority that the Muslims were 'blood of our blood and bone of our bone'. He sought complete identification with the Bengali people. 'I claim to be an Indian,' he asserted, 'and, therefore, a Bengali, even as I am a Gujarati.' Once he settled down to live in the village of Srirampur from 20 November 1946, he diligently took lessons in learning Bengali before the crack of dawn. He explained why he had made himself a Bengali. Bengal had produced not just Tagore and Bankim, but also, as he put it, 'the heroes of the Chittagong Armoury Raid, however misguided their action might have been in my eyes'.[17] He could not understand how there could be cowardice in a province with that lineage. Bengal might still solve the problem facing all of India.

Based in remote Noakhali, Gandhi consistently argued in favour of provincial rights. He admitted that Bose had been right in contending in 1939 that Assam was a special case and that the Gopinath Bardoloi ministry should not resign along with the other provincial governments. 'We look to the Congress,' Gandhi pointed out, 'and then we feel that if we do not follow it slavishly, something will go wrong with it. I have said that not only a province but even an individual can rebel against the Congress and, by doing so, save it.' The Mahatma had come a long way from imposing the discipline of the high command on provincial units. It was incumbent on the Congress and the League to make their policy 'appeal to the reason of the recalcitrant province or groups'.[18]

Between 7 January and 2 March 1946, Mahatma Gandhi undertook a 116-mile pilgrimage on foot through forty-seven villages of Noakhali and Tippera. Manu Gandhi sang his favourite hymn 'Vaishnava Janato' at the early morning prayers on the day he set out on his journey. At Bapu's suggestion the word Vaishnava would occasionally be replaced with Muslim and Isai during the singing of the chorus. In addition to bringing solace to those who had suffered, Gandhi candidly held forth on burning social and political questions of the day. On 20 January he reached the village of Shirandi where Amtus Salam was on the twenty-fourth day of her fast for the cause of Hindu–Muslim unity. He extracted a written pledge from Muslim leaders to maintain peace in the locality before advising her to break the fast with a sip of orange juice and to the chant of Koranic verses. The cause of communal riots, he bluntly said, was 'the idiocy of both the communities'. Five thousand people gathered to hear him on 22 January at Paniala, which had hosted an intercommunity dinner a few weeks ago. At Dalta on 23 January the Chowdhuris of the village gifted him the plot of land on which his prayer meeting was held. He was glad that on the auspicious birthday of Netaji he had received this gift and had the privilege of staying at the home of a Scheduled Caste friend, Rai Mohan Mali. He reminded his audience that Netaji was 'an Indian first and last' and that 'he fired all under him with the same zeal, so that they forgot in his presence all distinctions and acted as one man'. Bose had 'in his life verified the saying of Tulsidas that all becomes right for the brave'. The next day at Muraim Gandhi stayed in the house of Habibullah Patwari and addressed the largest gathering of his tour. In Kamalapur in Tippera on 21 February Gandhi was asked point-blank whether he, who had been advocating inter-caste marriages, also favoured inter-religious marriages. He honestly answered that there was a time when he had not done so, but had quite a while ago decided that 'an inter-religious marriage was a welcome event, whenever it took place'. It had to be based on 'mutual friendship, either party having equal respect for the religion of the other'.[19]

Gandhi devoted the month of March 1947 to the service of those who had suffered grievously in Bihar. As he moved from Bengal to Bihar, he disdainfully declined an urgent invitation to attend a

Congress Working Committee meeting in Delhi, saying 'that was not within his present beat'. On his arrival in Patna on 5 March, he stated categorically that what the Hindus of Bihar had done to the Muslims was 'infinitely worse' than the horrors in Noakhali.[20] Accompanied by Khan Abdul Ghaffar Khan, he visited ruined Muslim homes and asked Hindus to atone for their sins in the land of Tulsidas's *Ramcharitmanas*. No sooner had Gandhi started to restore some calm in Bihar than news came of the violence that had engulfed Punjab.

On Christmas Eve 1946, the young B.R. Nanda had sat sipping hot tea at a crowded table in Lorangs in Lahore. 'The crowded road, the thronged restaurant, the rippling laughter of pretty women in prettier clothes,' he recorded, 'this was the customary life of the gay town of Lahore.' He chatted with a Muslim friend about the Great Calcutta Killing, the Noakhali tragedy and the Bihar frenzy and they expressed satisfaction that their own province continued to be at peace. The 'Punjabi character', his friend claimed, was averse to the kind of hatred that appeared to have taken root in eastern India. Nanda made an accurate forecast that the tranquillity would last only as long as the Khizar Hayat Khan coalition government managed to stay in office.[21] In the eyewitness account he wrote in December 1947 titled *Punjab Uprooted*, he held Clement Attlee or rather the prime minister's 20 February statement to be directly responsible for the outbreak of the Punjab disturbances in March 1947.[22] It may have been more accurate to blame the responses of the Hindu Mahasabha, the Congress, the League and the Akali Dal to Attlee's declaration that the British would quit by June 1948 at the latest. The Mahasabha was the first off the mark, demanding the partition of Punjab and Bengal. Nehru followed suit. The Khizar government fell on 2 March. With Gandhi away in Bihar, the Congress Working Committee passed a momentous resolution on 8 March 1947, calling for the partition of Punjab. Nehru explained that the principle of partition might have to be extended to Bengal as well.[23]

At the very end of March Gandhi eventually came to Delhi and met Mountbatten. On 1 April he told the delegates to the Asian Relations Conference being held in the Purana Quila that he was in the capital as the viceroy's prisoner and Nehru's prisoner. He lamented that Indians did not know how to maintain peace. Speaking at the concluding session the next day, he expressed his embarrassment at the shameful carnage unfolding before their very eyes and begged the visitors from abroad to 'not carry the memory of that carnage beyond the confines of India'. Living among the Dalits of the city, Gandhi preached the message of peace. His prayer services typically included Koranic verses along with excerpts from other religious scriptures. When one or two members of the audience objected to the recitation from the Koran, Gandhi altogether refused to hold the prayers. He was prepared to die cheerfully with the name of Ram and Rahim on his lips. As a *sanatani* Hindu, he claimed to be a Christian, a Buddhist and a Muslim at the same time. Taking a stand against religious conservatives on all sides, he declared that he saw no reason 'why he should not read the *kalma*, why he should not praise Allah and why he should not acclaim Muhammad as the Prophet'. At the level of high politics, Gandhi broached the idea of letting Jinnah head the first government of free India to Mountbatten in the second week of April. Unable to persuade Nehru and Sardar Patel, he left for Bihar in mid-April. Before doing so he signed with Jinnah a joint appeal that read as follows: 'We denounce for all time the use of force to achieve political ends, and we call upon the communities of India, to whatever persuasion they may belong, not only to refrain from acts of violence and disorder, but also to avoid both in speech and writing, any word which might be construed as an incitement to such acts.'[24]

Gandhi insisted that he had acted as a true Hindu in his efforts to befriend the Muslims. To his critics, he cited Iqbal's famous line: *'Mazhab nahin sikhata apas mein ber rakhna.'* In both Noakhali and Bihar his motto was 'do or die'. 'My non-violence,' he explained, 'bids me dedicate myself to the service of the minorities.' It was this sense of mission that called him back from Bihar to Delhi at the end of April to take part in a Congress Working Committee meeting and parleys with Mountbatten and Jinnah in the first week of May. 'I feel sure,' Gandhi wrote to Mountbatten on his departure from Delhi for Bihar on 8 May, 'that the partition of Punjab and Bengal is wrong in every case, and a needless irritant for the Muslim League.' Non-partition of these provinces did not mean that the minorities there were to be neglected. Gandhi informed the viceroy that he had spent 'a very pleasant two hours and three quarters with Quaid-e-Azam Jinnah' on 6 May. They had disagreed on Pakistan, but Jinnah had been 'agreeably emphatic' about his commitment to non-violence.[25]

Between 9 May and 14 May 1947, in Sodepur, Gandhi explored the possibility of keeping Bengal united in a series of interviews with Sarat Chandra Bose, Abul Hashim and Husain Shaheed Suhrawardy. Gandhi told Hashim on 10 May that he had been trying to become a Bengali. His main reason for learning Bengali was to be able to read Tagore's poems in the original. When Hashim professed that Hindus and Muslims alike revered the poet, Gandhi responded that the spirit of the Upanishads bound Tagore to the whole of Indian culture. What would Hashim have to say, he asked, if Bengal wished 'to enter into a voluntary association with the rest of India'? On 12 May Gandhi gave Suhrawardy an undertaking in writing that so long as the Muslim League leader showed sincerity and undertook to preserve Bengal for the Bengalis—Hindus and Mussalmans—the Mahatma was prepared to act as 'his honorary private secretary'. Having heard that the plan for a united, sovereign Bengal had received Gandhi's blessings, Syamaprasad Mukherjee rushed to Sodepur on 13 May. Gandhi wanted Mukherjee to evaluate the scheme on its merits. 'An admission that Bengali Hindus and Bengali Mussalmans were one,' Gandhi told the Mahasabha leader, 'would really be a severe blow against the two-nation theory of the League.'[26]

Sarat Bose sent a detailed draft of the United Bengal plan to Gandhi on 20 May. Bapu responded from Patna on 24 May suggesting that 'every act of Government must carry with it the cooperation of at least two-thirds of the Hindu members in the Executive and the Legislature' and that there should be 'an admission that Bengal has a common culture and common mother tongue—Bengali'. He promised to discuss the draft with the Congress Working Committee and to telephone or telegraph if Sarat's presence was needed in Delhi. The plan was refined further in light of Gandhi's comments and a final version sent to Mountbatten through the good offices of George Catlin, a British MP, who was a guest of Sarat Bose.[27] On 22 May Patel asked Sarat Bose to 'take a united stand' with the Congress leadership on the partition of Punjab and Bengal. Sarat Bose retorted on 27 May, saying 'the united stand should be for a united Bengal and a united India'.[28] On 28 May, Mountbatten recorded two alternative broadcasts in London—broadcast A was to be used if both Punjab and Bengal were to be partitioned, and broadcast B if it appeared probable that Bengal would remain unified under the auspices of a new coalition government.[29] Once Mountbatten returned to India on 30 May, Nehru and Patel vetoed the Bengali exception, and so it was that broadcast A went on the air on 3 June 1947.

At his prayer meetings between 29 May and 2 June Gandhi had maintained that if the Congress or the British went back on the letter and spirit of the Cabinet Mission's paper of 16 May 1946, 'it would be a breach of faith'.[30] When the Congress Working Committee met to ratify the 3 June Partition plan, Gandhi remonstrated with Nehru and Patel that they had not informed him of the partition scheme before committing themselves to it. With the exception of Gandhi, Khan Abdul Ghaffar Khan, Jai Prakash Narain and Ram Manohar Lohia, no one spoke a word against partition at that meeting. In a last throw of the dice Gandhi suggested that the Congress and the League should work out the modalities of the partition and Pakistan without further British assistance now that Congress had conceded the principle of the partition.[31] His voice went unheeded since all his yes-men had now turned into no-men.

Once 15 August 1947 was set as the date for independence, Gandhi expressed his desire to spend that day in Noakhali. He did, however, take a detour to Kashmir and Punjab in early August. In Srinagar he made clear his view that the future of Kashmir 'should be decided by the will of the Kashmiris'. On 6 August in Lahore he told Congress workers that he was going to spend the rest of his life in East Bengal or West Punjab or, may be, the North West Frontier Province. Once he reached Bengal, he abandoned his plan of going to Noakhali on 11 August to work for 'the return of sanity' to Calcutta, 'this premier city of India'. On 13 August he moved into a Muslim home in the Beliaghata neighbourhood of Calcutta in the company of Suhrawardy. To those who distrusted the Muslim League leader, he said that he had known Suhrawardy since the Faridpur political conference where Deshbandhu Chittaranjan Das had taken him in the era of non-cooperation. Ignoring the celebrations in New Delhi, Gandhi chose to spend Independence Day fasting and praying with those who were poor and obscure. The information and broadcasting department of the Government of India asked him for a message. The Father of the Nation simply said that 'he had run dry'.[32]

Peace and camaraderie reigned in Calcutta on 15 August 1947. In an editorial titled 'Miracle or Accident' on 16 August, the first anniversary of the Great Calcutta Killing, Gandhi narrated how Hindus were taken to masjids and Muslims to mandirs at the dawn of freedom and both communities shouted 'Jai Hind' in unison. It was neither miracle nor accident, but the willingness of human beings to dance to God's tune. 'We have drunk the poison of mutual hatred,' Gandhi wrote, 'and so this nectar of fraternization tastes all the sweeter, and the sweetness should never wear out.'[33] Nanda was right when he wrote that peace came to Bengal on 15 August 'through the bowl of a beggar who begged from the citizens of riot-torn Calcutta for a little mutual forgiveness and goodwill'. He wondered if Gandhi's presence in Lahore in mid-August might have saved Punjab.[34]

It was Eid on 18 August 1947. While Punjab descended into anarchy upon the announcement of Radcliffe's award the day before, Hindus and Muslims wished each other 'Eid Mubarak' in Calcutta. On 21 August Gandhi was happy to note that the Indian and Pakistani flags were being flown side by side at his prayer meeting.[35] During the non-cooperation movement Gandhi and Shaukat Ali had chosen three national slogans: 'Allah-hu-Akbar', 'Bande Mataram' and 'Hindu–Mussalman ki Jai'.[36] Gandhi was delighted that the last cry was being revived. On 23 August he described 'Allah-hu-Akbar' as 'a soul-stirring religious cry' that had a noble meaning and urged Hindus to utter the cry with their Muslim friends. 'Bande Mataram', according to Gandhi was 'a purely political cry'. Tagore had resolved the controversy over the song in 1937 and many Bengalis had sacrificed their lives with that cry on their lips. As 'Bande Mataram' was sung at the prayer meeting on 29 August, Suhrawardy and other Muslims on the stage stood up to show their respect along with the rest of the audience. Gandhi alone remained seated because he believed standing up as a mark of respect for a national song was an unnecessary Western import and not a requirement of Indian culture.[37]

Calcutta had a brief relapse into violence at the end of August and the beginning of September. It required a fast by the Mahatma from 1 to 4 September 1947 to bring the errant Calcuttans into line. 'Can you fast against the goondas?' C. Rajagopalachari had asked, seeking to dissuade Gandhi. 'It is we who make the goondas,' Gandhi had replied. Having restored tranquillity in Calcutta, he was ready to leave for Delhi en route to Punjab on 7 September. He wrote his farewell message to Bengal in Bengali: 'Amar Jibani Amar Bani' (My Life Is My Message).[38]

On 10 September Gandhi made a forty-mile tour of Delhi which, he said in a nationwide broadcast, 'looked like a city of the dead'. Two days later he visited the Jama Masjid, where 30,000 refugees had congregated, and the Purana Quila, that had been transformed from being the venue of an Asian international conference to a refugee camp for 50,000 helpless people. 'If India fails,' Gandhi warned, 'Asia dies.'[39] The spirit of revenge and retaliation that vitiated the atmosphere in Delhi mortified him. Nanda had an insight into why it was so difficult to curb the post-Partition lawlessness in Delhi and Punjab. 'Communal passion is a passing emotion,' Nanda noted astutely, 'the vested interest in property is more permanent. When the first wave of blind violence had passed in West Punjab, the lure of loot was the chief motive of violence; calculated homicide succeeded indiscriminate violence; it was no longer a fanatic's leap in the dark but an adventurer's firm foothold on a house, a shop, or a factory.'[40] More recently, Ayesha Jalal has depicted Partition violence in Punjab as not about religion as faith but a scramble over *zar* (wealth), *zameen* (land) and *zan* (women) in the region's patriarchal society amid the crumbling ruins of the British Raj. That is what made separating at close quarters a colossal human tragedy.[41] Gandhi had an inkling of what was really going on when he commented: 'Irreligion masquerades as religion.'[42]

After Pakistan and India went to war over Kashmir Gandhi reiterated that the people of Kashmir must decide their own future 'without any coercion or show of it from within or without'. The rajas and maharajas of the princely states could at most serve as trustees. Whispers had reached his ears that Kashmir could be divided along religious lines with Jammu for the Hindus and the Valley for the Muslims. He could not countenance 'such divided loyalties and splitting up of Indian states into so many parts'. It was in such a grim domestic and international scenario that the first AICC session in post-Independence India convened from 15 to 17 November. Acharya Kripalani resigned as Congress president citing differences with the government of the day. Gandhi would have preferred to see the veteran socialist Narendra Deva as Kripalani's successor, but others favoured Rajendra Prasad who took charge. Addressing the AICC in camera, Gandhi spoke some home truths. 'No Muslim in the Indian Union,' he told the leaders of the party and government, 'should feel his life unsafe.' During his post-prayer discourse on 21 November he noted that as many as 137 mosques in Delhi had been damaged and said that he regarded 'all such desecration as a blot upon Hinduism'. Noticing a lack of warmth in welcoming Muslims into the Congress, he asked them to serve the party from outside just as he was doing.[43]

On 12 January 1948 Mahatma Gandhi announced his momentous decision to start an indefinite fast to try and bring about a reunion of hearts among all communities. His reward would be 'regaining India's dwindling prestige and her fast fading sovereignty over the heart of Asia and, therethrough, the world'. As he commenced his fast, 'When I Survey the Wondrous Cross' was sung followed by recitations from the Koran and Guru Granth Sahib and Hindu devotional songs. This was no ordinary fast. It was designed to avert a catastrophe and to assert that no one had a right to say India belonged to only the majority community and 'the minority community can only remain there as the underdog'. The fast was for the Muslim minority in India and both against Hindus and Sikhs of India and Muslims of Pakistan. Having conceded Pakistan, Gandhi did not want the Government of India to be mean-spirited in the sharing of the assets of undivided India. Even though Patel had ceased to be his 'yes-man', he did not want him to be singled out for censure and insisted on the Cabinet's collective responsibility. On 15 January 1948 the Government of India released Rs 55 crore that it had withheld from Pakistan on account of the outbreak of hostilities over Kashmir. 'It ought to lead to an honourable settlement, not only of the Kashmir question,' Gandhi said the next day, 'but of all the differences between the two dominions. Friendship should replace the present enmity.' However, it was only after receiving an iron-clad written declaration signed by leaders of all the major organizations to restore goodwill among communities in Delhi and beyond that Gandhi broke his fast on 18 January. There had been reports of the Rashtriya Swayamsevak

Sangh (RSS) fomenting trouble in different parts of the country, including Kathiawar and Rajkot in the Mahatma's own Gujarat. Gandhi did not fail to remind the representatives of the Hindu Mahasabha and the RSS that they could not be indifferent to violence in places other than Delhi. 'It would be a fraud upon God,' he warned, 'if they did so.'[44]

Far away in Lake Success, New York, Pakistan's Foreign Minister Zafrullah Khan informed the United Nations Security Council that 'a new and tremendous feeling and desire for friendship between India and Pakistan' was 'sweeping the subcontinent in response to the fast'. Gandhi himself was glad to be released from his duty in Delhi to be able to travel to Pakistan. He broke the fast to the chanting and singing of Japanese, Muslim, Parsi, Christian and Hindu scriptures and hymns and the recitation of the ancient mantra:

Om asato ma sadgamaya
Tamaso ma jyotirgamaya
Mrityorma amritam gamaya

Lead me from untruth to truth
From darkness to light
From death to immortality.[45]

The final week of the Mahatma's life was rich with symbolism redolent of India's unity. On 23 January 1948 Gandhi was 'very glad' to take note of Bose's birthday, even though he 'generally did not remember such dates' and 'the deceased patriot believed in violence', while he was wedded to non-violence. Bose, according to the Mahatma, 'knew no provincialism nor communal differences' and 'had in his brave army men and women drawn from all over India without distinction and evoked affection and loyalty, which very few have been able to evoke'. A lawyer friend had requested Gandhi for a good definition of Hinduism. He did not have any, but suggested that 'Hinduism regarded all religions as worthy of all respect'. Bose, according to him, was 'such a Hindu' and so, 'in memory of that great patriot', he called upon his countrymen to 'cleanse their hearts of all communal bitterness'. For Gandhi's generation 26 January was Independence Day. 'Let us permit ourselves to hope,' he said on that occasion, 'that though geographically and politically India is divided into two, at heart we shall ever be friends and brothers helping and respecting one another and be one for the outside world.' The next day he was taken inside the sanctum sanctorum of Chishti's shrine in Mehrauli where he was anguished to see the damage to the exquisite marble screens. He had come to make a pilgrimage, not a speech, and simply urged Hindus, Muslims and Sikhs to 'never again listen to the voice of Satan and abandon the way of brotherliness and peace'.[46]

On the morning of 30 January 1948, Gandhi did not neglect to do his daily Bengali writing exercise even though he had other pressing work, such as drafting a new constitution for the Congress.[47] The sound of the shots fired at the Mahatma that evening by a Hindu fanatic echoed across the length and breadth of this great land. 'The last few months of Gandhiji's life and the manner of his death,' Nanda wrote, 'constituted an epic struggle between an all-embracing humanism and sectarian fanaticism.'[48]

A seventeen-year-old girl was attending an interregional and inter-caste wedding of a Bengali bride and Malayali groom in Calcutta that evening when she heard the stunning news that Gandhiji had been shot dead. She tried to persuade herself that it must be a rumour. A pall of gloom slowly descended on the gathering and the guests quietly departed. Returning home, she heard the radio playing the song 'Samukhe Shanti Parabar' as the great soul began his journey across the ocean of peace.[49] Sarat Bose loved English literature and Shakespeare as much as he had hated British rule. On receiving the heart-rending news that the Mahatma was no more, he remarked wistfully, 'When comes such another'—he might have added, if ever another.[50]

WHY JINNAH MATTERS

On the death of Mohammed Ali Jinnah in September 1948 an Indian political leader paid him a rare, fulsome tribute describing him as 'one who was great as a lawyer, once great as a Congressman, great as a leader of Muslims, great as a world politician and diplomat and, greatest of all, as a man of action'. Despite having serious differences with the Quaid-e-Azam, Sarat Chandra Bose recalled that Jinnah, initially along with Mahatma Gandhi, once lent support to a last-ditch attempt to prevent Bengal's partition along religious lines.

On 8 March 1947 the Congress led by Jawaharlal Nehru and Vallabhbhai Patel passed a formal resolution calling for the partition of Punjab. It went against all the principles the Congress had stood for—at least since 1929, when in Lahore India's premier nationalist party had demanded a united and independent India. The then Congress president Nehru explained that even though the resolution mentioned only Punjab, Bengal too may have to be partitioned. Partition seemed to be a price worth paying for untrammelled power at a strong centre. Gandhi sought an explanation from his erstwhile lieutenants, but was elbowed aside.

As one Bengali paper put it, the Congress as much as the Hindu Mahasabha, beset by George Curzon's ghost, was ready to raise the matricidal Parashuram's axe to slice the motherland into two. The partition of the provinces of Punjab and Bengal at Nehru and Patel's behest, much like the partition of the province of Ulster in Ireland, permanently skewed subcontinental politics and left a poisoned postcolonial legacy. The refusal of the Congress high command to entertain a serious discussion on provincial rights also meant that the party's Muslim supporters in the North West Frontier Province led by the Frontier Gandhi, Khan Abdul Ghaffar Khan, were thrown to the wolves. History is a matter of interpretation and debate based on historical evidence; it is not a matter of opinion. While there may still be different points of view on the relative balance of forces that led to Partition, and Jinnah is by no means blameless in this regard, the role of Congress majoritarianism in shaping the final outcome of August 1947 has been well accepted in the best historical scholarship. South Asian historical writing has shed its statist biases and reached a certain level of maturity and sophistication in the last few decades. South Asian political discourse on historical figures and issues, by contrast, has remained utterly puerile six decades after Independence.

India was fortunate to possess a galaxy of great political leaders in the pre-Independence era with extraordinary accomplishments and all-too-human failings. Even those with magnificent contributions committed Himalayan blunders at crucial turning points of history. We do them no justice and fail to learn from their exemplary lives by replacing biography with iconography.

The reaction of the major political parties and a state government to the Bharatiya Janata Party's former external affairs minister Jaswant Singh's healthy predilection for historical interpretation over political deification is cause for some concern about the quality of our nationalism and democracy. The apparent need of our political class to continue demonizing the founding father of Pakistan reveals a sense of insecurity that sits uneasily with the self-confidence to which India could legitimately aspire. One can only hope that the political leaders are out of sync with the majority of the young population of this country.

The controversy over Jaswant Singh's book on Jinnah[1] where he held that the Congress was more responsible for Partition than the Quaid-e-Azam has also brought into sharp focus the strengths and weaknesses of India's democracy. The major strength is revealed in the vigorous public discussion of the issue in the print and electronic media. The key weakness is evident in the lack of genuine inner-party democracy and an anti-intellectual attitude that refuses to tolerate any expression of dissent. A particular political party's wish to self-destruct may to some extent be regarded as its own business. But resorting to an archaic law to ban a book affects the entire citizenry. The stance of both the major parties in Gujarat is unworthy of the region which gave birth to Gandhi and Jinnah.

I am not in agreement with those who say that the parties are obsessed with a non-issue, sixty-two years out of date. The issue which revisiting Partition brings to the fore is full of contemporary relevance. It is the search for a substantive rather than procedural democracy that protects citizens from majoritarian arrogance and ensures justice in a subcontinent where people have multiple identities.

Majoritarianism, whether in secular or saffron garb, continues to be a potential threat to Indian democracy. Regional rights were once thought to be a counterpoise to the anti-democratic tendencies of an over-centralized state. Regional parties run by petty and insecure dictators are proving to be as ruthless as the all-India parties in the suppression of internal dissent. In such a scenario freedom of speech and expression remains the best guarantee of the future of Indian democracy.

Fortunately, this freedom has deep roots in history. The political parties in pursuit of their narrow interests and short-term electoral advantages have set themselves squarely against India's long and weighty argumentative tradition. They are, therefore, bound to lose.

TRACK RECORD OF INDIA'S DEMOCRACY

'Like 1757 and 1857,' Ramachandra Guha writes in a forgivable overstatement, '1957 was also a year of momentous importance in the history of modern India.' That year the Indian republic held its second general elections, proving that the 1952 experiment had not been a flash in the pan. The regularity of a reference to the people on which political formation should rule India was now firmly established. The communist victory in the state of Kerala signalled the first successful regional electoral challenge to the Congress party's dominance at the Centre. The storm in Parliament over the investments of the Life Insurance Corporation of India in the firm of Haridas Mundhra gave the country its first full-blown financial scandal and an early indication of political corruption seeping steadily into the body politic.

Choosing 'the more primitive techniques of the narrative historian' over 'the methods of statistical social science', Guha gives us a lucid and lively chronicle of independent India's adventurous engagement with democracy. His choice of

---

Review of Ramachandra Guha, *India after Gandhi: The History of the World's Largest Democracy* (Picador, 2007).

techniques is fully vindicated in a book that is from beginning to end a genuine pleasure to read. With an eye for detail and a knack for finding the most telling anecdotes, Guha presents a grand panorama of the unfolding of sixty years of India's political history. It is a book worthy of a diamond jubilee.

In giving an overall assessment of the track record of India's democracy, Guha borrows a line from the Hindi comic actor Johnny Walker: '*Boss, phipty-phipty.*' The 'hardware' of democracy in the form of elections and a free media looks to be in pretty good shape. Its 'software', by contrast, has been infected and corrupted by viruses of the dynastic and criminal assortments. Presented with a spectacle of a glass half-empty and half-full, Guha is nevertheless prepared to raise a toast to India's half-impressive achievement.

The 50 per cent rate of success seems especially remarkable in the context of predictions by a motley array of Western doomsayers whom Guha sets up as straw men to be systematically demolished. The book opens with an unwarranted pessimistic premise about the prospects of Indian democracy and unity after 1947. Had the author turned in a serious fashion to consider India's precolonial and anti-colonial political thought and practice, such lowly expectations would have been dispelled. India has a long and rich history of the ethics of good governance and the ideal of uniting without destroying the autonomy of its many peoples. The 50 per cent rate of failure had much to do with independent India turning its back on that history in an ill-judged decision to rely on the instruments of an over-centralized state inherited from the colonial masters.

Both individuals and institutions are prominent actors in Guha's dramatic story. India's first prime minister was a majestic man prone to committing Himalayan blunders. Carried away by his starry-eyed admiration for Jawaharlal Nehru, the author seeks to throw a cloak of Teflon over the shoulders of his hero. Yet the Nehru jacket does not remain wholly unstained. Even if we leave out of account his foibles before Independence, the architect of India's parliamentary democracy equated communists and federalists with terrorists in the late 1940s, let the Gandhian Potti Sriramulu die of starvation in 1952, threw his friend Sheikh Abdullah into prison in 1953, turned a blind eye to human rights violations in Nagaland in 1956, acquiesced in the dismissal of Kerala's duly elected state government in 1959 and led India into a military debacle against China in 1962. Why should we consider his decision to release Abdullah in 1964 to be more significant than his resolve to incarcerate him for more than a decade? The only justification for doing so would be to persuade the custodians of Nehru's papers to let scholars and the public know the terms on which the ailing prime minister was prepared to solve the Kashmir riddle.

In answering the question why India has survived as a democracy and a unified entity, Guha gives much credit to a colonial institution—the much vaunted Indian Civil Service (ICS). It is well known that after Independence Nehru and Sardar Patel both embraced the bureaucracy they had castigated as being antithetical to democracy in the days of the anti-colonial struggle. Patel made somewhat better use of the steel frame of the Raj in integrating the princely states with the Indian Union. The civil service doubtless contained some very able individuals. Sukumar Sen, the chief election commissioner during the first two general elections, was, as Guha points out, an ICS man. Yet Guha refuses to recognize the extent to which the Congress party's marriage of convenience with the bureaucracy transformed Nehruvian socialism into a stifling form of statism. India's political economy has been breaking free of those shackles only since 1991.

Guha is as critical of Indira Gandhi as he is enamoured of her father. Nehru's 'halting yet honest attempts to promote a democratic ethos' were, in Guha's view, 'undone by his own daughter, and in decisive and dramatic ways'. The authoritarian streak in Indira Gandhi, clearly on display during the years of the Emergency, is well known. But in the 1969–73 period she had widened and deepened the democratic social base of the Congress party and in so doing had revived its electoral fortunes. The broad social coalition she conjured up in Uttar Pradesh, for example, has been only partially replicated recently by Mayawati, albeit under Dalit rather than Brahmin leadership. It is a trifle unfair to see Indira Gandhi's adviser P.N. Haksar's leftism as purely ideological and hers as crassly pragmatic, if not cynical.

In Guha's temporal scheme India in the first two post-Independence decades was a constitutional democracy, while in the last two decades it has become a populist one. The middle two decades, therefore, constitute the era of this transition. The book is much more engaging on the first rather than the second thirty-year time span. One reason for this is that it moves, by Guha's own admission, from history to 'historically informed journalism'. But there is also a second reason. As a self-professed liberal, Guha invests greater emotional and intellectual effort in his imagined golden age of constitutional democracy. He is not entirely oblivious of the oligarchical nature of Nehruvian democracy relying on provincial party bosses to bring in the vote. He recognizes India's gravest political failures to have been in the domains of education and health. He quotes B.V. Krishnamurti, a lecturer in Bombay, who noted the allocation for primary education in the Second Plan was 'absurdly low' in light of the constitutional obligation to provide free and compulsory education to all children up to the age of fourteen. But Guha is unable to squarely face the fact that the roots of India's biggest failures lay in the pathetic lack of public action in the heyday of constitutional democracy.

Guha's nostalgia, however, is not entirely misplaced. He is right in noting 'a rapid, even alarming decline in the quality of the men and women who rule India'. There is one major difference between 1947 and 2007. On 15 August 2007, members of India's political class will all be in celebratory mode. Sixty years ago Mahatma Gandhi had stayed away from the celebrations in New Delhi to quietly mourn the human tragedy of Partition in a Muslim neighbourhood of Calcutta. India after Gandhi has sorely missed the presence of a great soul prepared to abjure the lights of the capital to light up the darkness engulfing the lives of those who are poor and obscure.

LIMITS OF LIBERALISM

With *Recovering Liberties*, C.A. Bayly has made yet another magnificent and magisterial contribution to modern South Asian history. This book boldly opens up a conceptual domain for a new history of ideas that is global in scope and genuinely comparative and connective in its method.

In an earlier work, *Origins of Nationality in South Asia*, Bayly had offered keen insights into diverse forms of precolonial patriotism that connoted a link between land and people without the land being too closely delimited.[1] Love for regional homelands, often termed *watan* or *desh* in Indian languages, drew on both affective bonds informed by the languages of devotional religion and rational doctrines about legitimacy and good governance. The concept of space in precolonial patriotism could be simultaneously finite and infinite, restrictive and expansive. The name 'Hindustan' for India could, for instance, refer to the north Indian Gangetic plain or to the whole of the subcontinent with fuzzy boundaries. Precolonial patriotism was one of the sources of modern Indian nationalism.

'To imagine a society, even a nation,' Bayly contends in *Recovering Liberties*, 'one has to imagine other societies and other

---

C.A. Bayly, *Recovering Liberties: Indian Thought in the Age of Liberalism and Empire* (Cambridge University Press, 2012).

nations; to imagine a liberal order one must see it displayed, or denied, in the world.'² For Bayly, liberalism was not just the intellectual field in which nationalism took root but spoke more broadly to Indians' understanding of the modern world. In making his case, he has not so much decentred liberalism as liberated it from the narrow north European and negative contexts into which it has typically been confined. The book is strongest in interpreting Indian participation in the global liberal moment that stretched from the 1810s to the 1830s. Bayly might have further excavated the precolonial roots of Indian liberalism that would buttress his important point about the Indian espousal of liberalism being a conjunctural rather than a derivative phenomenon. His acknowledgement that Euro-American liberalism 'came to be grounded in, and modified by, pre-existing Indian discourses of virtue and good government' at the end of chapter 1 is too quickly overtaken by his formulation on the 'advent of liberalism in India' that forms the title of chapter 2.³

Bayly refuses to subscribe to the view that a brief liberal conjuncture in the early nineteenth century was swept aside by the onset of an authoritarian, colonial modernization of the Victorian era. He insists that Indian intellectuals believed they could 'rewrite the liberal discourse so as to strip it of its coercive colonial features'. In recasting liberalism as their own, Indians kept their distance from 'the utilitarianism and rationalism of the British variety' and were 'closer to the liberalism of France, Spain or Italy, or to American republicanism'.⁴ In the latter half of the nineteenth century South Asian intellectuals engaged with Auguste Comte's evolutionary humanism, Friedrich List's notion of national political economy and Giuseppe Mazzini's republican radicalism. If the engagement with Mazzini is to provide a window into the mind of late-nineteenth-century

Indian thinkers, it is important to ask whether they considered the Italian prophet to be a liberal. The 'L' word does not appear to figure in eulogistic life histories of Mazzini by Surendranath Banerjea in his speech to the Uttarpara Hitakari Sabha of 1876 or by Lala Lajpat Rai twenty years later.[5] Gandhi wrote a eulogy to Mazzini on his birth centenary in 1905 in *Indian Opinion*, but also pointed out in *Hind Swaraj* that 'India can fight like Italy only when she has arms'. He worried that to arm India on a large scale would be to Europeanize it.[6] Should the Indian fascination with the challenges faced by Italy of foreign rule and internal difference, and their overcoming through Mazzinian suffering and sacrifice be interpreted as the embracing by Indians of a southern European variant of liberalism?

Bayly correctly notes that Indian liberals were drawn to the religions of humanity espoused by Saint Simon, Comte and Mazzini.[7] Yet the humanistic religion that attracted Indian intellectuals did not draw on nineteenth-century European liberalism alone. With whom was Mazzini being compared? 'You must live in a high and holy atmosphere,' Banerjea told the youth of Bengal, 'fragrant with the breath of the gods. Burke, Mazzini, Jesus Christ, Buddha, Mohamed, Chaitanya, Ram Mohun Roy, Keshub Chunder Sen, must be your constant companions. Your souls must be attuned to the pathos and the music of *Bande-Matarama*.'[8] Between 1896 and 1898 Lala Lajpat Rai published five Urdu biographies in a series titled 'Great Men of the World'. The five were Mazzini, Garibaldi, Shivaji, Swami Dayanand and Sri Krishna.[9] The company that Mazzini was being made to keep might be cause for some doubt about any easy congruence between liberalism and religious universalism even though the two were undoubtedly tied in an intricate relationship missed by many scholars of European liberalism. There is a comparative evaluation of Mazzini and Shivaji by Lajpat Rai that might rescue Bayly's claim about late-nineteenth-century Indian liberalism. Lajpat Rai found Mazzini and also Washington to be 'more laudable' than Shivaji and was not prepared to admit that Shivaji had really established 'Swarajya'. 'Swarajya means,' he wrote, 'Government by the people and not by a sovereign.'[10]

Even if we accept Mazzini as a liberal and his Indian admirers as liberals, there was no shortage of contemporary critics of the latter. B.B. Majumdar followed up his chapter on the 'liberal school of political thought' with an equally detailed chapter on 'critics of the liberal thought'.[11] Many of them supported the principle of sovereignty as espoused by precolonial emperors. Qualitative changes in the exercise of sovereignty and power between 1857 and 1877 ensured that critics of the liberal thought were not to be limited to a handful of Bengalis or intellectuals from western India. The desacralization and deportation of the last Mughal emperor, Bahadur Shah Zafar, in 1858 necessitated the search for a Khalifa (Caliph) beyond the borders of Hind. This quest of Indian Muslims would receive dramatic support from Mahatma Gandhi between 1919 and 1922. Between 1907 and 1909 Veer Savarkar in his pre-Hindutva phase had no difficulty in spending his time in England writing a Marathi translation of the life of Mazzini and eulogizing the martyrs of the 1857 revolt at the same time.[12] In another colony, Vietnam, the revolutionary monarchism of Phan Boi Chau contended with the republican liberalism of Phan Chau Trinh in the same decade. The late nineteenth century and the turn of the twentieth century may have been characterized by lively debates about liberalism in Indian political thought, but may not have been unproblematically 'the age of liberalism'.

How far can we extend the temporal scope of Bayly's liberal conjuncture? Bayly claims that liberalism 'remained the dominant sensibility in India through to 1916'.[13] Already from the 1890s there were attempts in Indian political thought to light new lamps in place of the old lamp of liberalism lit from the flame of humanistic religion. In the Swadeshi conjuncture of 1905 a compelling and intellectually sophisticated critique was offered of the abstract nature of late-nineteenth-century liberal nationalism. Bipin Chandra Pal wrote of the new patriotism in India which was different from the period when Pym, Hampden, Mazzini, Garibaldi, Kossuth and Washington were 'the models of young India'. The old patriotism 'panted for the realities of Europe and America only under an Indian name'. 'We loved the abstraction we called India,' Pal wrote, 'but, yes, we hated the thing that it actually was.' But the new patriotism was based on 'a love, as Tagore put it . . . for the muddy weed-entangled village lanes, the moss-covered stinking village ponds, and for the poor, the starved, the malaria-stricken peasant populations of the country, a love for its languages, its literatures, its philosophies, its religions; a love for its culture and civilization'.[14] Pal's contemporary, Aurobindo Ghose, found the sources of an ethical polity infused with elements of federalism and democracy in India's precolonial past while deploring the mechanical turn of the centralized modern European nation-state.[15] It is a mistake, however, to characterize the Swadeshi movement and the 1919 uprisings as 'nativistic'.[16] What one finds in the early twentieth century is a sharper critical perspective on all the variants of European liberalism without abandoning the search for universalisms in easterly (Asian), westerly (Islamic) and northerly (Soviet) directions.

Bayly's broadening of the definition of liberalism to include its southern and central European variants enables a fresh interpretation of Indian political and economic ideas in the nineteenth century. Yet to stretch the age of liberalism into the twentieth century, he expands its meaning a little too liberally. This move enables him to save Hindu political figures, such as Madan Mohan Malaviya and Lala Lajpat Rai, whom he describes as 'spiritualized' or 'communitarian' liberals, from the taint of communalism accorded to them in secular South Asian historiography. However, there is a tendency in Bayly's later chapters to force his rather reluctant subjects to wear the liberal hat. A few examples will suffice. Ambedkar 'denied he was a liberal' but in Bayly's view he 'remained typical of late Indian liberalism in many ways'. M.N. Roy 'rejected the appellation of liberal', but, according to Bayly, 'he inherited fragments of the old liberal sensibility'. While 'rejecting the description liberal', S. Radhakrishnan is seen to have 'epitomized the neo-Vedantist humanist liberalism' discussed in the book. 'Ambedkar, Savarkar and Roy, let alone Iqbal and the Aga Khan,' Bayly acknowledges, 'would have been outraged by any attempt to put them within the same range of discourse and probably by any argument that classed them with the earlier liberals.'[17] The question is never asked as to why those Indians who set out to recover liberties, national as well as social, tended to shun the liberal label. Traces of liberalism can, of course, be found in those who did not self-define as liberals. Bayly is on the mark in suggesting that Subhas Chandra Bose was 'the last inheritor' of both Swadeshism and Mazzinian liberal nationalism.[18] One simply wishes that Bayly had directly addressed the deep Indian unease with the liberalism of empire.

Bayly offers the most comprehensive coverage to date of the ideas of Indian political thinkers in the modern era. It is impossible for any single historian to do more in the span of a single book. He is more self-assured in analysing the ideas of Hindu rather than Muslim political leaders and intellectuals. Despite his declared intention not to 'hive them off into a separate category', that is what Bayly ends up doing with Indian Muslims by accepting uncritically the rather bizarre theories about Sayyid Ahmad Khan and his contemporaries expounded within a small, closed circle of Oxbridge intellectual historians.[19] The book generally concentrates on the English writings of key Indian thinkers with the exception of a few Hindi tracts from northern India. It opens the way for other histories of ideas drawing on the vast corpus available in regional South Asian languages.

Bayly has done a great service to the cause of a new history of ideas by taking seriously political speeches and tracts, and moving the field well beyond the early 'linguistic turn' that looked at the nexus between the nation and the novel. There was a plethora of Indian Kropotkins whose pamphlets and manifestos deserve serious study. Bayly has demonstrated that the new history of ideas must not neglect institutions and practice, but even more importantly it must encompass the study of moral sentiments. One of Bayly's characters, Surendranath Banerjea, a true liberal and believer in the religion of humanity, had put it in these words: 'The qualifications of the orator are moral rather than intellectual . . . The equipment of the orator is . . . moral, and nothing will help him so much as constant association with the master-minds of humanity, of those who have worked and suffered, who have taught and preached great things, who have lived dedicated lives, consecrated to the service of their country and of their God.'[20]

OUR NATIONAL ANTHEM

On 27 December 1911, at the annual session of the Indian National Congress, Rabindranath Tagore's freshly composed song 'Jana Gana Mana' was performed, offering thanks for the divine benediction showered so generously on our country and our people. It had pleased Providence to guide Bharat's destiny and to give succour to its suffering populace. The poet's lyrics sang a paean to the expression of this divine glory that had many attributes—the 'Janaganamangaldayak', the Giver of grace, was at the same time the 'Janagana-aikya-bidhayak'—the One who crafted unity out of India's religious and regional diversity. The eternal Charioteer was also the 'Janaganapathparichayak'—navigating for His followers a most difficult path.

Patan-abhyudaya-bandhur pantha, jug-jug dhabita jatri
He chirasarathi taba rathachakre mukharita path dinratri
Darun biplab majhe taba shankhadhwani baje
Sankatdukhatrata.

The gender of this divinity is uncertain. The 'janaganadukhatrayak' appears in feminine form.

Duhswapne atanke raksha korile anke
Snehamayee tumi mata.

A song that so brilliantly fuses together an invocation to divine sovereignty with an intimation of popular sovereignty may seem with hindsight to have been a natural selection as a national anthem. Yet there is reason to ponder how Tagore, a patriot who was a powerful critic of nationalism, came to be accepted as the author of two national anthems of India and Bangladesh.

When Netaji Subhas Chandra Bose inaugurated the Free India Centre in Europe on 2 November 1942, the green, saffron and white tricolour of the Indian National Congress was adopted as the national flag. 'Jana Gana Mana Adhinayak Jaya He'—was chosen by Netaji as the national anthem—a choice that would be ratified by the Indian constituent assembly after Independence. He had played a key role in resolving the controversy surrounding the later verses of the other song, 'Bande Mataram', in 1937. He was open to considering Muhammad Iqbal's song 'Sare Jahan se Achha Hindustan Hamara'—proclaiming the excellence of India compared to the whole world—but in the end the decision was in favour of Tagore.

Dinendranath Tagore had written down the musical score of 'Jana Gana Mana' in 1918. An elaborate orchestration of the song was done in Hamburg, Germany, in September 1942. On the occasion of the inauguration of the Deutsche-Indische Gesellschaft in Hamburg on 11 September 1942, a German orchestra played for the first time Tagore's song as India's national anthem. In 1971 Krishna Bose found the bill for the orchestration of 'Jana Gana Mana' in the archives of Hamburg's Rathaus. It had cost 750 Reichmarks. Bose spoke of the bonds of poetry and philosophy between the two countries at the function. He did not neglect to mention how Tagore's visits to Germany in the 1920s had strengthened cultural ties between the two countries.

Netaji made his final public appearance in Berlin at a big ceremony to observe Independence Day on 26 January 1943, before his epic submarine voyage to Asia. The Independence Pledge of the Indian National Congress was read out. Berlin's Radio Orchestra played 'Jana Gana Mana' as India's national anthem with great panache. Those in India who listened clandestinely to the broadcasts of Azad Hind Radio were enthused to hear it.

The Azad Hind government proclaimed by Netaji in Singapore on 21 October 1943 inculcated a spirit of unity among all Indians with a subtle sense of purpose. 'Jai Hind' was chosen from the very outset as the common greeting or salutation when Indians met one another. Hindustani, an admixture of Hindi and Urdu, written in the Roman script, became the national language, but given the large south Indian presence, translation into Tamil was provided at all public meetings. A springing tiger, evoking Tipu Sultan of Mysore's gallant resistance against the British, featured as the emblem on the tricolour shoulder-pieces on uniforms. Gandhi's charkha continued to adorn the centre of the tricolour flags that Indian National Army soldiers were to carry in their march towards Delhi.

A simple Hindustani version of Tagore's song 'Jana Gana Mana Adhinayak Jaya He' became the national anthem. As a Bengali, Netaji went out of his way to ask Abid Hasan to get the national anthem rendered in the national language of India. The lyricist Mumtaz Hussain composed the Hindustani song in three verses rather than five and Ram Singh Thakur wrote down a band score based on the original tune. Mumtaz Hussain did not attempt a translation, but sought to capture the spirit of

Tagore's song. 'Jaya He' naturally became 'Jai Ho', long before A.R. Rahman made 'Jai Ho' famous the world over. The first verse that mentioned several place names bore a strong resemblance to the Bengali lyrics. A comparison of the verses evoking unity gives a clear sense of the similarities and differences between the Bengali original and the Hindustani version.

> *Aharaha taba ahwan pracharita, shuni taba udar bani*
> *Hindu Bouddha Sikh Jaina Parasik Mussalman Christani*
> *Purab pashchim ashe taba singhasan-pashe*
> *Premhar hoy gantha.*

The Azad Hind version went thus:

> *Sab ke dil me preeti basaye teri mithi bani*
> *Har sube ke rahne wale har mazhab ke prani*
> *Sab bhed aur pharak mitake sab god mein teri ake*
> *Gunthe prem ki mala.*

In 1911 the British moved the capital from Calcutta to Delhi. Little did our colonial masters know that in the same year a song had found utterance in this city that would be acknowledged in Delhi as the national anthem once the tricolour replaced the Union Jack. But the song did not travel along the Grand Trunk Road from Calcutta to Delhi. It traversed 'Patan-abhyudaya-bandhur pantha'—the entire global itinerary of India's struggle for freedom—to eventually find its home in every Indian heart.

We can only speculate on how Tagore would have felt about the November 2016 order compelling Indian citizens to stand to receive divine benediction for their country. But history has recorded Gandhi's perspective on the matter. Soon after

Independence and Partition as 'Bande Mataram' was sung at his prayer meeting on 29 August 1947, in Calcutta, Hindu and Muslim leaders on the stage including Suhrawardy stood up to show their respect along with the rest of the audience. The Mahatma remained in his characteristic seated pose. He was firm in his belief that standing erect in reverence for a national song was a Western custom, not in tune with Indian culture.

SPEECHES IN THE LOK SABHA

THE TRUE MEANING OF BHARATAVARSHA
Lok Sabha, 11 June 2014

Mr Chairman, Sir, carrying a little flame of India in my heart I have come to India from abroad to be of some little service to my motherland at a critical turning point in our history . . . (*Interruptions*).

I am honoured to be able to deliver my maiden speech in this august House as part of the debate on the President's address. It is a time-honoured convention for a maiden speech not to be interrupted and I would appeal to my fellow members to listen quietly while I speak.

We are most grateful to our Rashtrapatiji for coming down from Raisina Hill to address us in the Central Hall of Parliament. We only wish the new government had utilized this ceremonial occasion better to give us and the country a clear enunciation of policies instead of a recitation of pious wishes. We share with the government a commitment to build a strong India that will command the highest respect around the world.

We commend the prime minister for his initiative in inviting the leaders of SAARC countries to his swearing-in ceremony. We need a generous and an imaginative foreign policy towards our neighbours so that regional problems do not impede our legitimate ambition to play a major role on the global stage. One of the biggest challenges of the twenty-first century will be for India and China to peacefully manage their simultaneous rise. But I was sorry to see my good friend Shri Rajiv Pratap Rudy being too starry-eyed in his admiration of China. China is, after all, a one-party dictatorship and an authoritarian State. Our developmental path should be better based on our own democracy. We agree with the government that Japan can be our valuable partner in building world-class infrastructure across Asia. As a historian, I am glad that the government recognizes our soft-power potential. When Rabindranath Tagore set out on his voyage to South East Asia he had followed the civilizational trail of India's entry into the universal. Tagorean universalism can serve us well in this contemporary phase of global interconnections. Since Sushmaji, our minister of external affairs, is present in the House, I would like to say that we will extend our hand of cooperation in her conduct of foreign policy.

Mr Chairman, Sir, it is true that the federal spirit animating our polity in the past has been sadly diluted in recent years. The great Swadeshi leader Bipin Chandra Pal had pointed out in his book, *The Soul of India*, [that] the legendary king Bharata—after whom our country Bharatavarsha is named—had been described in the ancient texts as *rajchakravarti*. He took pains to explain that the term did not mean emperor but simply a king at the centre of a circle of kings. That was the model for great princes and king of kings in ancient times. He also pointed out that in the age of Muslim sovereigns Indian polity, always of a federal type, became even more pronouncedly so. The age of monarchy has passed, in this era of democracy the central government must learn to behave like a government at the centre of a circle of state governments. We welcome the Centre's promise of cooperative federalism. When the central government siphons off the bulk of a state's revenues in the form of debt interest, surely it violates the federal spirit. I call upon the central government in its reply to this debate to spell out what policies it will adopt to provide relief to debt-trapped states that are suffering because of the irresponsible profligacy of previous regimes. For no fault of their own these states, including mine, cannot pursue their developmental agenda towards poverty elimination, a concept which was first enunciated by a great Gujarati leader Dadabhai Naoroji in the nineteenth century.

I must also strenuously object to the patronizing claim made by this government that it will bring the 'Eastern region of the country on par with the Western region in terms of physical and social infrastructure'. I quote from the President's speech. Here I differ slightly from my friend Shri Bhartruhari Mahtab. I do want Odisha to prosper. I consider myself as half Oriya because my grandfather was born in Cuttack. But the fact is that the western and the northern regions lag behind the eastern and the southern regions in terms of every conceivable index of human development and social infrastructure, especially education and health. The gender imbalance, that is, the ratio of women to men, is far worse in the north and west of our country than in the east and the south. The western region has much to learn from the eastern region in this sphere of innovative projects and programmes . . . (*Interruptions*) For example, the visionary Kanyasree scheme of West Bengal Chief Minister Mamata Banerjee presages the central government's Beti Bachao, Beti Padhao campaign. Her highly successful Jal Dharo, Jal Bharo programme for water security holds lessons for the proposed Pradhan Mantri Krishi Sinchayee Yojana . . . (*Interruptions*)

RAJIV PRATAP RUDY: What kind of a speech is this? (*Interruptions*)

SUGATA BOSE: You have mentioned all these in the President's speech . . .

The central government would be well advised to follow West Bengal's lead in becoming an enabler for modern madrasa education with a minimum of state interference. There has been a new sunrise in the east that can light up the path to India's future.

Of greatest concern to us on the federal question is what the government has had to say on the issue of infiltration and illegal immigrants. This is a highly sensitive matter bearing on relations with our neighbours on which the states must be fully consulted and taken into confidence. We must never allow, West Bengal will never permit, the language of citizenship to be used as a façade for anti-minority prejudice. We also want to know the mechanisms through which states can contribute to the formulation of the proposed National Education Policy. I agree with Dr Thambi Durai who is in the Chair today and who spoke from here yesterday that the states must play a pre-eminent role in the field of education. The huge disparity in funding for state and central universities and educational institutions must be bridged in the interests of our youth and youth development. It will not suffice to simply build IITs and IIMs in various states. We have to build world-class universities on the solid foundation of primary and secondary school education.

Mr Chairman, Sir, permit me to say a heartfelt word or two about the government's plan to clean the River Ganga, a noble and worthy project. We hail from the great delta where the mighty tributaries of the Ganga flow into the sea. We have grown up singing Dwijendralal Roy's song, 'Patitodharini Gange, ogo ma, patitodharini Gange'. Even the worst sinner, it is said, can find redemption with a dip in its holy waters. The river is our mother in Bengal as much as it is for the residents of Benares. You will be happy to know that our poet Kazi Nazrul Islam did not write just about the Ganga. He sang: *Ganga Sindhu Narmada Kaberi Jamuna oi, bohia cholechche ager mato, koi re ager manush koi?* The Ganga and the other great rivers flow on as before, where are the human beings of yesteryears? That poetic lament laced with nostalgia is probably more poignant now than it was in Nazrul Islam's time. But it is the lines sung in the immortal voice of Bhupen Hazarika that are haunting me today: *Bistirna duparer asankhya manusher hahakar shuneo, nishabde nirabe o Ganga tumi, Ganga boichcho keno?* The term 'hahakar' was used by Sushmaji. If we cannot hear the hahakar, the cries of despair of the Dalit women subjected to brutal violence in the Gangetic plains, we cannot claim to be true representatives of the people of India.

And far away from the Gangetic plains, we mourn the death of Mohsin Sheikh, the young computer engineer in Pune. He belonged to the so-called aspirational class whose dreams for the future had been fired by the election campaign of the ruling party. He did not live to see the *achche din*, the good times, which this government promises to usher in. His only fault was that he wore his identity in his headgear and attire as he returned home after praying to the Almighty. Hockey sticks that had once done our nation proud in the world of sports were used as weapons to bludgeon the expression of diversity.

The composition of the 16th Lok Sabha does not reflect the rich diversity of India as well as it should. That is why it is our special duty and responsibility to give voice to the needs and aspirations of underrepresented minorities. If you truly want to be the harbinger of good times, I would say to the government, do not confuse uniformity with unity, majoritarianism with democracy. In his famous essay 'Bharatbarsha', Rabindranath had alerted us: 'Where there is genuine difference, it is only by respecting that difference and restraining it in its proper place, that it is possible to achieve unity. Unity cannot be achieved by issuing legal fiats that everybody is one.' Only by nurturing a healthy reverence for cultural difference can we invite everyone to unite at the feet of the Mother: *'Eso he Hindu, eso Musalman, eso he Parasi, Bouddha, Christian, milo ho Mayer charane.'*

I will just leave you with an image when the revolutionary leader Netaji Subhas Chandra Bose went from Bengal to Gujarat at Haripura to preside over the Indian National Congress.... (*Interruptions*) He and Mahatma Gandhi together fused the vision of a modern industrial future with the idyll of agrarian India. Jawaharlal Nehru and Patel were also there.... (*Interruptions*) Let us follow their lead and say to the Mother that we will work that she may prosper and suffer that she may rejoice.... (*Interruptions*)

Mr Chairman, I am done.

FISCAL FEDERALISM
Speech on the Central Budget, 17 July 2014

I rise to offer a critique of the central budget presented to us a week ago. We know that it is the hon'ble finance minister's first budget and he has been at some pains to explain that he had only forty-five days to prepare it. So we ought not to be too harsh in our assessment of his financial proposals. An author had once sent his first book manuscript to the legendary Dr Johnson for his comments. Upon reading it Dr Johnson had remarked that it contained some good things and some new things. But the good things in it were not new and the new things were not good. I am afraid we must pass a similar verdict on the finance minister's maiden budget.

Far from being 'the most comprehensive action plan' to achieve his goal of macroeconomic stabilization, the budget identifies a destination to be reached in three or four years without providing any clear roadmap on how to get there. Reduction of the fiscal deficit to 3 per cent of GDP by 2016–17 is a laudable, if ambitious, target. The budget sets a direction, but is hopelessly vague about how we might navigate towards that goal. The finance minister notes in an apparent tone of disapproval that the decline in the fiscal deficit from 5.7 per cent in 2011–12 to 4.5 per cent in 2013–14 was achieved by reducing expenditure rather than by enhancing revenue. Yet his government, which is ideologically committed not to raise taxes, is silent about what it might do to widen the tax base to increase revenues other than to stealthily deploy information technology. It is evident there will be spending cuts even though that intention is cloaked in the garb of setting up an Expenditure Management Commission. I hope the minister will spell out in his reply to this debate the status of this commission and whether its recommendations will be binding on the government. I would urge him not to reduce the food subsidy for the poor. He should ensure that the fertilizer subsidy benefits peasant smallholders and does not get siphoned off by the fertilizer manufacturers and rich farmers.

If the principles of federalism and democracy appeal to him, the finance minister would do well to curb his impatience and not shut down the debate on the goods and services tax (GST). In principle, we are in favour of the introduction of a GST as we believe it will be good for small- and medium-scale enterprises across our vast and diverse land. However, this should not be done at the cost of the states' revenues. A couple of years ago we reduced the rate of the central sales tax, having received a false promise of compensation by the Centre. The perfidy of the central government resulted in a loss of as much as Rs 4300 crore to West Bengal's exchequer. The concerns of the states must be fully addressed and iron-clad constitutional guarantees provided by the Centre before taking the momentous step of introducing a GST.

Genuine cooperative federalism demands not just a fair basis of sharing tax revenues but a proper sharing of the powers of taxation by the states and the Centre. I understand that this government admires Pandit Madan Mohan Malaviya after whom it has named one of its new schemes. So let me remind the treasury benches what that far-sighted patriot and member of the central legislative assembly of the pre-Independence era had to say on this subject. He told the Decentralization Commission of 1908: 'The unitary form of government which prevails at present should be converted into a federal system. The provincial governments should cease to be mere delegates of the supreme government, but should be made semi-independent governments.' In his Lahore Congress presidential address of 1909 he declared: 'What is needed is that the Government of India should require a reasonable amount of contribution to be made [for Imperial purposes] and should leave the rest of the revenues to be spent for Provincial purposes.'

Infrastructure, health and education must be the three pillars on which India should build its edifice of development over the next decade. I applaud the government's clear-eyed vision so far as investment in infrastructure is concerned. The allocations for roads and power stations, airports and seaports, are impressive and probably the best that could be done in the current fiscal situation. Government outlays will not be enough and we will have to achieve macroeconomic stability in order to attract global funds to meet our infrastructure needs. I am dismayed, however, by the government's myopia in not seeing that a healthy and educated populace is imperative for sustained economic growth and development. 'To those who say you haven't looked at the social sector,' the finance minister retorts in a newspaper interview, 'I say we haven't scrapped any programme.' What a negative thing to say! The country is in the grip of a full-scale public health crisis, which will not be solved by simply setting up AIIMS-like institutions in different states. A 4.2 per cent nominal increase in the allocation for the Health and Family Welfare Department masks a 4.4 per cent decrease in real terms if one adjusts for the 8.6 per cent inflation during the last financial year.

The biggest disappointment of the budget lies in the miserliness shown towards education, especially primary and secondary school education. The manifesto of the ruling party had proclaimed that spending on education would be raised from 3 per cent to 6 per cent of GDP that is the norm in much of Asia and ought to be a matter of national consensus in India. Where is the finance minister's roadmap towards realizing that objective? The budget has managed to put the country in reverse gear on the education front with a decrease in real-term allocation of 3.2 per cent in this sector so vital for the future of our younger generation. Pandit Malaviya would not have been pleased with this sorry state of affairs even if you have provided Rs 500 crore for new teachers' training in his name.

On the face of it, higher education fares a bit better than school education in the government's scale of priorities with the announcement of another Rs 500 crore for establishing five new IITs, five new IIMs, and one Humanities Centre named after Jai Prakash Narain. So we can expect nearly Rs 50 crore to be spent on brick and mortar in eleven new locations this year. But has adequate attention been given to the requirement of human resources, including faculty, for these new educational institutions? And is this the best strategy to achieve both broad access and excellence in the field of higher education? Why not invest similar amounts in ten of the most promising established colleges and universities, both central and state, that may have gone into some decline of late, but can be turned around through visionary leadership and judicious, strategic investment. This is precisely what China has done to have at least half a dozen of their best universities break into the league of the world's top one hundred.

I would like to put in an earnest plea to not misuse the name university that must have something universal about it to educate well-rounded future citizens of India. By all means, set up an institution to promote sports in Manipur, but call it an academy, not a university. I can understand the need for a railway training polytechnic or horticultural institutes, but to call them universities is to make a mockery of the idea of a university. I am sad, of course, that one of the horticultural universities—I would name them institutes—is not being set up in Bengal. If I could invite Shri Arun Jaitley to my constituency, I am sure he would be convinced that the most delicious fruits and vegetables come from places called Baruipur, Sonarpur and Bhangar that could serve as wonderful locations for an innovative horticultural institute.

I can quite understand that Rs 100 crore would be a sensible amount to allocate for single institutions of this kind. However, flagship nationwide schemes featuring in the government's agenda announced with much fanfare in the President's address need to be backed by significant resources and call for much larger outlays. 'It is a shame,' the finance minister says, 'that the apathy towards [the] girl child is still quite rampant in many parts of the country.' It is a far bigger shame and a sign of far greater apathy that he has set aside a paltry Rs 100 crore for the Beti Bachao, Beti Padhao Yojana. West Bengal's Kanyasree scheme has state budgetary support to the tune of Rs 1000 crore. The provision of Rs 100 crore for the modernization of madrasas is a mere pittance. I call upon the finance minister to increase each of these allocations tenfold straight away to show a modicum of respect to women and minorities. There is yet another Rs 100 crore set aside for ghat development and beautification of the riverfront in seven cities from Kedarnath to Patna. The Ganga does not stop flowing at Patna, but we in Bengal would not wish to claim a share of that minuscule figure.

In conclusion, a final word about a budgetary item of symbolic value. I refer to the allocation of Rs 200 crore to cast the Iron Man of India in an iron mould. I wonder what Sardar Vallabhbhai Patel would have made of it. I have a sneaking suspicion that the hero of the Bardoli satyagraha would have preferred to donate that amount towards rural development that has suffered a budgetary cut of 3.2 per cent in real terms. And his even greater elder brother Vithalbhai Patel, who held the flag of Indian freedom aloft in Europe with Subhas Chandra Bose in the early 1930s, would have excoriated the government for wasteful expenditure in the same way as he held the British accountable when he spoke eloquently in these precincts as a member and president of the central legislative assembly. To honour the Patel brothers and other noble figures of that generation we need to follow their ideals, not worship them in iron or stone.

In this time of rampant food inflation, we must be grateful to our finance minister for presenting a prosaic budget. But we Bengalis are incorrigible. One of our poets had bid farewell to poetry as in the kingdom of hunger the world had turned prosaic and even the full moon looked like a flaming roti. But he said it in poetry: *'Kabita tomay dilam ajke chhuti, Khudhar rajye prithibi gadyamoy, purnima chand jeno jhalsano ruti.'*

THE INDIA—BANGLADESH BORDER
Lok Sabha, 7 May 2015

Deputy Speaker, Sir, I rise to support, on my own behalf and on behalf of the All India Trinamool Congress, the Constitution (119th Amendment) Bill which, after an amendment is passed, will become the 100th Constitution (Act Amendment).

At the outset, I would like to congratulate our minister of external affairs for bringing forward this historic legislation before this House and also for making a statesmanlike speech in opening this discussion and debate.

Our external affairs minister referred to the Radcliffe Award of 1947. The roots of the problem that we are going to solve in this Parliament later today go back to the tragic Partition of 1947. The irony of that partition was captured best by the poet W.H. Auden in his poem 'Partition' where he wrote about Radcliffe.

Radcliffe was not a good surgeon. Partition was often referred to as a surgical operation. Not only did he bring misery to the people on either side of the lines that were drawn in 1947 but like any bad surgeon, he left swabs inside the patient. These were the enclaves that are going to be exchanged today. We call these 'Chhit Mahal' in the local parlance in West Bengal.

As I speak today, my mind goes back to 1971, a date to conjure with in South Asian history. I was merely a high school student, not even in college. I used to go with my paediatrician father, Dr Sisir Kumar Bose, to the Bongaon border where millions of refugees had come from what was then the Eastern Wing of Pakistan. I had seen poverty in Kolkata. But I had never seen the kind of human misery that I witnessed in 1971 in the refugee camps around Bongaon town. But there was something else. I also used to visit the Netaji Field Hospital in a village called Bakchara where the brave, wounded soldiers of Bangladesh's Mukti Bahini used to be brought across the border and public-spirited doctors and surgeons from Kolkata would operate upon them. That is the only time in my life that I have seen operations being conducted in the open and there was not even any saline. I have seen *daber jal*, coconut water, being used in place of saline. These Mukti Yoddhas sacrificed their all. Our Indian soldiers made huge sacrifices. What we witnessed in 1971 was a glorious freedom struggle against one of the most brutal military crackdowns in modern history. After the victory of 16 December 1971, Sheikh Mujibur Rahman, Bangabandhu, came back, and I remember, on the 17th of January, my father met him in Dhaka. What was the border like? He just drove across in an ambulance carrying medical supplies for newly independent Bangladesh. That was the kind of border we saw in 1971. People wanting to help each other to live a life of dignity.

Then, of course, in 1974, our external affairs minister has referred to the historic agreement made between Bangabandhu Sheikh Mujibur Rahman and our great prime minister, Indira Gandhi. It is a pity that forty-one years have passed before this Parliament could ratify that agreement. Today, the words of Bangabandhu, his historic speech on the 7th of March, are ringing in my ears, when he said, '*Rakta jakhan diyechhi, rakta aro debo e desher manushere mukto koirya chharbo, Inshallah.*' 'Since we have given blood, we will give more of it, Inshallah, we will free the people of this land.' In other words, he offered to give more sacrifice in blood so that the people of East Bengal could be free. He brought freedom to the people of Bangladesh.

We have to look at this 1974 agreement and the protocol signed in 2011 between Prime Minister Manmohan Singh and Prime Minister Sheikh Hasina. I had the privilege of meeting the prime minister when they gave an award to my father posthumously, just two years ago. I find this is what is really historic and what is really positive about this Bill that has been brought by this government. We have a carefully balanced Bill; we are protecting and promoting the national interest, the states' interest, and the human interest. The national interest, because this Bill, once it is passed later today by this House, will bring about a revolutionary transformation in the relations between India and Bangladesh. I agree with the external affairs minister that we will be able to rekindle the spirit of 1971. After that, when you go to ask the people of Bangladesh and the Government of Bangladesh for trade and transit facilities, they will respond to you in a positive manner. So, that national interest has been supreme. I know, earlier this week, there was a little temptation to falling prey to the narrow party-partisan interests but what is important today is that the people of Assam also rose to the occasion and the temptation was resisted. National interest was put above party-political interests.

Secondly, states' interests have been protected. It was a real privilege for me to work on the Standing Committee on External Affairs with Dr Shashi Tharoor of the Congress, Mohd. Salim of the CPI(M), my own colleague, Mumtaz Sanghomita of the Trinamool Congress, and so many of the BJP members and the members of the other parties belonging to the ruling coalition. It shows the value of the standing committee system in our parliamentary democracy. In the unanimous report that we tabled in this House on the 1st of December 2014, we protected the states' interests. This is what we said about the earlier history. We said, closer consultations at the highest political level between the central government and state governments would have been desirable. The committee, while appreciating the efforts to keep the state governments on board, would therefore suggest the government effectively coordinate with them on all matters and resolve the lacunae, if any, relating to the actual implementation of the accord on the ground.

I am very glad, I am truly happy, I have to tell the external affairs minister, that she has conducted consultations at the highest political level as we had wanted, she has spoken several times with our leader, the chief minister of West Bengal, Mamata Banerjee. We had also said, the committee expects that the central government and the state government of West Bengal will arrive at a consensus on the issue relating to the rehabilitation package. All the humanitarian issues should be resolved in advance including assistance from the central government in this regard.

I trust, as the external affairs minister has assured on the floor of this House, that the rehabilitation package which has been sent to her by the government of West Bengal led by Chief Minister Mamata Banerjee on the 6th of December 2014, will be available to the state so that we can build infrastructure and also give a true life of dignity to those in the enclaves who have been leading a miserable existence for the last sixty-seven years. That is the most important aspect of this Bill. We are protecting the human interest.

I am delighted today that our veteran, elder statesmen Advaniji, Murli Manohar Joshiji are sitting here this afternoon as we are debating this Constitution Amendment Bill. I am remembering our visionary former prime minister, Atal Bihari Vajpayee. It is because, what we are going to do today is to be a solution of an intractable problem, a solution that is going to be found in the spirit of *insaniyat*. Under the sign of insaniyat, human beings are taking precedence over territory, small amounts, small pieces of territory that are only going to be notionally exchanged between the two sovereign States of India and Bangladesh.

Mr Deputy Speaker, Sir, I would like to say that sometimes I hear certain justifications for this agreement. I can understand that the ruling party, in order to satisfy their recalcitrant constituents in a certain province, may often have to make those kinds of arguments. I often hear that this particular piece of legislation and the final settlement of the land boundary between India and Bangladesh will help us resolve the problem of illegal immigration, of smuggling across the borders and so on. That may well be a by-product of the settlement that we are going to reach with Bangladesh. But let us remember that this historic piece of legislation is actually meant for the benefit of the law-abiding citizens of India and Bangladesh. Once the entire boundary is demarcated, I would like to see that innocent law-abiding citizens of India and Bangladesh should be able to cross the border with dignity. I would urge our external affairs minister to have consultations with the home minister so that a whole series of integrated checkposts can be set up along the India–Bangladesh border. It is because we want the ordinary people to be able to cross without difficulty. We want music to flow across the border that separates the two Bengals. We want theatre groups from the two Bengals to come to each other and to have their performances. I have spent a lot of time as a student in Bangladesh going about all the districts, working in district record rooms. I have seen how much the people of Bangladesh admire Deshbandhu Chittaranjan Das, Sarat Chandra Bose and Netaji Subhas Chandra Bose. I have seen the best performance of D.L. Roy's *Shahjahan* play on a stage in Dhaka, not on this side in Kolkata, even though we have great theatre personalities and theatre groups in West Bengal and some of them actually now belong to our party, the All India Trinamool Congress.

So, I would like to say that let us gift this historic piece of legislation to the people of the two Bengals and also to someone whose birth anniversary, *Ponchishe Boishakh*, we are going to celebrate all over the country in two days' time. Ponchishe Boishakh is either on the 8th of May or the 9th of May. He not only wrote the national anthems of our two countries, India and Bangladesh, but all of the songs that he wrote during the Swadeshi movement of 1905 were inspirational for the Mukti Yoddha of Bangladesh in 1971.

'*Aji Bangladesher hridoy hote kakhan aponi, tumi ei aparup rupe bahir hole janani, ogo Ma, tomai dekhe dekhe ankhi na fire.*' You know, we cannot turn our eyes from her. We have always envisioned our state Bengal and also Bharatavarsha as the Mother. That is the spirit. In those days, we used to recite Jibanananda Das's poetry—*Banglar mukh ami dekhiachi, tai ami prithibir roop khunjite jai na aar.* We have seen Bengal's face, that is why we do not need to go out and find beauty in the rest of the world. So, that is what I am being reminded of here today.

Finally, I would simply like to say that there is one song. Of course, there were many other songs that were referred to by Ahluwaliaji, Bhupen Hazarika's famous song 'Ganga amar ma, Padma amar ma'. But let us remember that during the heyday of the Swadeshi movement, Rabindranath Tagore wrote a very beautiful song—'Amra milechhi aj mayer dake'—We have actually gathered here at the call of the Mother. We are answering the call of the Mother in passing this historic legislation in the Lok Sabha today.

On behalf of everyone in this House, it is such a great moment to see that we have risen above all political party differences. We have protected the national interest, the states' interest and the human interest today. So, let us—as has happened in the Rajya Sabha—rise to the full stature of this House and unanimously pass this Constitution Amendment Bill. Let the message go out to the whole of South Asia that we want peace and development for the poor and obscure, who live all across this great subcontinent.

With these few words, I conclude. Thank you.

AGAINST INTOLERANCE, TOWARDS CULTURAL INTIMACY
Lok Sabha, 1 December 2015

Madam Speaker, the word 'intolerance' is a mere euphemism for a wave of unreason, injustice and inhumanity that has been unleashed across our country during the last few months.

My friend Mr Venugopal has already given a comprehensive catalogue of the incidents that have taken place. So, I will not repeat that catalogue. In order to confront the challenges that face our country today, a powerful message needs to go out from this Lok Sabha, the House of the People, that reason *(aql)* will be our only torch, justice *(insaf)* our only worship and humanity *(insaniyat)* our only religion. As the minorities face the cold winds of exclusion from the powers that be today, it is pertinent to recall what Dr Ambedkar said on the question of minority protection while introducing the draft Constitution on 4 November 1948. I will quote only one of the most important sentences from that historic speech: 'It is for the majority to realize its duty not to discriminate against minorities.'

Whatever might be Rajnath Singhji's reservation about the term 'secularism', its use or misuse, will he as the home minister at least perform this duty enjoined on us by the architect of our

Constitution? If we wish to truly honour the lead author of our Constitution on his 125th birth anniversary, let us pledge today collectively never to make our minorities feel insecure in this great land of ours.

Had the Hon'ble Speaker allowed this humble historian to say a few words in the discussion on the Constitution, I would have just said something about the concept of constitutional morality that our home minister referred to towards the end of his speech. Dr Ambedkar invoked the concept of constitutional morality described by Grote, the historian of Greece, as: 'A paramount reverence for the forms of the Constitution, enforcing obedience to authority acting under and within these forms yet combined with the habit of open speech and unrestrained censure of those very authorities as to all their public acts.'

Constitutional morality, Dr Ambedkar told us, is not a natural sentiment. It has to be cultivated and the people have to learn it. He followed up this contention with a debatable proposition. He said: 'Democracy in India is only a top-dressing on an Indian soil, which is essentially undemocratic.' In today's climate, who knows, some would probably label him unpatriotic or anti-national for having said so. But if we are a mature democracy, we will ponder over his remark and embrace the value of constitutional morality as respect for forms and processes that enable us to negotiate and then rise above differences, differences which Grote described or characterized as 'the bitterness of party contest'. This Lok Sabha needs to transcend the bitterness of party contest.

In the course of the Constituent Assembly debates, Zairul-Hassan Lari pointed out that constitutional morality was a value that not just citizens but also the government must learn. The spirit underlying the Constitution and not just the words must guide the government. When will this government begin to appreciate that it can learn much more from the criticism of its opponents than from the eulogy of its supporters? I urge this government to listen to the voices of our most brilliant thinkers, writers, historians, scientists, artists and activists and not let loose their hounds in the social media on them whenever they express their concern or anguish. Do not be sarcastic about them by calling them our wonderful intellectuals.

To be absolutely clear, we are not saying that India is intolerant. We are saying that followers, supporters and even some members of this government are spreading a virulent form of prejudice and bigotry. The refusal to unequivocally condemn and take exemplary action against the offenders on the part of the leader of this government must be seen as out of sync with the concept and the value of constitutional morality. Our poet Kazi Nazrul Islam had sung *'Hindu na ora Muslim oi jigyashe kon jan? Kandari balo dubichhe manush santan mor Ma'r'*. The duty of the captain of a ship is to treat his passengers in crisis equally as human beings, as children of the mother.

Intolerance is bad, Madam Speaker, but tolerance is not good enough. I agree with Shrimati Supriya Sule: Should we just be tolerating one another? No, that is not my idea of India. We have to aspire for something much higher. We must cultivate the value of cultural intimacy, *saanskritik sannidhya*, among our diverse communities. That was the foundation of Netaji Subhas Chandra Bose's political philosophy. He said to the Maharashtra Provincial Conference as early as 1928, 'Democracy is by no means a Western institution; it is a human institution.' He wanted to see a federal republic of India after Independence. He warned Indians not to become a queer mixture of political democrats and social conservatives. He spoke in unequivocal terms about building political democracy on the pedestal of a democratic society. He spoke about not just the depressed classes, the working classes but also the women of India. He regretted that different communities in India were too exclusive. 'Fanaticism is the greatest thorn in the path of cultural intimacy,' he told his audience, 'and there is no better remedy for fanaticism than secular and scientific education.' That was the first occasion Subhas Chandra Bose used the term 'secular'. For him, secularism was not hostile to religion or religiously informed cultural differences, but he felt that it could help foster cultural intimacy, saanskritik sannidhya, among India's diverse religious communities.

Madam Speaker, a few days ago, I saw a beautiful photograph of our prime minister paying homage to Netaji and the noble martyrs of the Indian National Army in Singapore. Our chief minister, Mamata Banerjee, had offered her tribute during her visit to Singapore last year. Who were these martyrs? They were Hindu, Muslim, Sikh and Christian soldiers who dined together before they went to war together, and their blood mingled in the battlefields around Imphal and Kohima so that India may be free.

The original martyrs' memorial had been blown up by Mountbatten's forces. The Singapore government, very generously, built a new memorial fifty years later in 1995. What was the name of the INA officer who had built the original martyrs' memorial? His name was Cyril John Stracey. He was a wonderful Christian and an Anglo-Indian officer of the INA, and the motto of INA, 'Itmad, Ittefaq, Kurbani', was emblazoned on the memorial.

On 16–17 January 2016 we, in Kolkata, will be observing the 75th anniversary of Netaji's 'Mahanishkraman', that is, his great escape from India. Sisir Kumar Bose drove him out from Kolkata, but who received him in Peshawar? His name was Mian Akbar Shah, a great freedom fighter of the North West Frontier

Province. Who was Netaji's only Indian companion on the perilous submarine voyage from Europe to Asia that took ninety days? His name was Abid Hasan from the Hyderabad Deccan. Who was the commander of the First Division of the INA which fought in India's Northeast? His name was Muhammad Zaman Kiani. Who hoisted the Indian tricolour in Moirang near Imphal in 1944? His name was Shaukat Malik. Who was Netaji's only Indian companion on his final flight in 1945? His name was Habibur Rahman. What were the names of the three officers who were put on trial at the Red Fort seventy years ago? Their names were Prem Kumar Sahgal, Gurbaksh Singh Dhillon and Shah Nawaz Khan.

We have observed an anniversary of the Constitution and the birth anniversary of Dr B.R. Ambedkar. I think that we ought to be observing the seventieth anniversary of the Red Fort trials that began on 5 November 1945 and ended on 31 December 1945, and these three men were sentenced to deportation for life, but the British could not implement that sentence. In those days, you will remember, Madam Speaker . . . *(Interruptions)* or the older generation will certainly remember that there was a slogan:

'Lal Quile se aye awaz Sahgal, Dhillon, Shahnawaz'

HON. SPEAKER: We do study it in history lessons. *(Interruptions)*

Mahatma Gandhi visited the INA prisoners in the Red Fort and he was told that in the INA they recognized no differences of creed or religion, but here the British are serving us Hindu tea and Muslim tea separately. So, Mahatma Gandhi asked: 'Why do you suffer it?' and the reply came: 'No, we do not. We mix Hindu tea and Muslim tea exactly half and half and then serve. The same with food.' We have to rekindle that spirit of the winter of 1945 in India today.

Madam Speaker, our fight against intolerance is essentially a fight against unreason, injustice and inhumanity. In conclusion, let me make a fervent appeal concerning a sensitive issue that has led to a tragic loss of lives in recent months. We do, of course, have Article 48 as part of the many Directive Principles of the State on the subject of agriculture and animal husbandry urging steps for prohibiting the slaughter of cows. Yesterday, Shrimati Lekhi made a reference to this Directive Principle in the course of her fiery speech. But it cannot, under any circumstances, be used as a sordid pretext to take precious human life. Dr Ambedkar would have been horrified to see this happen.

In my maiden speech delivered in June 2014 I had mourned the death of Mohsin Sheikh, the computer engineer in Pune. This happened days after the new government took power. Today, I mourn the death of Mohammad Akhlaq and others who have been victims in recent months of the poison of religious hatred. In the name of bygone generations that have welded the Indian people into a nation, I invoke the noble meaning of the word *akhlaq*. What does 'akhlaq' mean? It means ethics, and I urge those who hold the reins of power in our country today, especially our prime minister and our home minister, Shri Rajnath Singh, to uphold the fundamental right to life and liberty of all our citizens and abide by 'akhlaq', the ethics of good governance that have informed the very best of Indian political thought and practice through the ages. Thank you, Madam Speaker.

FREE OUR UNIVERSITIES, FREE OUR STUDENTS
Lok Sabha, 24 February 2016

Madam Speaker, I rise to speak in this highly charged and sensitive debate as someone who has been a teacher at universities for three and a half decades. I hope that my colleagues in this august House will have the patience to listen to me. This is after all a forum for debate and discussion, as the President reminded us only yesterday.

Just over a month ago, a Dalit research scholar at Hyderabad Central University, Rohith Vemula, tragically took his own life. The death of a bright young Dalit scholar is not new in Indian universities. The Thorat Committee that was appointed in 2007 to investigate the growing number of suicides among students in elite educational institutions discovered that of the twenty-three suicide cases nineteen were Dalits, two tribals and one Muslim. This alarming figure should have raised several questions of academic justice and freedom that our nation needed to seriously ponder.

Rohith Vemula left us a poignant message when he chose to leave this unfair world. In 'the only letter' that he was going to write, he told us: 'I always wanted to be a writer— a writer of science. Like Carl Sagan. I love science . . . stars.' Rohith today is not dead. He lives up in the heavens as a star 'of purest ray serene' to serve as a beacon light to posterity.

Rohith's tragedy should have stirred our collective conscience, including that of our government. Unfortunately, we have a heartless government that refuses to listen to the cries of despair coming from the marginalized sections of our society. Instead of assuring social justice to all, the ruling party wishes to use the student unrest in our universities to claim a monopoly on nationalism and tar all of their critics with the brush of 'anti-nationalism'.

Madam Speaker, I am not a communist. In fact, I won this seat in the Lok Sabha by defeating a prominent communist candidate. But I stand today in support of the right to freedom of expression by young students who may be inspired by Marx as well as Ambedkar. Madam Speaker, I am a nationalist. I believe in a kind of nationalism that instils a spirit of selfless service in our people and inspires their creative efforts. But I know that nationalism can be a truly Janus-faced phenomenon and I deplore the brand of nationalism espoused by members of the treasury benches that I find narrow, selfish and arrogant.

Following the unrest in Hyderabad there were incidents that took place in Jawaharlal Nehru University (JNU), a university named after our great first prime minister. Earlier this month at one or two events on that campus very disturbing slogans were raised and deeply troubling posters were put up. We unequivocally condemn those slogans and posters. However, we strongly oppose the attempt being made to portray the entire university as a hub of anti-national activities and the onslaught of State forces on academic freedom. We were horrified to witness the scenes of students, teachers and journalists being assaulted within the court premises of Patiala House. It was not the students but the black-coated storm troopers affiliated with the ruling party who defiled and desecrated the image of Mother India.

The reverberations of the JNU incidents were felt in my home state, especially in Jadavpur University. There too unfortunate slogans were heard in the streets around the campus. But in contrast with what happened in the nation's capital, the West Bengal state administration led by Mamata Banerjee and the university administration knew how to defuse tension and to not unnecessarily escalate a crisis. It knew how not to overreact. After all, the idea of India is not so brittle as to crumble at the echo of a few slogans.

You cannot be a true nationalist if you are opposed to freedom. It is not a crime to seek freedom from caste oppression, freedom from class exploitation, freedom from gender discrimination. We must give our students and youth the freedom to think, the freedom to speak, the freedom to be idealistic and, yes, the freedom to make mistakes and learn from them. What must be avoided at all costs is the criminalization of dissent. *(Interruptions).*

I heard the speech given by Kanhaiya Kumar on YouTube. *(Interruptions).* I heard the speech given by Kanhaiya Kumar on YouTube. I agreed with many things that he said. I disagreed with some of the things that he said. I agreed with him when he extolled Ambedkar's commitment to constitutional rights and constitutional morality. I agreed with him when he expressed admiration for our great revolutionaries like Bhagat Singh, Ashfaqullah, Sukhdev and Rajguru. He, of course, said that the RSS took no part in our freedom struggle. There too he was right . . . *(Interruptions)* But as a teacher I would have liked to have a discussion with him about history and I would have pointed out to him that even the communists had actually taken part in the freedom struggle but also betrayed the freedom struggle at crucial moments during the 1942 movement and during the Azad Hind movement led by Netaji Subhas Chandra Bose. So, we condemn the vigilantism of self-appointed protectors of the nation who are trying to create a climate of fear. *(Interruptions)*

HON. SPEAKER: Shri Kalyan Banerjee, you are disturbing the member from your own party. He is speaking very well. Please take your seat.

Madam Speaker, as I have said, I stand for the right to free expression of my communist friends and they will be speaking in this House soon afterwards. But we condemn the acts of vigilantism by self-appointed protectors of the nation which foments a climate of fear and I believe that students, teachers and university personnel must all be permitted to express opinions freely even if they conflict with the government's political stances and the government must end the witch-hunt for anti-nationals and the shameful scapegoating of university students. Why? It is because we believe that this witch-hunt is meant to distract the nation from issues necessary to the nation's development such as employment opportunities and poverty alleviation. We insist that no group within the Indian polity or in its diaspora is the univocal spokesperson for the nation. History shows us that State-sponsored or State-condoned campaigns against so called anti-nationals lead to authoritarian rule and the destruction of democratic principles. If universities and students are attacked, then the legacy of our anti-colonial freedom struggle and of democratic reconstruction is gravely undermined.

Madam Speaker, we learn our lessons in nationalism from great figures like Mahatma Gandhi, Jawaharlal Nehru and Subhas Chandra Bose and those of us who are from Bengal are also inspired by what we have been taught about patriotism and nationalism by figures like Swami Vivekananda, Rabindranath Tagore, Deshbandhu Chittaranjan Das, Bipin Chandra Pal and Aurobindo Ghose. I was wondering whose definition of nationalism might be acceptable to my friends in the treasury benches. I thought that at least I would try by citing before them the example of Aurobindo.

The issue of Kashmir kept coming up in the speech given by Shri Anurag Thakur. Now, it is incumbent on all of us who are the elected representatives of the Lok Sabha to give a greater sense of belonging to the Union of India among the people of Jammu and Kashmir and all of our far-flung states. The issue is, what kind of Indian Union do we want?

What did Aurobindo say about this? Aurobindo touched upon 'the secret of the difficulty in the problem of unifying ancient India'. And he cited ancient texts. He said that the rishis from the Vedic age onwards propounded 'the ideal of the Chakravarti, a uniting imperial rule, uniting without destroying the autonomy of India's many kingdoms and peoples from sea to sea'. The ruler was meant to establish a suzerainty. The 'full flowering' of this ideal Aurobindo found in 'the great epics'. The Mahabharata narrates the legendary and quasi-historic pursuit of this ideal of empire which even 'the turbulent Shisupala' is represented as accepting in his attendance at Yudhisthira's *dharmic* Rajasuya sacrifice. The Ramayana too presents 'an idealized picture of such a Dharmarajya, a settled universal empire'. It is in Aurobindo's words, 'not an autocratic despotism but a universal monarchy supported by a free assembly of the city and provinces and of all the classes that is held up as the ideal'. He goes on to say that according to his ideal, unification 'ought not to be secured at the expense of the free life of the regional peoples or of the communal liberties and not therefore by a centralized monarchy or a rigidly unitarian imperial State'.

Now we are not a monarchy any more. We are a democracy but the nationalism that is being talked about from the other side of the House represents centralized despotism and it is talking about a rigidly unitarian imperial State.

I mentioned Rabindranath Tagore. Tagore composed our national anthem. But he was also a powerful critic of nationalism. He knew that nationalism could be both a boon and a curse. He wrote beautiful patriotic songs during our Swadeshi movement. But then he also saw that nationalism could lead to the carnage of war in Europe during the First World War. And that is why, when he travelled the world in 1916, he first went to Japan and then the United States of America, he gave lectures on nationalism and it was a powerful critique of nationalism that we find in those lectures. These lectures were published in a little book titled *Nationalism*, by Macmillan in 1917.

I sometimes fear that those who are defining nationalism so narrowly will end up one day describing Rabindranath Tagore, the composer of our national anthem, as anti-national if they read some of the sentences in his book on nationalism . . . *(Interruptions)*

We always had different visions of nationhood and it is really a debate and discussion about what should be an ideal form of the Union of India that has animated the thought of all the great figures that I have talked about. Chittaranjan Das of course had debates with Rabindranath Tagore but they were respectful towards each other. Deshbandhu Chittaranjan Das felt that you could have a nationalism where you are very proud of Bengal, your region, but you can still be a very proud Indian nationalist at the same time. All of this has to flower in the garden of internationalism.

I know that Anurag Thakur tried to quote Netaji Subhas Chandra Bose even though he confused the two great Bengali luminaries, Netaji and Rabindranath Tagore, the patriot and the poet. When I said that the nationalism that they represent is narrow, selfish and arrogant, I was, in fact, quoting from Netaji Subhas Chandra Bose. He spent a number of years in exile—from 1933 to 1936—in Europe. As he was leaving and coming back to India to be imprisoned here, he pointed out the new German nationalism that he had witnessed in Europe was narrow, selfish and arrogant.

Then, in 1937 when Japan invaded China and at that time the Indian National Congress sent a medical mission to China, at that time too Netaji Subhas Chandra Bose said that we must pursue national fulfilment in every direction, but not at the cost of imperialism, and not at the price of self-aggrandizement. So, we must understand that nationalism can have a liberating aspect. That is what inspired generations of our freedom fighters. But nationalism in its narrow form can also be extremely oppressive. This is a topic and a concept on which we ought to be able to have healthy debates.

The President, speaking to us yesterday, pointed out that this government is trying to repeal many obsolete laws. There are many colonial-era laws that need to be done away with from our statute book. I venture to suggest that the law on sedition is one of them. This was a law that was deployed to persecute our freedom fighters. We ought to be able to have a discussion with our children, with our students, with our youth. We ought not to be subjecting them to trumped-up charges of sedition based on very dubious evidence, based on morphed visual evidence. We ought not to be doing this to our students and to our youth today.

I have said what I have wanted to, because it is not always necessary to make a long speech in order to stand for academic freedom. Free our universities, free our students, let our youth dream a glorious future for our country. I have mentioned that Tagore wrote this beautiful little book on nationalism. At the end of the book he printed an English rendering of a Bengali poem that he had composed on the last day of the nineteenth century. It says:

> The last Sun of the century sets amidst the blood-red clouds of the West and the whirlwind of hatred. The naked passion of self-love of nations, in its drunken delirium of greed, is dancing to the clash of steel and the howling verses of vengeance. Keep watch India. Let your crown be of humility, your freedom the freedom of the soul. Build God's throne daily upon the ample bareness of your poverty. And know that what is huge is not great and pride is not everlasting.

From this poem, I would like to simply underline three phrases. Let us not be deluded by the naked passion of self-love of nations, let our freedom be the freedom of the soul and let us remember the admonition of the great sentinel that what is huge is not great and pride is not everlasting.

Thank you very much.

KASHMIR: CRUCIBLE OF CONFLICT, CRADLE OF PEACE

Lok Sabha, 20 July 2016

Mr Deputy Speaker, Sir. First of all, I would like to express my gratitude to the Home Minister Shri Rajnath Singh for being present in the House at this late hour to listen to us on this very sensitive topic of peace and security in Kashmir.

I entirely agree with my good friend M.J. Akbar that every text has a context and that we can learn lessons from history in order to address the contemporary situation in Jammu and Kashmir. Muzaffar Hussain Baig in his long and passionate speech gave his own reading of Kashmiri history. Since, unlike M.J. Akbar and Muzaffar Hussain Baig, I cannot claim Kashmiri parentage, I hope that this academic historian's interpretation will be accepted as impartial, and on the basis of that I want to make a very constructive proposal for the Government of India to consider.

As the tragedy unfolded over the last twelve days, I picked up a book of history written by a former Kashmiri student of mine, Dr Chitralekha Zutshi, and found these lines that she quoted from a late-eighteenth-century writer:

> The garden of Kashmir became a wound of pain,
> The master's pleasure became the people's indigence,
> They fell upon the soul of Kashmir,
> As voracious dogs set loose.
> The doors, walls, roofs and streets,
> And every soul complained like a doleful flute.
> The hearts of the tyrants were as hard as stone,
> They were too implacable to feel the people's pains.

These lines were written about the tyrannical rule of the Afghans in Kashmir from 1752 to 1819 by Saiduddin Shahabadi in his late-eighteenth-century history of Kashmir titled *Bagh-i-Suleiman* (Solomon's Garden). Since then, unfortunately, many managers of colonial and postcolonial States have been guided by territorial greed and have not felt the people's pain. The time has now come, if it is not long overdue, to feel and respond to the people's pain and embrace insaniyat or humanity, just as Atal Bihari Vajpayeeji had, as the guiding principle in the quest for just peace in this crucible of conflict.

In my view, Kashmiri expressions of regional identity, at their best, have always been compatible with universal humanity. Who gave the Kashmiris their regional identity? They were the great devotional preachers like Lal Ded or Nund Rishi, Sheikh Nooruddin. They preached in the regional vernacular and created a close mesh between language and religion. They were not that different from the *bhakti* preachers, like Mirabai, in other regions of India. They taught the people to creatively accommodate their differences.

Now, a namesake of our current minister of state for external affairs, another Akbar, conquered Kashmir in 1586. But that was no ordinary conquest. Akbar only claimed the highest manifestation of sovereignty and he left many other local and regional sovereigns in place. Of course, his son, Jahangir, was completely captivated by the beauty of the Kashmiri landscape and that created stereotypical images of the region. We have had our modern Jahangir in the form of Jawaharlal Nehru, but what we need to remember today is that Kashmir is not just a landscape. There are people who inhabit that beautiful Valley.

What the British did was to have a kind of monolithic sovereignty of their own in the British Indian provinces and then they had many princely rulers, and there was the Dogra ruler of Jammu and Kashmir for 100 years—1846 to 1947. Since the British guaranteed his sovereignty, he could be somewhat tyrannical. He need not grant patronage to the religious and cultural sites of all his subjects. So, some of his Muslim subjects were disaffected. The first mass movement took place in 1931 as a result of that kind of negation of understanding the needs of the people.

In the contemporary period, of course, since the late 1940s, the old historic state of Jammu and Kashmir has been divided into our own state and one-third has been under Pakistani occupation and a slice has been given away by Pakistan to China. I think there was an element of truth in what Muzaffar Baig Sahab was saying. It was in the 1950s, 1960s, early 1970s that successive Congress regimes had whittled down Article 370. It became a shadow and a husk of what it originally was in 1952–53. It was a certain kind of denial of democracy and also a negation of genuine federal autonomy that led in 1989 to the beginning of the insurgency. I will not go through the history of the insurgency. There was the JKLF [Jammu Kashmir Liberation Front], supposedly a secular formation to begin with, but already by 1994, the balance of power shifted into the hands of the Hizbul Mujahideen; after that, there were groups like the Lashkar-e-Taiba and the Jaish-e-Mohammad, trained in terror by Pakistan, which attacked our military and civilian targets alike. All that I will say is that it is a story of brutalization that should hold the salutary lesson that tactics of terror generally prove self-defeating for the cause that they try to promote. Conversely, it is futile to seek an end to the cycle of terrorism without addressing the roots of injustice—real and perceived—that nourish it.

Our former prime minister, Shri Atal Behari Vajpayee, had the vision and statesmanship to understand the complexity of the Kashmir problem. Can we forget that he released Hurriyat leaders from prison in the spring of 2000? He declared a Ramzan truce later that winter. He showed that his government was capable of goodwill to try and grasp the Kashmir nettle. I would urge the current Government of India to follow in Shri Vajpayeeji's footsteps and open a comprehensive political dialogue with all shades of opinion in Jammu and Kashmir.

Now if the British government headed by John Major and Tony Blair could talk to Martin McGuinness, the de facto head of the Irish Republican Army to reach the Good Friday Agreement of 1998, there is no reason why we cannot speak to those who are deeply alienated while maintaining our own commitment to the unity and integrity of India. There will, of course, be no shortcuts in this process. We must have a people-centred approach; we should not treat Kashmir as a real-estate dispute; and also we have to let Kashmiris talk to one another. The demographic composition of Kashmir is very complex. That is why no simple plebiscitary solution is possible there. We all know that in order to ensure rule by religiously defined majorities, Bengal and Punjab were partitioned in 1947 and also Ulster in Ireland was partitioned. And those of us who know the human toll of this expedient decision to partition would want to keep census-takers and map-makers with an old colonial mindset as far away as possible from the drawing board of a Kashmir peace process.

I now come to the constructive proposal that I want to offer this government. More than a decade ago, Sumantra Bose—who, for reasons of transparency, I should say is my younger brother—wrote a book called *Kashmir: Roots of Conflict, Path to Peace* [Cambridge, Mass.: Harvard University Press, 2003] where he suggested that in the search for a peace-building framework, we could take a leaf or two out of the book of the Irish peace process. Now, the Irish experiment occasionally runs into rough weather but it has proceeded much further than is the case of the subcontinent. We can modify it to suit our conditions. Vajpayeeji had been willing and eager between 2000 and 2004 to open new channels of communication with a wide array of groups in Kashmir, even those who had been shunned earlier as separatists. He also did a major rethink on our earlier stance of negotiations with Islamabad as there seemed to be no prospect of long-term peace in Kashmir without bringing Pakistan on board. It is very easy to blame the neighbouring country. But, even Satan cannot enter until he has found a flaw. So, we should look inwards and remove that flaw that we might have so that that does not happen. We need to talk to our own Kashmiri citizens once again. Let Kashmiris talk to one another, give the regional peoples of Jammu, Ladakh and Kashmir Valley a chance to arrive at an adjustment of their claims and counterclaims. The people of Kashmir have a long history of knowing how to live with differences. We do not need to force them into communitarian ghettos.

The history of ancient, medieval, early modern India is replete with instances of rajas, maharajas, *maharajadhirajas*, shahs and *shehanshahs* reigning in relative peace, having shared sovereignty along different layers of the Indian polity. An emperor was only a king at the centre of a circle of kings. Today, the Centre needs to be a democratically elected central government at the Centre of a circle of state governments. The best speeches today that I have heard have been from leaders of regional parties, whether it is Shri Tathagata Satpathy speaking for the Biju Janata Dal [BJD] or the person who spoke on behalf of the Yuvajana, Shramika, Rythu [YSR] Congress Party. We have a chance now to completely renegotiate the federal equation and have a new kind of a political centre which, I believe, will be a federal union that will be a long-lasting and stronger union. So, I would like to suggest to this government that we in India learnt the concept of unitary sovereignty from the British. In 1947 we were not able to layer and share sovereignty and sadly we divided the land.

A drastic redefinition of sovereignty preceded the Good Friday Agreement in Ireland and also paved the way for Scottish and Welsh autonomy. And this ideational change was not easy to achieve. If the British can rethink the idea of sovereignty and share it, I do not see why we cannot do so. Let us take a leaf out of that book. The British gave up absolutist claims of sovereignty over Northern Ireland, yielded political space to new democratic arenas which hold lessons for comparable conflicts. Of course, Brexit is going to create all kinds of problems now in Northern Ireland, but it [the Good Friday Agreement] was a good move.

Our best political theorists who lived in the precolonial period, who led our anti-colonial struggle, would have had no argument over the concept of layered and shared sovereignty. They knew its theory and practice. There is no reason why we should be beset by the ghosts of Curzon and Mountbatten and cling to a colonial definition of sovereignty. We can do much better if we rely on our own political traditions in building an

Indian Union which young people in the northern and also the northeastern extremities of our vast country will proudly want to be part of and certainly not want to leave.

So, I want this House, this Lok Sabha, to rise up to the full stature of its statesmanship and try its level best to turn Kashmir, which has been a crucible of conflict, into a cradle of peace. Thank you, Mr Deputy Speaker, for letting me speak.

ACKNOWLEDGEMENTS

On the occasion of the fiftieth anniversary of South Asian independence and partition I gave the G.M. Trevelyan Lecture on 'Nation, Reason and Religion' in one of the Mill Lane lecture rooms in Cambridge at the invitation of Chris Bayly. His passing has left a huge void in the historical profession. I remember him fondly for the example he set in academic collegiality and intellectual mentorship. My debts to many outstanding scholars are duly recorded in the endnotes. The ideas in all of the essays published in this book were initially tried out in conversations with my former and current graduate students and in lectures delivered to undergraduates. I am deeply grateful to all of them. In particular, I have had insightful discussions on nationalism and cultural difference with Semanti Ghosh. Kris Manjapra, now associate professor at Tufts University, helped in thinking through the question of cosmopolitanism and patriotism. Mou Banerjee put some of the older essays composed with obsolete software into acceptable digital format and provided helpful suggestions on content and style.

The title essay 'The Nation as Mother' was originally written for a Tufts conference. I have had the good fortune for several years of jointly teaching a course on the history and economics of India and South Asia with Amartya Sen at Harvard. That enriching experience has undoubtedly influenced this book. I have had numerous stimulating conversations with Homi Bhabha in formal and informal settings. The Lok Sabha has been for me a classroom with a difference. I wish to record a special word of gratitude to all those who listened to my speeches delivered in Parliament and sent me thoughtful and encouraging responses.

Ranjana Sengupta of Penguin Random House India persuaded me to undertake this project and has been of immense help throughout the editorial and publication process. I would also like to thank Arpita Basu for her careful copy-editing of the manuscript.

My mother, Krishna Bose, has been a matchless inspiration as a writer, teacher and parliamentarian. I have benefited from my brother Sumantra Bose's works on comparative politics. The arguments put forward in this book, especially on the complex relationship between nation and religion as well as the vexed question of sovereignty, have been honed over decades of brainstorming with Ayesha Jalal.

NOTES

Introduction

1. Rabindranath Tagore, *Nationalism* (Westport, Conn.: Greenwood Press, 1973; originally published New York: Macmillan Company, 1917), p. 127.
2. Ibid., pp. 133, 57.
3. Ibid., pp. 24, 149.
4. Ibid., pp. 35–36, 58, 95, 103.
5. Ibid., p. 138.
6. Chittaranjan Das, presidential speech at the Bengal Provincial Conference, April 1917, and Bipin Chandra Pal, *Nationality and Empire: A Running Study of Some Current Indian Problems* (Calcutta: Thacker, Spink and Co., 1917), cited and discussed in Semanti Ghosh, *Different Nationalisms: Bengal, 1905-1947* (Delhi: Oxford University Press, 2017), pp. 120–37.
7. Ayesha Jalal, 'Exploding Communalism: The Politics of Muslim Identity in South Asia', in Sugata Bose and Ayesha Jalal (eds.), *Nationalism, Democracy and Development: State and Politics in India* (Delhi: Oxford University Press, 1997), pp. 76–103.
8. Tagore, *Nationalism*, pp. 139–40, 147.

The Nation as Mother

1. Earlier versions of this essay were presented at the seminar on 'Languages, Literatures and Societies in South Asia' at the University of Pennsylvania and at St Antony's College, University of Oxford. I am grateful for comments by Ranajit Guha, David Ludden, Ayesha

Jalal, Sumathi Ramaswamy, Gayatri Chakravorty Spivak and David Washbrook. I have benefited from the important theoretical and historical work on nationalism by Partha Chatterjee even though my disagreements with certain key aspects of his method and conclusions will be evident. Needless to say, I bear sole responsibility for any errors and for any contentious arguments and interpretations I have chosen to advance.
2. Bipin Chandra Pal, *The Soul of India: A Constructive Study of Indian Thoughts and Ideals* (Calcutta: Yugayatri Prakashak, 4th edition, 1958), p. 134.
3. Surendranath Banerjea's challenge to Curzon's confident assertion about the done deal of partition was phrased in these terms.
4. *Millat*, 28 Chaitra, 1353; 11 April 1947, p. 2.
5. Those who are not steeped in Puranic mythology may wish to refer to Sudhir Chandra Sarkar (ed.), *Pouranic Abhidhan* (A Dictionary of the Puranas, Calcutta: M.C. Sarkar and Sons, 1963), pp. 289–92.
6. Aurobindo Ghose, 'Rishi Bankim Chandra', in *Bande Mataram*, 16 April 1907. Aurobindo overlooked the contributions of Bhudeb Mukhopadhyay who preceded Bankim in crafting the image of the mother in nationalist fiction. Of course, Bhudeb missed the 'fated moment' and did not have the same impact on Bengali nationalist consciousness as 'Rishi Bankim' (the sage Bankim).
7. I have read Aurobindo's translations of this poem in verse and prose in *Karmayogin*, 20 November 1909, and have borrowed from him. But I have made quite a few changes in an attempt to give a more accurate and simpler rendering of the Bengali original.
8. There is mention of this in Rabindranath Tagore, *Jibansmriti*, in *Rabindra Rachanabali*, vol. 17 (Calcutta: Visva-Bharati, 1965), pp. 348–53.
9. Cf. Tapati Guha-Thakurta, *The Making of a New 'Indian' Art: Artist, Aesthetics and Nationalism in Bengal, c. 1850–1920* (Cambridge: Cambridge University Press, 1992), pp. 255, 258.
10. See Ashis Nandy, *The Intimate Enemy: Loss and Recovery of Self under Colonialism* (Delhi: Oxford University Press, 1983).
11. Sara Suleri, *The Rhetoric of English India* (Chicago: University of Chicago Press, 1992), pp. 16–17.
12. Tanika Sarkar, 'Nationalist Iconography: Image of Women in 19th Century Bengali Literature', *Economic and Political Weekly*, 21 November 1987, p. 2011.
13. Pal, *Soul of India*, pp. 102–05, 108–09.

14. Carolyn Merchant, *The Death of Nature: Women, Ecology and the Scientific Revolution* (San Francisco: Harper and Row, 1980), pp. 2–3.
15. See Benedict Anderson, *Imagined Communities: Reflections on the Origin and Spread of Nationalism* (London: Verso, 1991), p. 141.
16. I am grateful to Ranajit Guha and Gayatri Chakravorty Spivak for encouraging me to take a sceptical view of Pal's ideological construction.
17. Sarkar, 'Nationalist Iconography', p. 2012.
18. Khana cut off her tongue rather than utter pearls of wisdom that cast her husband into the shade.
19. Jung's observation that 'the consequence of increasing Matriolatry was the witch hunt' in the European Middle Ages was not wholly irrelevant to Bengal in terms of social consequence. But the psyche underlying the collective worship of the Virgin Mary was qualitatively different from the adoration of the Mother Goddess.
20. Sister Nivedita, Swami Vivekananda's famous Irish disciple, stressed this point in 'The Function of Art in Shaping Nationality: "Notes" on "Bharatmata"', in *The Modern Review,* February 1907, cited in Guha-Thakurta, *The Making of a New 'Indian' Art,* p. 255.
21. Partha Chatterjee, *Nationalist Thought and the Colonial World: A Derivative Discourse?* (London: Zed Press, 1986), p. 42.
22. Partha Chatterjee, *The Nation and Its Fragments: Colonial and Postcolonial Histories* (Princeton and Delhi, 1994), pp. xi, 6, 9. Chatterjee is quite on target in underlining the attempt in nationalist discourse to separate the two domains. But he then makes a discursive shift to rather unquestioningly utilize this dichotomy in his own analysis. I discuss Chatterjee's assertion about the unviability of difference in the material domain of the state in the section entitled 'Nation and State' below.
23. Chatterjee, *Nationalist Thought,* pp. 43, 50–51.
24. Ibid., pp. 61, 73, 79.
25. Jasodhara Bagchi, 'Positivism and Nationalism: Womanhood and Crisis in Nationalist Fiction—Bankimchandra's *Anandamath*', in 'Review of Women's Studies', *Economic and Political Weekly,* October 1985. What is not clear, however, in Bagchi's analysis is the extent to which Bankim may or may not have been conversant with the various shifts in Comtean thought.
26. Pal, *Soul of India,* pp. 109–10. Pal was, of course, conversant with nineteenth-century European philosophy. While comparing Christian Trinity and Hindu Purusha-Prakriti, he wrote: 'To quote a well-known saying of one of your own European philosophers, in every act

of knowledge or reason, "the self separates itself from itself to return to itself to be itself". And if this be the logic of rational life, and if the Ultimate Reality, by whatever name called, whether God, or Allah, or Brahman, or Isvara, be intelligent and self-conscious, then you must posit in the very Being of that Reality an element of differentiation which, without cancelling the Divine Unity, supplies the object of Divine thought, through which the Divine realises his own consciousness. The Ultimate Reality being infinite, the object through which that Reality can realise its infinite reason, must also be infinite. As it is true of the rational, so also is it true of the emotional and the volitional life. Love also demands, with a view to realise itself, an object not different from, yet not absolutely identified with, the lover.' Pal, p. 111.

27. As Sara Suleri puts it, '. . . if colonial studies is to avoid a binarism that could cause it to atrophy in its own apprehension of difference, it needs to locate an idiom for alterity that can circumnavigate the more monolithic interpretations of cultural empowerment that tend to dominate current discourse'. Suleri, *Rhetoric of English India*, p. 4. For a powerful, if occasionally strident, Marxist critique of the indigenist (among other) fallacies of 'colonial discourse theory', see Aijaz Ahmad, *In Theory: Classes, Nations, Literatures* (London: Verso, 1992).

28. See Sarvani Datta, 'The Songs of Dwijendralal Roy: Its Sources and Lyrics' (MPhil diss., University of Calcutta, 1989).

29. Partha Chatterjee provides some insightful glimpses into the variations between the written and spoken word as well as the role of the theatre in middle-class nationalism in *The Nation and Its Fragments*, pp. 7–8, 55–58. Poetry has not received the same attention as prose from students of nationalism. The novel was arguably *the* literary vehicle that transmitted the content and forms of 'Western' nationalism to colonial settings. Poems and songs, despite borrowings of Western forms, represented alternative modes of expression that might suggest a different accent on the question of derivation in particular and the languages of nationalism in general.

30. Chatterjee, *Nationalist Thought*, p. 51. In *The Nation and Its Fragments*, however, he advances an argument about the 'subalternity of an elite', referring to the Calcutta middle class, p. 37.

31. Sarkar, 'Nationalist Iconography', p. 2012.

32. The relevant lines from the song 'Durgama giri kantar maru' are *Jatir athaba jater karibe tran, kandari balo dubichhe manush santan mor ma'r*. Kazi Nazrul Islam, *Nazrul Rachanabali* (Dhaka: Bangla Academy, 1993), pp. 288–89.

33. Sri Aurobindo, *The Spirit and Form of Indian Polity* (Calcutta: Arya Publishing House, 1947), pp. 86, 89. This volume consisted of chapters extracted from 'A Defence of Indian Culture', a series of essays written in response to William Archer's strictures upon Indian culture and civilization and published in *Arya* in 1918–21.
34. Dinesh Gupta to his *boudi* (sister-in-law), 18 June 1931; see also Dinesh Gupta to his mother, 17 June 1931 and 30 June 1931. Originally published in *Benu*, a Bengali monthly literary magazine, in 1931, these letters have been quoted in full in Sailesh De, *Benoy, Badal, Dinesh* (Calcutta: Biswas Publishers, 1970), pp. 154–56, 158.
35. See Subhas Chandra Bose to Jawaharlal Nehru, 17 October 1937, in Sisir Kumar Bose and Sugata Bose (eds.), *The Collected Works of Netaji Subhas Chandra Bose*, vol. 8, *India's Spokesman Abroad 1933–37* (Calcutta: Netaji Research Bureau, and Delhi: Oxford University Press, 1994). pp. 226–27; and Jawaharlal Nehru to Subhas Chandra Bose, 20 October 1937 (Nehru Memorial Museum and Library).
36. Rabindranath Tagore to Subhas Chandra Bose, 19 October 1937, and Tagore's press statement on 'Bande Mataram', 30 October 1937, cited in Nepal Majumdar, *Rabindranath o Subhaschandra* (Calcutta: Saraswati Publishers, 1987), pp. 56–57, 59–60. Nearly three decades prior to this direct political intervention, Tagore had subtly subverted the blind adoration of the mother-nation on the part of Gora, the hero of the most 'nationalist' of his novels, through a revelation of his Irish parentage. See Rabindranath Tagore, *Gora* (English translation, Madras: Macmillan, 1924).
37. See Majumdar, pp. 60–66.
38. Chatterjee, *Nationalist Thought*, pp. 55, 58.
39. Chatterjee, *Nation and Its Fragments*, pp. 113–15. One interesting dimension of these alternative regional histories of Bengal (written mostly by Hindus) is that they contain generally favourable assessments of the rule of independent Muslim sultans and nawabs of Bengal.
40. Sri Aurobindo, 'Desh o Jatiyata', in *Dharma o Jatiyata* (Pondicherry: Sri Aurobindo Ashram, 1957, originally written in 1920), pp. 80–83.
41. The complete Bengali original of this letter from Pradyot Bhattacharya to his mother is reproduced in Sailesh De, *Ami Subhas Balchi*, vol. 1 (Calcutta: Rabindra Library, 1970), pp. 316–19.
42. *Anandabazar Patrika*, 20 August 1939.
43. See Ayesha Jalal, *Democracy and Authoritarianism in South Asia: A Comparative and Historical Perspective* (Cambridge: Cambridge University Press, 1995), pp. 16–22.

44. Chatterjee, *Nationalist Thought*, pp. 49, 51.
45. Edward W. Said, *Culture and Imperialism* (New York: Alfred A. Knopf, 1993), pp. 217–19.
46. Pal, *Soul of India*, pp. 62–63, 65, 92.
47. Aurobindo, *Spirit and Form of Indian Polity*, pp. 77–78, 91.
48. See Chatterjee, *Nation and Its Fragments*, pp. 6–9.
49. See Partha Chatterjee's brilliant analysis in *Nationalist Thought*, chapter 4. It could be argued, however, that Gandhian thought was 'derivative' of certain nineteenth-century misperceptions of India's ancient 'village communities'.
50. See M.K. Gandhi, *Hind Swaraj*, in *The Collected Works of Mahatma Gandhi*, vol. 10 (New Delhi: Publications Division, Government of India, 1958), pp. 26, 32–38.
51. Mahatma Gandhi to Jawaharlal Nehru, 5 October 1945, in Jawaharlal Nehru, *A Bunch of Old Letters* (Delhi: Oxford University Press, centenary edition, 1989), pp. 505–06.
52. Chittaranjan Das, 'Swaraj Scheme, January 1923', in *The Oracle*, vol. IV, no. 1, Jan 1982, pp. 63–80. This remarkable 'constitution' held that the 'ordinary work' of a 'Central Government should be mainly advisory'. It called for 'a maximum of local autonomy, carried on mainly with advice and coordination from, and only a minimum of control by, higher centres . . .'
53. Rabindranath Tagore, 'Bharatbarsher Itihas', *Bharatbarsha*, in *Rabindra Rachanabali*, vol. 4 (Visva-Bharati, Santiniketan, 1965), p. 382.
54. *Anandabazar Patrika*, 20 August 1939.
55. Sarat Chandra Bose, *I Warned My Countrymen* (Calcutta: Netaji Research Bureau, 1968), p. 196.

Nation, Reason and Religion

1. I would like to thank Ayesha Jalal for inspiring the ideas that inform this lecture even though she does not share my starry-eyed admiration of Gandhi.
2. Jawaharlal Nehru, *Towards Freedom* (Boston: Beacon Press, 1958), p. 32.
3. David Cannadine, *G.M. Trevelyan: A Life in History* (London: Fontana Press, 1993), p. 92.
4. Nehru, *Towards Freedom*, pp. 34–36, 38.
5. Dipesh Chakrabarty, 'Radical Histories and the Question of Enlightenment Rationalism', *Economic and Political Weekly*, 8 April 1995, pp. 751–59.

6. Benedict Anderson, *Imagined Communities: Reflections on the Origin and Spread of Nationalism* (London: Verso, 1991), p. 11.
7. G.M. Trevelyan, *English Social History*, p. 353, and *British History in the Nineteenth Century*, p. vii, cited in Cannadine, G.M. Trevelyan, p. 202.
8. Thomas Babington Macaulay, 'Gladstone on Church and State', in G.M. Young (ed.), *Macaulay: Prose and Poetry* (Cambridge, Mass.: Harvard University Press, 1952), pp. 609–60, quotations from pp. 636–38.
9. Partha Chatterjee, 'Our Modernity', in *The Present History of West Bengal* (Delhi: Oxford University Press, 1997), p. 204.
10. Rajnarayan Basu, *She Kal aar E Kal*, in Brajendranath Bandyopadhyay and Sajanikanta Das (eds.) (Calcutta: Bangiya Sahitya Parishad, 1956), cited in Chatterjee, 'Our Modernity', in *Present History*, p. 198.
11. Chatterjee, ibid., pp. 200, 210.
12. Partha Chatterjee, *The Nation and Its Fragments: Colonial and Postcolonial Histories* (Delhi: Oxford University Press, 1994), p. 110.
13. I have undertaken an elaborate critique of this position elsewhere. See my 'Nation as Mother: Representations and Contestations of "India" in Bengali Literature and Culture', in Sugata Bose and Ayesha Jalal (eds.), *Nationalism, Democracy and Development: State and Politics in India* (Delhi: Oxford University Press, 1997), pp. 50–75.
14. Ramabai Ranade (ed.), *Miscellaneous Writings of the late Hon'ble Mr. Justice M.G. Ranade* (Delhi: Sahitya Akademi, 1992), p. 190.
15. Chatterjee, 'Our Modernity', in *Present History*, p. 199.
16. Ranade (ed.), *Miscellaneous Writings of... M.G. Ranade*, pp. 193–94.
17. Lala Lajpat Rai, *Writings and Speeches*, vol. 1 (Delhi: University Publishers, 1966), p. 47.
18. Aurobindo Ghose, 'New Lamps for Old', in Haridas Mukherjee and Uma Mukherjee, *Sri Aurobindo's Political Thought (1893-1908)* (Calcutta: Firma K.L. Mukhopadhyay, 1958), pp. 103–04.
19. Ibid., pp. 108–09.
20. Cited in R.F. Foster, *Modern Ireland, 1600-1972* (London: Allen Lane, 1988), p. 454.
21. Cited in Ayesha Jalal, 'Exploding Communalism: The Politics of Muslim Identity in South Asia', in Bose and Jalal (eds.), *Nationalism, Democracy and Development*, p. 87.
22. For a fuller treatment of the history of this period see the relevant chapters in Sugata Bose and Ayesha Jalal, *Modern South Asia: History, Culture, Political Economy* (London: Routledge, and Delhi: Oxford University Press, 1997), pp. 107–25.

23. See 'The Moment of Manoeuvre: Gandhi and the Critique of Civil Society', in Partha Chatterjee, *Nationalist Thought and the Colonial World: A Derivative Discourse* (Minneapolis: University of Minnesota Press, 1993), pp. 85–130. The quoted phrases appear on p. 93.
24. 'Mr Andrews' Difficulty', *Young India*, 21 July 1920, in Mahatma Gandhi, *Young India 1919-1922* (Madras: S. Ganesan, 1922), pp. 151–52.
25. 'Khilafat', *Young India*, 12 May 1920, in ibid., p. 158.
26. 'Why I Have Joined the Khilafat Movement', *Young India*, 28 April 1920, in ibid., p. 154.
27. Ibid., p. 153. See also 'Pledges Broken', *Young India*, 19 May 1920, in ibid., pp. 159–62.
28. 'Mr Andrews' Difficulty', *Young India*, 21 July 1920, in ibid., pp. 152–53.
29. 'The Khilafat', *Young India*, 23 March 1921, in ibid., pp. 178–79.
30. 'The Question of Questions', *Young India*, 10 March 1920, in ibid., p. 145.
31. 'The Turkish Question', *Young India*, 29 June 1921, in ibid., pp. 180–81.
32. 'Three National Cries', *Young India*, 8 September 1920, in ibid., pp. 442–43.
33. 'Hindu-Muslim Unity a Camouflage', *Young India*, 20 October 1921, in ibid., p. 419. Gandhi had not, however, wanted to make the stopping of cow-killing a condition for lending Hindu support to the Khilafat claim. See 'Khilafat and the Cow Question', *Young India*, 10 December 1919, in ibid., pp. 141–43.
34. 'The Inwardness of Non-Co-Operation', *Young India*, 8 September 1920, in ibid., p. 237.
35. 'Hindu-Mahomedan Unity', *Young India*, 25 February 1920, in ibid., pp. 397–400.
36. 'Hindu-Muslim Unity', *Young India*, 20 October 1921, in ibid., p. 421.
37. 'The Meaning of the Moplah Rising', *Young India*, 20 October 1921, in ibid., pp. 675–78.
38. 'Hindu-Muslim Unity', *Young India*, 28 July 1921, in ibid., p. 417.
39. 'Ireland and India', *Young India*, 15 December 1921, in ibid., pp. 621–22.
40. Ayesha Jalal, 'Territorial Nationalism and Islamic Universalism: South Asian Critiques of the European Nation-State', paper presented at the Institute of Advanced Study, Berlin, June 1997. I owe the insights into religion and rights to her latest work, *Self and Sovereignty: Individual and Community in South Asian Islam since 1850* (London: Routledge, 2000).
41. See Mohamed Ali's statement in R.M. Thadani, *The Historic State Trial of the Ali Brothers* (Karachi, 1921), pp. 63–87. I am grateful to Ayesha Jalal for bringing Mohamed Ali's line of contestation to my

attention. For a much more detailed analysis which does full justice to Muslim conceptions of rights as well as sovereignty during the Khilafat movement, see Ayesha Jalal, *Self and Sovereignty*, chapter 5.

42. Nehru, *Towards Freedom*, pp. 104–05.
43. Subhas Chandra Bose, *The Indian Struggle: 1920-1942*, Sisir Kumar Bose and Sugata Bose (eds.) (Calcutta: Netaji Research Bureau, and Delhi: Oxford University Press, 1997), pp. 102, 112.
44. Sisir Kumar Bose and Sugata Bose (eds.), *The Essential Writings of Netaji Subhas Chandra Bose* (Calcutta: Netaji Research Bureau, and Delhi: Oxford University Press, 1997), pp. 3–4, 67–68, 86.
45. Nehru, *Towards Freedom*, p. 117.
46. M.A. Jinnah to Jawaharlal Nehru, 17 March 1938, in Jawaharlal Nehru, *A Bunch of Old Letters* (Delhi: Oxford University Press, 1986), p. 278.
47. Chatterjee, *Nationalist Thought*, pp. 113, 115.
48. Mulk Raj Anand, *Letters on India* (London: Labour Book Service, 1942), p. 9.
49. Bose and Bose (eds.), *Essential Writings of Netaji Subhas Chandra Bose*, pp. 11–12, 199–200.
50. Sisir Kumar Bose and Sugata Bose (eds.), *The Collected Works of Netaji Subhas Chandra Bose*, vol. 10, *The Alternative Leadership May 1939–January 1941* (Calcutta: Netaji Research Bureau, and Delhi: Oxford University Press, 1998), pp. 98–126.
51. Ibid., pp. xiii–xiv.
52. Ibid., p. 216.
53. Abid Hasan, *The Men from Imphal* (Calcutta: Netaji Research Bureau, 1995), p. 11.
54. Ibid., pp. 7–9.
55. Manuscript (archives of the Netaji Research Bureau, Calcutta).
56. 'India and Ireland', in Narayana Menon (ed.), *On to Delhi or Speeches and Writings of Subhas Chandra Bose* (Bangkok: Indian Independence League, 1944), p. 117. Bose had visited Ireland in early 1936 and knew Irish nationalists, including De Valera. He had also met De Valera in London in January 1938.
57. 'At Bahadur Shah's Tomb', in ibid., p. 90.
58. Text of speech delivered by His Excellency Dr Ba Maw, in ibid., p. 128.
59. Subhas Chandra Bose, 'The Great Patriot and Leader', in *Blood Bath* (Lahore: Hero Publications, 1947), p. 65.
60. See Moti Ram, *Two Historic Trials in Red Fort: An Authentic Account of the Trial by a General Court Martial of Captain Shah Nawaz Khan, Captain P.K. Sahgal and Lt. G.S. Dhillon and the Trial by a European Military Commission of Emperor Bahadur Shah* (New Delhi, 1946).

61. See Ayesha Jalal's G.M. Trevelyan Seminar, 27 November 1997, 'Nation, Reason and Religion: The Punjab's Role in the Partition of India' in this issue.
62. See the use of the concept of *Ausgleich* by the founder of Sinn Fein, Arthur Griffith, in his *The Resurrection of Hungary* (London: Whelan & Son, 1904).
63. Rabindranath Tagore, 'The Sunset of the Century', in *Nationalism* (Westport, Connecticut: Greenwood Press, 1973, originally published New York: Macmillan, 1917), pp. 157–59. In 1921 Tagore was sharply critical of the unreason inherent in the Gandhian ritual of spinning in 'The Call of Truth', in *The Modern Review*, 30, 4 (1921). For Gandhi's defence of his own position and his tribute to Tagore, see 'The Great Sentinel', *Young India*, 13 October 1921, in *Young India*, pp. 668–75.

Instruments and Idioms of Colonial and National Development

1. An earlier version of this essay was presented at the workshop on 'Historicizing Development', the first of three in the Social Science Research Council series on 'Development Knowledge and the Social Sciences', held on 10–12 December 1993, at Emory University, Atlanta. I am grateful to the workshop organizers and participants, especially Fred Cooper, Randall Packard and Michael Watts, for their helpful comments.
2. 'The Tiger Steps Out' is the caption of the next 'Survey of India', published three and a half years later, *The Economist*, 1991:5.
3. Interview of Vaclav Klaus, then finance minister of Czechoslovakia and later prime minister of the Czech Republic, with Sarmila Bose, *Anandabazar Patrika*, April 1990, cited in Bose, 'To Market, To Market: Economic Reform and Industry in India and Eastern Europe', mimeograph (Warwick Manufacturing Group, 1993).
4. Sukhamoy Chakravarty, *Development Planning: The Indian Experience* (Delhi: Oxford University Press, 1987).
5. Amartya Sen, 'Indian Development: Lessons and Non-Lessons', *Daedalus*, vol. 118, no. 4, 1989, pp. 369–92. Quote from p. 371.
6. On the distinction between 'means enhancement' and 'means use', see Sen, ibid., pp. 373–80.
7. Romesh C. Dutt, *Economic History of India*, vol. 2, *In the Victorian Age* (London: K. Paul, Trench, Trubner, 1904).
   Dadabhai Naoroji, *Poverty and Un-British Rule in India* (London: Sonnenshein, 1901).

8. Mahatma Gandhi, *The Collected Works of Mahatma Gandhi* (New Delhi: Publications Department, Government of India, 1958), pp. 22–23.
9. David Ludden, 'India's Development Regime', in Nicholas Dirks (ed.) *Colonialism and Culture* (Ann Arbor: Michigan University Press, 1992), pp. 247–87. Quote from p. 263.
10. Ibid., p. 249. Ludden defines a development regime as 'an institutionalized configuration of power within a state system ideologically committed to progress that draws its material sustenance from the conduct of development', p. 252.
11. Ibid., p. 262. Emphasis added.
12. On the lasting legacy of the centralized colonial state apparatus in postcolonial South Asia, see Ayesha Jalal, *Democracy and Authoritarianism in South Asia: A Comparative and Historical Perspective* (Cambridge: Cambridge University Press, 1995), pp. 16–22.
13. I am quoting from p. 57 of Partha Chatterjee's essay 'Development Planning and the Indian State', pp. 51–72, in Terence Byres (ed.) *The State of Development Planning in India* (Delhi: Oxford University Press, 1993).

    A slightly modified version of the same essay appears as the chapter entitled 'The National State' in Chatterjee, *The Nation and Its Fragments* (Princeton: Princeton University Press, 1993). Chatterjee does not use the word 'idiom', which I have introduced to clarify the aspects of legitimacy and instrumentality in the exercise of development planning.
14. Chatterjee, 'Development Planning and the Indian State', p. 52.
15. Partha Chatterjee, *Nationalist Discourse and the Colonial World: A Derivative Discourse?* (London: Zed Books, 1986).
16. Ludden, 'India's Development Regime', p. 263.
17. Sisir Kumar Bose and Sugata Bose (eds.), *The Collected Works of Netaji Subhas Chandra Bose*, vol. 9, *Congress President, Speeches, Articles and Letters, January 1938–April 1939* (Calcutta: Netaji Research Bureau, and Delhi: Oxford University Press, 1995), pp. 43–48.
18. Ibid., pp. 15–16.
19. 'I hope you will accept the Chairmanship of the Planning Committee,' Subhas Chandra Bose wrote to Jawaharlal Nehru on 19 October 1938. 'You must if it is to be a success.' See Jawaharlal Nehru, *A Bunch of Old Letters* (Delhi: Oxford University Press, centenary edition, 1989), p. 301.

    The fifteen-member committee consisted of five scientists (Nazir Ahmed, V.S. Dubey, J.C. Ghosh, A.K. Saha and Meghnad

Saha); four industrialists/businessmen (Walchand Hirachand, Ambalal Sarabhai, A.D. Shroff and Purushottamdas Thakurdas); three economists (Radhakamal Mukherjee, K.T. Shah and M. Visvesvaraya); and three politicians (N.M. Joshi, a labour leader; J.C. Kumarappa, a believer in Gandhian village communities; and Jawaharlal Nehru).

20. 'The other day I have had a long and interesting discussion with Dr Meghnad Saha about Scientific Planning for Indian Industry; I am convinced about its importance and as you have consented to act as the President of the Committee formed by Subhas for the guidance of the Congress, I would like to know your views on the matter,' wrote Rabindranath Tagore to Jawaharlal Nehru on 19 November 1938. See Nehru, *A Bunch of Old Letters*, p. 304.
21. Chatterjee, 'Development Planning and the Indian State', pp. 51–72, in *The State of Development Planning in India*, cited from p. 54.
22. Ashis Nandy, *The Intimate Enemy: Loss and Recovery of Self under Colonialism* (Delhi: Oxford University Press, 1983).
Nandy, 'The Political Culture of the Indian State', *Daedalus*, vol. 118, no. 4, 1989, pp. 1–26.
Chatterjee, *Nationalist Discourse and the Colonial World*, pp. 85–130.
23. Mahatma Gandhi, *The Collected Works of Mahatma Gandhi* (New Delhi: Publications Department, Government of India, 1958), vol. 3, pp. 332, 341.
24. Chatterjee, *Nationalist Discourse and the Colonial* World, p. 93.
25. Chittaranjan Das, 'Swaraj Scheme, January 1923', *The Oracle*, vol. IV, no. 1, January 1982, reprint, pp. 63–80.
26. I have engaged in a more detailed discussion of alternative models of nation and state in anti-colonial thought in Sugata Bose, 'Nation as Mother: Representations and Contestations of "India" in Bengali Literature and Culture', in Sugata Bose and Ayesha Jalal, *Nationalism, Democracy, and Development: State and Politics in India* (Delhi: Oxford University Press, 1996), pp. 50–75.
27. Santimay Chatterjee (ed.), *Collected Works of Meghnad Saha* (Calcutta: Saha Institute of Nuclear Physics, and Bombay: Orient Longman, 1987), vol. 2, pp. 431, 445.
28. Ibid., vol. 2, p. 533.
Meghnad Saha was elected to Parliament in 1952 from Calcutta by defeating the Indian National Congress as an independent candidate with the support of the leftist parties. Of particular interest is his pamphlet 'Rethinking Our Future: An Objective Review of the Report of the Planning Commission and Its Industrial Programme'

(S. Chatterjee, 1987, pp. 532–637). In addition to his trenchant criticisms of India's postcolonial development policies, he denounced the Congress government's reneging on its long-standing promise of linguistic reorganization of states in the name of the state's integrity and administrative convenience (S. Chatterjee, 1993, vol. 3, pp. 528–54). He also dissented from the state's decision to 'concentrate' nuclear physics research, calling for a more decentralized structure so as not to 'smother all fundamental research and choke the growth of knowledge' (S. Chatterjee, 1993, vol. 4, p. 175).

29. A.F. Robertson, *People and the State: An Anthropology of Planned Development* (Cambridge: Cambridge University Press, 1984), p. 20.
30. Sukhamoy Chakravarty, *Development Planning: The Indian Experience* (Delhi: Oxford University Press, 1987), pp. 3, 14.
31. Ibid., p. 28.
32. Amartya Sen, 'Development: Which Way Now?', *The Economic Journal*, vol. 93, no. 372, 1983, pp. 745–62.
33. Akhil Gupta, 'Agrarian Populism in the Development of a Modern Nation (India)', in Frederick Cooper and Randall M. Packard (eds.), *International Development and the Social Sciences: Essays on the History and Politics of Knowledge* (Berkeley: University of California Press, 1997), pp. 320–44.
34. Chakravarty, *Development Planning*, p. 38.
35. Kaushik Basu, 'Indian Economy: Performance and Policy', in R.A. Choudhury, Shama Gamkhar and Aurobindo Ghose (eds.), *The Indian Economy and Its Performance since Independence* (Delhi: Oxford University Press, 1990), p. 108.
36. Ibid, p. 110.
37. Sen, 'Indian Development', pp. 369–92. Quote from p. 374.
38. Ibid., p. 387.
39. Ibid., pp. 369–92. Quote from p. 384.
40. Jagdish N. Bhagwati, *India in Transition: Freeing the Economy* (Oxford: Oxford University Press, 1993).
41. Sen, 'Indian Development', pp. 369–92. Quote from p. 388.
42. Pranab Bardhan, *The Political Economy of Development in India* (Delhi: Oxford University Press, 1985), pp. 61, 65, 73–74.
    Pranab Bardhan, 'A Political Economy Perspective on Development', in Bimal Jalan (ed.), *Indian Economy: Problems and Prospects* (Delhi: Viking, 1992), pp. 324–27.
43. Ashis Nandy, *Science, Hegemony and Violence: A Requiem for Modernity* (Tokyo, Japan: United Nations University, 1988).

Frédérique Apffel-Marglin and Stephen Marglin (eds.), *Dominating Knowledge: Development, Culture, and Resistance: Studies in Development Economics* (New York: Oxford University Press, 1990).
44. Ludden, 'India's Development Regime', p. 279.
45. Ashis Nandy, 'The Political Culture of the Indian State', *Daedalus*, vol. 118, no. 4, 1989, p. 25.
46. Ludden, 'India's Development Regime', p. 278.
47. Ibid., p. 266.
48. Pranab Bardhan, 'The State against Society: The Great Divide in Indian Social Science Discourse', in Bose and Jalal (eds.) *Nationalism, Democracy and Development*, pp. 184–95.
49. For a more elaborate statement of an argument about ways to re-evaluate nationalism, reinvigorate democracy and reconstitute development, see Bose and Jalal (eds.) *Nationalism, Democracy and Development*.
50. Jean Drèze and Amartya Sen, *India: Economic Development and Social Opportunity* (Delhi: Oxford University Press, 1995), pp. 179–204.

The Spirit and Form of an Ethical Polity

1. An earlier version of this essay was given as the Sri Aurobindo Memorial Oration at the Centre for Human Values, Indian Institute of Management, Calcutta, on 12 August 2005.
2. Bejoy Krishna Bose, *The Alipore Bomb Trial* (Calcutta: Butterworth, 1922), pp. 140–41.
   Chittaranjan Das served as Aurobindo Ghose's defence counsel in 1909. Das later rose to become the pre-eminent leader of the Indian nationalist movement between 1917 and 1925, and was given the honorific title 'Deshbandhu' ('Friend of the Country').
3. P.C. Ray, *Life and Times of C.R. Das* (London and Calcutta: Oxford University Press, 1927), p. 62.
4. Bose, *Alipore Bomb Trial*, p. 111.
5. Sumit Sarkar, *The Swadeshi Movement in Bengal, 1903-1908* (New Delhi: People's Publishing House, 1973), pp. 315–16.
6. Ashis Nandy, *The Illegitimacy of Nationalism: Rabindranath Tagore and the Politics of Self* (Delhi: Oxford University Press, 1994), p. 7.
7. Andrew Sartori, 'The Categorical Logic of a Colonial Nationalism: Swadeshi Bengal, 1904-1908', *Comparative Studies of South Asia, Africa and the Middle East*, 23: 1 & 2, 2003, p. 272.
8. C.A. Bayly, *The Origins of Nationality in South Asia* (Delhi: Oxford University Press, 1998) and 'Liberalism at Large: Giuseppe Mazzini

and Nineteenth Century Indian Thought', Tufts University, 7 April 2005.
9. Benedict Anderson, *Imagined Communities: Reflections on the Origin and Spread of Nationalism* (London: Verso, 1991); Partha Chatterjee, *Nationalist Thought and the Colonial World: A Derivative Discourse* (Minneapolis: University of Minnesota Press, 1993).
10. Kris Manjapra's important doctoral research at Harvard University on intellectual encounters between Germany and India is based on this approach.
11. Ranajit Guha, 'Nationalism and the Trials of Becoming', *The Oracle*, vol. XXIV, no. 2, August 2002, pp. 12, 15, 17–20.
12. K.R. Srinivasa Iyengar, *Sri Aurobindo* (Calcutta: Arya Publishing House, 1945), p. 119.
13. The viceroy had divided this province proud of its linguistic and cultural unity largely along religious lines. The anti-partition agitation grew into the Swadeshi (own country) movement with the goal of winning 'swaraj' (self-rule).
14. Iyengar, *Sri Aurobindo*, pp. 124–27.
15. Sri Aurobindo, *The Doctrine of Passive Resistance* (Calcutta: Arya Publishing House, 1948), pp. 27–30.
16. Ibid., pp. 62, 65, 78.
17. Bipin Chandra Pal, 'The New Patriotism', in *Swadeshi and Swaraj: The Rise of New Patriotism* (Calcutta: Yugayatri Prakashak, 1954), pp. 17–20.
18. Biman Behari Majumdar, *History of Political Thought: From Rammohun to Dayananda (1821-84)*, vol. 1, *Bengal* (Calcutta: University of Calcutta, 1934), pp. 284–320.
19. Aurobindo, *Doctrine of Passive Resistance*, pp. 81, 83–85, 87–88.
20. *Speeches of Aurobindo Ghose* (Chandernagore: Prabartak Publishing House, 1922), p. 7.
21. Iyengar, *Sri Aurobindo*, pp. 149–50.
22. Ibid., p. 160.
23. *Speeches*, pp. 10–12, 15, 27, 35–39.
24. Ibid., pp. 65, 70, 75.
25. Ibid., p. 108.
26. Dipesh Chakrabarty, 'Radical Histories and the Question of Enlightenment Rationalism: Some Recent Critiques of Subaltern Studies', *Economic and Political Weekly*, 8 April 1995, p. 753.
27. *Speeches*, pp. 86–87, 90–93, 100–01, 108.
28. Sri Aurobindo, *The Ideal of the Karmayogin* (Calcutta: Arya Publishing House, 1945), pp. 6, 20–22, 26–27, 30–32.

29. Iyengar, *Sri Aurobindo*, p. 213.
30. Aurobindo, *Ideal of the Karmayogin*, p. 61.
31. *Speeches*, pp. 225, 231.
32. Sarkar, *Swadeshi Movement*, p. 316.
33. Sri Aurobindo, *Views and Reviews* (Madras: Sri Aurobindo Library, 1946), p. 7.
34. Sri Aurobindo, *The Renaissance in India* (Calcutta: Arya Publishing House, 1946), p. 81.
35. Sri Aurobindo, *The Significance of Indian Art* (Pondicherry: Sri Aurobindo Ashram, 1953).
36. Sri Aurobindo, *The Spirit and Form of Indian Polity* (Calcutta: Arya Publishing House, 1947), pp. 3–5, 22.
37. Ibid., pp. 10–15, 42, 45, 47–48.
38. Ibid., pp. 16–18, 34, 62.
39. Ibid., pp. 65–66, 75.
40. Ibid., pp. 72, 76–78.
41. Ibid., pp. 78–80, 86–87.
42. Ibid., pp. 88–89.
43. Ibid., pp. 90–91. In the late seventeenth century Ramdas's philosophy of regional patriotism and Shivaji's statecraft had formed the basis of a Maratha 'Swarajya' (independent kingdom). The Marathas emerged in the eighteenth century as a strong regional power in western India led by the Peshwas and seemed the most likely inheritors of the Mughal imperial mantle. The Sikh Khalsa (literally, the pure) had established a powerful regional kingdom in the Punjab.
44. Sisir Kumar Bose and Sugata Bose (eds.), *The Collected Works of Netaji Subhas Chandra Bose*, vol. 1, *An Indian Pilgrim* (Calcutta: Netaji Research Bureau, 1997), p. 112.
45. Guha, 'Nationalism', p. 20.
46. This point is conceded a little too easily in Partha Chatterjee, *The Nation and Its Fragments* (Delhi: Oxford University Press, 1994), pp. 1–7.
47. Aurobindo, *Spirit and Form*, p. 91.

Different Universalisms, Colourful Cosmopolitanisms

1. Rabindranath Tagore, 'Africa'.

> Across the ocean that very moment at dawn and dusk
> Church bells rang out in their neighbourhoods in the name of a benign God

> Children played in their mother's laps
> Poets sang paeans to beauty.
> Today when on the western horizon
> The twilight hour is stifled by stormy winds,
> As beasts emerge from secret caves
> To proclaim by their ominous howls
> The death of the day,
> Come, poet of the fatal hour,
> In the fading light of this sombre evening,
> Stand at that ravished woman's door,
> Ask for her forgiveness,
> In the midst of civilization's savage delirium,
> May it be your last auspicious utterance.
> (Trans. Sugata Bose)

2. Sugata Bose, *A Hundred Horizons: The Indian Ocean in the Age of Global Empire* (Cambridge, Mass.: Harvard University Press, 2006), pp. 267–70.
3. Homi Bhabha, *The Location of Culture* (New York: Routledge, 2004); Engseng Ho, *The Graves of Tarim: Genealogy and Mobility across the Indian Ocean* (Berkeley: University of California Press, 2006); Anthony Appiah, *Cosmopolitanism: Ethics in a World of Strangers* (New York: W.W. Norton, 2006).
4. I am drawing and elaborating upon Saranindranath Tagore's threefold classification of these philosophical streams. See Saranindranath Tagore, 'Rabindranath Tagore's Conception of Cosmopolitanism', forthcoming *University of Toronto Quarterly*.
5. Martha Nussbaum, 'Patriotism and Cosmopolitanism', in Joshua Cohen (ed.), *For Love of Country: Debating the Limits of Patriotism* (Boston: Beacon Press, 1996), pp.4–17.
6. Gopal Gandhi (ed.), *A Frank Friendship: Gandhi and Bengal* (Calcutta: Seagull, 2008), p. 336.
7. Hilary Putnam, 'Must We Choose between Patriotism and Universal Reason?', in Cohen (ed.) *For Love of Country*, pp. 91–97.
8. My concept of colourful cosmopolitanism is to be distinguished from Nico Slate's notion of coloured cosmopolitanism to describe solidarity among coloured peoples of the world. Colourful cosmopolitanism is meant to evoke a kind of cosmopolitanism that springs from vernacular roots and is compatible with the best traditions of anti-colonial nationalism. There is nothing 'partial' about colourful cosmopolitanism, contrary to Appiah's imposition of this limitation on rooted cosmopolitanism.

9. Charles Maier, 'Consigning the Twentieth Century to History: Alternative Narratives for the Modern Era', *American Historical Review*, 105, no. 3, June 2000, 807–31.
10. Erez Manela, *The Wilsonian Moment: Self-Determination and the International Origins of Anticolonial Nationalism* (New York: Oxford University Press, 2007); for a critique see the review by Rebecca E. Karl in *American Historical Review*, 113, no. 5, December 2008, pp. 1474–76.
11. Ayesha Jalal, *Self and Sovereignty: Individual and Community in South Asian Islam since 1850* (London: Routledge, 2000), pp. 187–261.
12. Bose, *A Hundred Horizons*, p. 161.
13. Jalal, *Self and Sovereignty*, pp. 43–101.
14. Nayanjot Lahiri, 'Bodh-Gaya: An Ancient Buddhist Shrine and Its Modern History', in Timothy Insoll (ed.), *Case Studies in Archaeology and Religion* (Oxford: Archaeopress), pp. 33–44.
15. Bose, *A Hundred Horizons*, p. 170.
16. Martin Lewis and Karen Wigen, *The Myth of Continents: A Critique of Metageography* (Berkeley: University of California Press, 1997).
17. Cited in Bose, *A Hundred Horizons*, pp. 108–09.
18. Deshbandhu Chittaranjan Das, 'Bengal and the Bengalees', in *Brief Survey of Life and Work, Provincial Conference Speeches, Congress Speeches* (Calcutta: Rajen Sen and B.K. Sen, n.d.), pp. 31–32, 1919–24. There are similarities between Das's views on the relationship between nationalism and universalism and those of Aurobindo Ghose. See Sugata Bose, 'The Spirit and Form of an Ethical Polity: A Meditation on Aurobindo's Thought', *Modern Intellectual History*, April 2007.
19. 'The Turkish Question', *Young India*, 29 June 1921, in Mahatma Gandhi, *Young India 1919–1922* (Madras: S. Ganesan, 1922), pp. 180–81.
20. Deshbandhu Chittaranjan Das, 'Swaraj and Dominion Status', in *Brief Survey of Life and Work*, p. 337.
21. The current whereabouts of this painting are unknown.
22. Nirad Chandra Chaudhuri, 'Nandalal Basur Ekti Chhabi', first published in *Bangasree*, 6 June 1933, reprinted in *Nirbachita Prabandha* (Calcutta: Ananda, 2000), pp. 277–80.
23. Nandalal Bose, *Vision and Creation* (Calcutta: Visva Bharati, 1999), p. 235.
24. Ibid.
25. Sisir Kumar Bose and Sugata Bose (eds.), *The Essential Writings of Netaji Subhas Chandra Bose* (Calcutta: Netaji Research Bureau and Delhi: Oxford University Press, 1997), pp. 175–90.
26. Sonya Rhie Quintanilla (ed.), *Rhythms of India: The Art of Nandalal Bose* (San Diego: San Diego Museum of Art, 2008).

27. Nandalal Bose to Kanai Samanta, February 1943, in Nandalal Bose, *Vision and Creation*, p. 269.
28. Sisir Kumar Bose and Sugata Bose (eds.), *The Collected Works of Netaji Subhas Chandra Bose*, vol. 12, *Chalo Delhi: Writing and Speeches 1943–1945* (Calcutta: Netaji Research Bureau and Delhi: Permanent Black, 2007), pp. 79, 161–62.
29. See Nirad Chandra Chaudhuri, 'Nandalal Basu', first published in *Nutan Patrika*, 14 February 1936, and reprinted in *Nirbachita Prabandha*, pp. 281–82; 'Nandalal Basu: Chitrakar', first published in *Kathasahitya*, April 1966, and reprinted in *Nirbachita Prabandha*, pp. 281–88; and 'Nandalal Bose', first published in *The Statesman*, 1943, and reprinted in *The East Is East and the West Is West* (Calcutta: Mitra and Ghosh, 1999), pp. 22–25.
30. On the concept of a different universalism, see Bose, *A Hundred Horizons*, pp. 233–71. On vernacular cosmopolitanism, see Bhabha, *The Location of Culture*, pp. ix–xxv.
31. See Kris Manjapra, 'The Mirrored World' (PhD diss., Harvard University, 2007).

Unity or Partition

1. Mohandas Karamchand Gandhi to Sarat Chandra Bose, 6 June 1947, reproduced in Sisir Kumar Bose, *Sarat Chandra Bose: Remembering My Father* (Kolkata: Netaji Research Bureau, and New Delhi: Niyogi Books, 2014), p. 211.
2. D.G. Tendulkar, *Mahatma: Life of Mohandas Karamchand Gandhi, 1947–1948*, vol. 8, (Bombay: Vithalbhai K. Jhaveri and D.G. Tendulkar, 1954), pp. 6, 9–12, 18–20.
3. Ibid., pp. 14–15.
4. Tendulkar, *Mahatma, 1945 1947*, vol. 7, pp. 8–9; Ayesha Jalal, *The Sole Spokesman: Jinnah, the Muslim League and the Demand for Pakistan* (Cambridge: Cambridge University Press, 1985), p. 128.
5. Tendulkar, *Mahatma*, vol. 7, p. 16.
6. Ibid., pp. 24, 35, 50, 60, 78.
7. Ibid., pp. 98–99.
8. Ibid., pp. 107–09.
9. *Young India*, 20 October 1921, cited in Sugata Bose, 'Nation, Reason and Religion'.
10. Tendulkar, *Mahatma*, vol. 7, p. 110.
11. Ibid., pp. 134–36.

12. Jalal, *Sole Spokesman*, p. 194.
13. Tendulkar, *Mahatma*, vol. 7, pp. 142, 144–45.
14. Ibid., pp. 244, 262, 269–70.
15. Sugata Bose, *Agrarian Bengal: Economy, Social Structure and Politics, 1919-1947* (Cambridge: Cambridge University Press, 1986), pp. 223–29.
16. Tendulkar, *Mahatma*, vol. 7, p. 296.
17. Ibid., pp. 298, 301, 305–06, 334.
18. Ibid., pp. 337–38, 362.
19. Ibid., pp. 355, 366–67, 369, 370–71, 399–402.
20. Ibid., pp. 407, 411.
21. B.R. Nanda, *Witness to Partition: A Memoir* (New Delhi: Rupa & Co, 2003), pp. 33–34.
22. Ibid., p. 40.
23. Jalal, *Sole Spokesman*, pp. 237–39.
24. Tendulkar, *Mahatma*, vol. 7, pp. 426–32, 437, 444.
25. Ibid., pp. 454, 460, 462, 464. See also, Nirmal Kumar Bose, *My Days with Gandhi* (Calcutta: Nishana, 1953), pp. 218–22.
26. Tendulkar, *Mahatma*, vol. 7, pp. 465–67; Bose, *My Days with Gandhi*, pp. 224–35.
27. Bose, *My Days with Gandhi*, pp. 235–36; Sisir Kumar Bose, *Sarat Chandra Bose*, pp. 210, 212–13; Sisir Kumar Bose, *Subhas and Sarat: An Intimate Memoir of the Bose Brothers* (New Delhi: Aleph, 2016), pp. 236–38.
28. Jalal, *Sole Spokesman*, pp. 280–81.
29. Bose, *Sarat Chandra Bose*, p. 214; Bose, *Subhas and Sarat*, p. 238.
30. Tendulkar, *Mahatma*, vol. 7, p. 482.
31. Rammanohar Lohia, *Guilty Men of India's Partition* (Allahabad: Kitabistan, 1960), pp. 9–11.
32. Tendulkar, *Mahatma*, vol. 8, pp. 77, 81, 84, 87–88, 95.
33. Tendulkar, *Mahatma*, vol. 8, pp. 96, 97–98.
34. Nanda, *Witness to Partition*, pp. 81, 165.
35. Tendulkar, *Mahatma*, vol. 8, pp. 102, 109.
36. *Young India*, 8 September 1920, cited in Sugata Bose, 'Nation, Reason and Religion'.
37. Tendulkar, *Mahatma*, vol. 8, pp. 110–11, 118.
38. Tendulkar, *Mahatma*, vol. 8, pp. 121–22.
39. Tendulkar, *Mahatma*, vol. 8, pp. 135–38, 160–62.
40. Nanda, *Witness to Partition*, p. 70.
41. Ayesha Jalal, *Self and Sovereignty: Individual and Community in South Asian Islam since 1850* (London: Routledge, 2000), pp. 504–62.
42. Tendulkar, *Mahatma*, vol. 8, p. 190.
43. Ibid., pp. 197, 222, 233, 238, 275.

44. Ibid., pp. 299, 303, 306–08, 314–16, 320.
45. Ibid., pp. 322–23, 329.
46. Ibid., pp. 335–36, 338, 344.
47. Ibid., p. 346.
48. Nanda, *Witness to Partition*, p. 162.
49. Krishna Bose, *Lost Addresses: A Memoir of India, 1934-1955* (New Delhi: Niyogi Books, 2014; first published as *Harano Thikana*, Kolkata: Ananda, 2013), p. 133.
50. Bose, *Subhas and Sarat*, p. 242.

Why Jinnah Matters

1. Jaswant Singh, *Jinnah: India, Independence, Partition* (New Delhi: Rupa, 2009).

Limits of Liberalism

1. C.A. Bayly, *Origins of Nationality in South Asia* (Delhi: Oxford University Press, 1998).
2. C.A. Bayly, *Recovering Liberties: Indian Thought in the Age of Liberalism and Empire* (Cambridge: Cambridge University Press, 2012), p. 150.
3. Ibid., pp. 41–42.
4. Ibid. pp. 3–4.
5. Surendranath Banerjea, 'Joseph Mazzini', in *Speeches of Surendranath Banerjea* (Calcutta: Indian Association, 1970), pp. 1–23; Lala Lajpat Rai, 'Great Men of the World I: Giuseppe Mazzini', in B.R. Nanda (ed.), *The Collected Works of Lala Lajpat Rai*, vol. 1 (Delhi: Manohar, 2003), pp. 283–310.
6. Mahatma Gandhi, 'Mazzini', in Raghavan Iyer (ed.) *The Moral and Political Writings of Mahatma Gandhi*, vol. 1, *Civilization, Politics and Religion* (Oxford: Clarendon Press, 1986), pp. 105–06.
7. Bayly, *Recovering Liberties*, p. 110.
8. Surendranath Banerjea, *A Nation in Making* (Bombay: Oxford University Press, 1925, 1963), p. 130.
9. Rai, 'Great Men of the World', in *Collected Works of Lala Lajpat Rai*, pp. 283–444.
10. Lala Lajpat Rai, *Shivaji: The Great Patriot* (Delhi: Metropolitan, 1980), p. 69.
11. Biman Behari Majumdar, *History of Political Thought: From Rammohun to Dayananda (1821-84)*, vol. 1, *Bengal* (Calcutta: University of Calcutta, 1934), pp. 284–320.

12. Government of Bombay, *Source Material for a History of the Freedom Movement in India (Collected from Bombay Government Records), 1885-1920*, vol. 2 (Bombay: Government of Bombay, 1958), p. 439.
13. Bayly, *Recovering Liberties*, p. 245.
14. Bipin Chandra Pal, 'The New Patriotism', in *Swadeshi and Swaraj: The Rise of New Patriotism* (Calcutta: Yugayatri Prakashak, 1954), pp. 17–20.
15. Sugata Bose, 'The Spirit and Form of an Ethical Polity: A Meditation on Aurobindo's Thought', *Modern Intellectual History*, April 2007, pp. 129–144.
16. Bayly, *Recovering Liberties*, p. 173.
17. Ibid., pp. 305, 311, 319–20.
18. Ibid., p. 329. See also Sugata Bose, *His Majesty's Opponent: Subhas Chandra Bose and India's Struggle against Empire* (Cambridge, Mass.: The Belknap Press of Harvard University Press, 2011).
19. Bayly, *Recovering Liberties*, p. 232. Faisal Devji, on whose speculations Bayly tends to rely, completely misses the dialogic historical context of Muslim thought in the late nineteenth century in his 'Apologetic Modernity', *Modern Intellectual History*, April 2007, pp. 61–76. For a work that studies Muslim thought in its interplay with colonial, Hindu and Sikh discourses, see Ayesha Jalal, *Self and Sovereignty: Individual and Community in South Asian Islam since 1850* (London: Routledge, 2000).
20. Banerjea, *A Nation in Making*, p. 130.

INDEX

Abdullah, Sheikh, 155
Abedin, Jainul, 123
academic freedom, 202
Advani, Lal Krishna, 190
'Africa', 107
agrarian populism, 75
agricultural: indebtedness, 68; stagnation, 74
Akali Dal, 137
Akbar, M.J., 209
Akbar, Mughal emperor, 103, 210–11
Akhlaq, Muhammad, 200
Ali, Maulana Mohamed, 44, 47–50, 51, 131, 134
Ali, Shaukat, 47, 49, 131, 134, 142
Alipore bomb trial (1909), 85, 94
All India Trinamool Congress, 187, 189, 192
Ambedkar, B.R., 164, 196, 199, 200, 202, 203
Anand, Mulk Raj, 53
Anderson, Benedict, *Imagined Communities*, 35
Andhras, 102
Andrews, C.F., 46
Annapurna and Rudra, 123

Annapurna and Shiva, 123
Appiah, Anthony, 108
Arya, 97–98
Aryavarta, 26
Ashfaqullah, 203
Asian Relations Conference, 138
Asiatic Association, Shanghai, 121
Asoka, 100
Ataturk, Kemal, 120
atomization, 28, 71
Attlee, Clement, 137
Auchinleck, Claude, 57
Auden, W.H., 187
Aufklarung, 41–42
Aurangzeb, 16
Ausgleich, 58
authoritarian rule, 204
autocratic despotism, 205
Azad Hind movement, 204
Azad Hind Radio, 169
Azad, Maulana Abul Kalam, 133

Ba Maw, 56
Babri Masjid, xiii
Bagchi, Jasodhara, 11
Bahadur Shah Zafar, 56–57, 162

Baig, Muzaffar Hussain, 209, 211
balance-of-payments crisis, 82
Bande Mataram (journal), 89, 91, 93
Bande Mataram, 3, 14–19, 48, 142–43, 168, 171
Banerjee, Kalyan, 204
Banerjee, Mamata, 177, 190, 198, 203
Bangadarshan, 3
Bangladesh, 21; War, 188–89
Bardhan, Pranab, 78, 81
Bardoli satyagraha, 186
Bardoloi, Gopinath, 135
Basu, Kaushik, 76
Basu, Rajnarayan, 39–40
Bayly, C.A., 87, 159–65; *Origins of Nationality in South Asia*, 159; *Recovering Liberties*, 159–60
Beachcroft, C.P., 85
Bengal: famine, 123–24; Government Plan (1945), 73; political discourse, 4
Bengal Provincial Conference (1917), 118; (1924), 52; (1925), 120
Bengali, Bengalis, 134–35; Hindus, 18–19, 29, 140;— mother complex, 6, 15; identity, 129; Muslims, 15–16, 140
Bentinck, William, 37
Beti Bachao, Beti Padhao Yojana, 177, 185
Bhabha, Homi, 108
Bhagat Singh, 203
Bharata, King, 26, 176
Bharatavarsha, 4, 26, 175–80
Bharatiya Janata Party (BJP), 150, 189

Bharatmata (painting of Abanindranath Tagore), 5, 7, 9, 21–22, 116
Bharatmata, 19, 122; concept of, 4
Bhattacharya, Pradyot, 22–23
Biju Janata Dal (BJD), 214
Blair, Tony, 212
Bolshevik internationalism, 111
Bombay National Union, 93
Bombay Plan (1944), 73
Bongaon refugee camps, 188
Bose, Krishna, 168
Bose, Nandalal, 116–17, 120–25
Bose, Sarat, 105, 127, 139–40, 148, 149, 192
Bose, Sisir Kumar, 188, 198
Bose, Subhas Chandra, 18–19, 23, 29, 51–52, 54–57, 67–68, 88, 105, 186, 192, 197–8, 204, 206–7
Bose, Sumantra, 213
Brahmin theocracy, 98
British Colonial Development and Welfare Act (1940), 64
British Empire, British rule in India, x–xii, 25, 33, 37, 67, 73, 102; divide and rule policy, 54; imperialism, 53, 56; ruling classes, 36
Buddha, 161
Buddhism, 113–14
bureaucracy, 155

Cabinet Mission, 58, 127, 132–33, 141
Caitanya-Janani (Birth of Caitanya), 121
Cannadine, David, 33
capitalism, 62, 65, 66, 83
caste conflicts, xi, 70, 203

Catlin, George, 140
Cavendish, Lord, 86
Chaitanya, 161
Chakravarti, ideal of, 102, 205
Chakravarty, Amiya Kumar, 120
Chakravarty, Dipesh, 35, 40, 95
Chatterjee, Partha, 24, 27, 39–41, 45, 53, 65, 69–70; *The Nation and Its Fragments*, 9, 20–21; *Nationalist Thought and the Colonial World*, 9–12, 20
Chattopadhyay, Bankim Chandra, 3–4, 10, 14–16, 18, 19, 21, 135; *Anandamath*, 3, 15
Chattopadhyay, Kedar Nath, 120
Chattopadhyay, Suniti Kumar, 120
China, 62, 76, 117, 120, 121, 211; authoritarian state, 176; education, 184; famine (1958–61), 77; and India war (1962), 155; invasion by Japan, 122–24, 207
Chittagong Armoury Raid, 135
Christianity, 1, 37, 38
Chungking, 124
Church and State in Europe and India, 35–38
civil disobedience movement, 53, 122
civil society, 70, 81; Western concept, 28, 45
class exploitation, 203
class, nation and, 12–14
collective conscience, 202
collective selfishness, 96
Collins, Michael, 58

colonial and national development, historical origins of the concept of, 64–72
colonial rule, economic consequences, x
colour prejudice, 126
communal: electorates (1909), 44; freedom and self-determination, 100–1; violence during partition, 133–38, 141–44
communalism, xiii, 21, 52, 86
Communist Party of India-Marxist (CPI-M), 189
communitarian conflicts, 43–44, 53, 81, 113, 164, 213
Comte, August, 11, 160
Congress/Indian National Congress, 2, 3, 18, 23, 43, 29–31, 44, 53, 54, 64, 65, 122, 129, 132, 133, 140–41, 144–45, 147, 149, 156, 189, 167, 168, 169, 180, 206, 211; All India Congress Committee (AICC), 19, 51, 127–28, 129, 144; majoritarianism, 150–51; role in Partition of Indian Subcontinent, 21, 150–51; Working Committee (CWC), 127, 137, 138, 139, 140
Congreve, Richard, 11
Constitution of India, 25, 147, 195–96, 199; (119th Amendment) Bill, 187, 191, 193
constitutional morality, 196–97, 203
Cornwallis, Lord, 66
cosmic balance, 6

Cosmopolitanism, xiii, 96, 107–26
cow slaughter issue, 43, 48, 200
Craig, James, 54, 58
Cripps, Stafford, 132
cultural: imperialism, 101, 125; intimacy, 195–200; nationalism, 7
Curzon, George, 1, 89, 149, 214

Dalit women, 179
Dandi March (Bapuji), 122
Darwinian revolution, 36
Das, Chittaranjan, xi, 28, 85, 118–20, 142, 192, 205, 206; Bengal Pact, 51–52; Constitution (1923), 71
Das, Jibanananda, 192
Datta, Michael Madhusudan, 40
Dayanand, Swami, 161
De Valera, 53, 56
decentralization, 28, 35, 71
Decentralization Commission (1908), 183
decolonization, 35, 81, 83
democracy, 28, 80, 151, 180, 176, 196, 197; track record, 153–57
Desai, Bhulabhai, 128, 129
Devi (1960), 9
Dey, Mukul, 120
Dharma, 99–102. See also religion
Dharmarajya, 27, 102, 205
Dhillon, Gurbaksh Singh, 129, 199
distinctiveness, xiii, 119
Durai, Thambi, 178
Dutt, Romesh C., x, 64

Earth as Prakriti, conception of, 6
economic liberalization, xiii, 82
education, 178, 184

engendering the nation, 2–9
ethical polity, spirit and form of, 85–106
ethics and politics, 97
European: 'enlightenment', 27; forms of the nation-state, 27; imperialism, 114; racism and totalitarianism, 97; rationalism, 38
Expenditure Management Commission, 182
external shocks, 75

female principle as Shakti, 7
Fenollosa, Ernest Francisco, 115
First War of Indian Independence (1857), 34, 50
fiscal deficit, 181
fiscal federalism, 181–86
fission and fusion, 29
Five Year Plan, Second (1955), 74; Third, 74
food inflation, 186
foreign policy, 175–76
freedom struggle, xi, 203–4
Fry, Roger, 125

Gandhi, Indira, 75–76, 156, 188
Gandhi, M.K., xii, xiv, 5, 18, 28, 64, 67, 69–71, 73, 75–76, 83, 86, 90, 95, 105–6, 109, 112–14, 119–20, 122, 125, 149, 151, 157, 161–62, 169, 170–71, 180, 188, 199, 204; assassination, 147–48 ; his last stand, 1945–48, 127–48; reason and Hindu-Muslim unity, 45–51
Gandhi, Manu, 135
Ganga, 18, 178–79, 185, 192

Garibaldi, 33–34, 91
gender discrimination, 203
George, Lloyd, 46
Ghose, Aurobindo, xi, 3, 16, 21, 27, 34, 43–44, 85–106, 205
Ghose, Barindra Kumar, 85
Gladstone, 36–38
Good Friday Agreement, 212, 214
goods and services tax (GST), 182
Government of India Act (1935), 83
Great Calcutta Killing, 137, 142
Grote, 196
Guha, Ramachandra, 153–57
Guha, Ranajit, 88, 105
Gupta, Dinesh, 17–18
Guptas, 101, 102

Haksar, P.N., 156
Harijan, 130
Hasan, Abid, 55, 169, 199
Hashim, Abul, 139
Hasina, Sheikh, 189
Hazarika, Bhupen, 179, 192
Hind Swaraj, 28, 45, 64, 161
Hindu: communalism, 18; communitarianism, 113; identity and politics, 53; majoritarianism, political compulsions, 53; Muslim unity, 131, 136;—Gandhi's reason and, 45–51; nationalism, 22, 40; religious symbolisms, 44; universalism, 113
Hinduism, 35, 38, 52, 96, 144, 147

Hindu Mahasabha, 2, 30–31, 137, 140, 146, 149
Hindustani, 128, 169–70
Hishida, Shunso, 116
Hizbul Mujahideen, 211
Hore, Somnath, 123
Howard, John, 37
human development, 177
human rights violations in Nagaland, 155
humanism, xi, 27, 86, 147, 160
humanitarian issues, 190
Hussain, Mumtaz, 169

identity politics, 113–14
illusion, 40
imagined community, 87
Immigration Act (1924), 120–21
import-substituting industrialization, 79
India-Bangladesh border issue, 187–93
Indian Civil Service (ICS), 155
Indian National Army (INA), 55, 56, 57, 124, 129–32, 198–99
Indian Opinion, 161
Indian Science News Association, 67
industrialization, 67–69, 74, 79
information technology, 182
internationalism, 108
intolerance, 195–200
Iqbal, Muhammad, 45, 139, 168
Irish: British imperialism, 56, 58; Catholics, 37; peace process, 212–13; Republican Army, 212; revolutionaries, 56
Islam, 17–18, 38, 45, 46–47, 74
Islam, Kazi Nazrul, 15, 179, 197

Jadavpur University, 203
Jahangir, 211
Jaish-e-Mohammed, 211
Jaitley, Arun, 185
Jalal, Ayesha, 50, 57, 144
Jamal, Abdul Karim, 116
Jammu and Kashmir Liberation Front (JKLF), 211
Japan, x, 115–17, 120–22, 176; invaded China (1937), 122, 124, 206, 207; nationalism, ix, 123–24
Jaswant Singh, 150–51
Jawaharlal Nehru University, 202–3
Jinnah, Mohammed Ali, 52–54, 128, 133, 138–39, 149–52
Johnson, Dr, 181
Joshi, Murli Manohar, 190
justice and righteousness, 46, 75, 92, 109, 114, 150–51, 195, 201–2

Kakuzo, Okakura, 115–16
Kampo, Arai, 117
Kanhaiya Kumar, 203
Kant, Immanuel, 39, 41–42
Kar, Surendranath, 120
Karmayogin, 96
Kashmir issue, 144, 155, 205, 209–15; complex demographic composition, 212; Kashmiri expressions of regional identity, 210
Khan Abdul Ghaffar Khan, 122, 137, 141, 150
Khan, Aga, 164
Khan, Khizar Hayat, 137
Khan, Liaquat Ali, 128

Khan, Sayyid Ahmad, 165
Khan, Shah Nawaz, 129, 199
Khan, Zafrullah, 146
Khilafat movement, 45–46, 47–48, 50, 53, 119, 131
Kiani, Mohammed Zaman, 55, 199
Klaus, Vaclav, 62
Komagatamaru, 117
Konarak sculptures, 117
Kripalani, Acharya J.B., 144
Krishnamurti, B.V., 156
Kumarappa, J.C., 69

Lajpat Rai, Lala, 42, 52, 161, 162, 164
Lal Ded, 210
Lari, Zairul-Hassan, 196
Lashkar-e-Taiba, 211
Lele, Bishnu Bhaskar, 93
Lenin, Vladimir, 111
Lewis, Arthur, 74
liberalism; in domestic politics of Britain, 34; limits of, 159–65; and religious universalism, 161
liberalization policies (1991), 61–62, 77, 79, 82
Life Insurance Corporation of India (LIC), 153
linguistic communities, 21, 45, 56
linguistic region, nation and, 20–23, 44
Lohia, Ram Manohar, 141
Ludden, David, 65, 80

Macaulay, Thomas Babington, 36–38
macroeconomic: inefficiencies, 78; stabilization, 181
Madrasas, modernization, 178, 185

Mahabharata, 102, 205
mahajati (great nation), 29
Mahalanobis, P.C., 62, 73
Maharaja Sadan, 23
Mahtab, Bhartruhari, 177
Maine, Henry, 70
Major, John, 212
majoritarianism, xii, xiii, 53, 82, 150, 151, 179
majorities and minorities, 38; political representation, 113; religion based notions, 44–45
Majumdar, B.B., 162
Malaviya, Pandit Madan Mohan, 164, 182, 184
Mali, Rai Mohan, 136
Malik, Shaukat, 199
Mandela, Nelson, 125
Manjapra, Kris, 88
Manmohan Singh, 189
Mao Zedong, 62
Mappila rebellion (1921), 49
Marathas, 101, 104
Marx, Karl, x, 202
Marxist, 35, 87, 88; internationalism, 88
Matribhakti, 8
Mauryas, 101, 102
Mazzini, Giuseppe, 91, 95, 160–63
McGuinness, Martin, 212
Millat (Nation), 2, 31
minorities, 38, 44, 52, 58, 113, 128, 134, 139, 145, 179, 185, 195–96
Mirabai, 210
modernity, 35, 80; anti-colonial, 39–45; versus tradition, 67
Modi, Narendra, xiv
monarchy, 99, 176, 205–6

Montagu-Chelmsford reforms, 47
Moran, D.P., 44
Motherland-Deshmata, concept of, 6
mother-nation, 21, 22; equation with Durga, 19–20; political cult, 16
Mountbatten, Louis, 1, 127, 138–41, 198, 214
Mughal Empire, 16, 101, 104
Mukherjee, Syamaprasad, 140
Mukhopadhyay, Prabhat, 9
Mukti Bahini, 188
Mukundadas, Charankabi, 8–9
Mundhra, Haridas, 153
Muslim conquest, 103
Muslim, Muslims l, 2, 18, 43–48, 50, 53, 55, 56, 119, 137, 140, 149, 162, 165; and Hindus, 18, 49, 51, 112, 120, 129, 131, 132, 134, 137, 139, 142–45, 147; and nation's equation with goddess, 15; rule, 26; separate electorates for, 51
Muslim League, 54, 129, 132–34, 139, 141

Nanak, Guru, 103
Nanda, B.R., 137, 142, 143, 147
Nandy, Ashis, 5, 70, 80, 86, 94
Naoroji, Dadabhai, x, 64, 177
Narain, Jai Prakash, 141, 184
Narendra Deva, 144
nation: and class, 12–14; and gender, relationship, 5, 8; and linguistic region, 20–23; reason and religion: India's independence in International perspective, xii, 33–60; and

religious community, 14–20; and state, 23–30
national anthem, 167–71
national development: instruments and idioms of colonial and, 33–60; and the postcolonial state, 72–79
National Education Policy, 178
National Planning Committee, 64, 68–69, 73
nationalism: authoritarian conception, 24; and universalism, 114; vernacular languages, 7
nationalist thought and colonial knowledge, 9–12
nationality and human community, contradiction, 27
Nature Philosophy of the Hindus, 6
Nature-Mother equation, 6–7, 20
Nehru, Jawaharlal, 5, 18, 29, 33–34, 51–52, 62, 67–75, 105, 133, 137–38, 141, 149–50, 154–56, 180, 204, 211; versus Gandhi, 67, 83
Nehruvian: centralism, xii; democracy, 75, 156; India, 62; misdiagnosis of the cause of Hindu-Muslim disunity, 52; modernism, 72–73; secularism, xiii; socialism, 155
Nivedita, Sister, 115–16
Noakhali riots, 134–37, 141
non-cooperation movement, 48, 53, 114, 119, 131, 134, 142
Nooruddin, Sheikh, 210
North West Frontier Province (NWFP), 133, 141, 150

Norton, Eardley, 86
Nund Rishi, 210

Orientalism, 98
Ottoman empire, 112

Pakistan, 127–28, 132, 141, 142, 146, 151, 188, 213; demand for, 133, 139; war over Kashmir, 144–45; occupied part of Kashmir, 211
Pal, Bipin Chandra, xi, 1, 6–7, 11, 25–27, 89, 91, 95, 163, 176, 205
Palestine, 47, 58
Parashuram myth, 2
Parnell, Charles, 54, 86, 89
Partition: of Bengal, 1, 29–30, 58, 89, 137, 139–40, 149–50; Congress's compromise on, 21, 151; of Indian Subcontinent, xii, xiv, 1, 34, 123, 187; of Punjab, 57–58, 137–40, 144, 149–50; or unity, Mahatma Gandhi's last stand (1945–48), 127–48
passive resistance (*satyagraha*), 89–90, 93, 111–12
Patel Vithalbhai, 186
Patel, Vallabhbhai, 138, 140–41, 145, 149–50, 155, 180, 186
patriotism, xii, xiii, 3, 85, 87, 91, 92, 97, 103, 105, 108–10, 115, 130, 159, 163, 204
Patwari, Habibullah, 136
Penn, William, 37
Phan Boi Chau, 162
Phan Chau Trinh, 162
Planning Commission, 68, 78
political economy, 10, 66, 155, 160

politics of multi-religious societies, 111
politics, xiv, 13, 14, 21, 34, 38, 44, 53–54, 66, 68–70, 80, 82–83, 88–89, 94, 97–98, 100–1, 111–13, 138, 150
poverty alleviation, 75–76, 177, 204
Pradhan Mantri Krishi Sinchayee Yojana, 177
princely states, integration into Indian union, 155
provincial autonomy, 132–33
public health crisis, 183
Punjab disturbances (1947), 137, 142
Purusha and *Prakriti*, dialectic of, 11

Queen's Proclamation of 1858, 38, 50
quit India movements, 53, 131

racialities and provincialities, 26
racism, 97, 125–26
Radcliffe Award (1947), 142, 187
Radhakrishnan, S., 164
Rahman, A.R., 170
Rahman, Habibur, 199
Rahman, Sheikh Mujibur, 188
Rajagopalachari, C., 143
rajchakravarti, 26, 176
Rajendra Prasad, 144
Rajguru, 203
Ram, Parashuram and Mother India, 30–31
Ramayana, 2, 102, 205
Ramdas, 104
Ranade, Mahadev Govind, 41, 42
rashtrashakti. *See* state power

Rashtriya Swayamsevak Sangh (RSS), 145–46, 203
rational reform, regional revival and intimations of anti-colonial modernity, 39–45
Ray, Satyajit, 9
Reading, Rufus Isaacs, 49
reason *(aql)*, 11, 20, 108–9, 135, 195, 213; and development, 67–68, 80; and emotion, 35; Gandhi's reason and Hindu-Muslim unity, 45–51; and religion, xii, xiii, 33–59; science and, 71; of state, 79; versus unreason, 67
regional, 102–4, 153, 159, 165, 175, 205; autonomy, 29, 71, 101; diversity, 167; as faith, 111–12; Hindu communalism, 18; identity, 210–11; nationalism as, 106; parties, 82, 151, 214; patriotism, 87, 105; political movements, xiii; rights, 151
religion, x–xi, xiv, 1, 16–18, 20, 22, 86, 91, 93–96, 103–4, 114, 128, 131, 136, 144, 147, 159, 161, 163, 165, 195, 198; and British history, 36; and language, 210; nation, reason and, xii–xiii, 33–59; and politics, 38, 98, 100–1, 111–12
religious: communities, 20, 29, 44–46, 49, 55, 56, 58, 71–72, 87, 104, 112–13, 129; differences, 54, 199; identity, 114; majoritarianism, xii, xiii, 82; minorities, 58; nationalism, 34; oppression and intolerance,

100; prejudices, 114; reforms, xii; sensibility and religious bigotry, xiii, 41, 44; universalism, 88, 112
Romulus, 26
Roy, Dwijendralal, 4, 12, 178, 192
Roy, Kamini, 8
Roy, M.N., 164
Roy, Ram Mohun, 161
Rudy, Rajiv Pratap, 178

SAARC, 175
sacrifice, doctrine of, 96–97, 105
Sagan, Carl, 202
Saha, Meghnad, 67, 73
Sahgal, Prem Kumar, 129, 199
Said, Edward, 98
St. Bartholomew, 44
Salam, Amtus, 136
Salim, Mohammad, 189
Samyavada (socialism), 29
Sanatana Dharma, 95
Banerjea, Surendranath, 95, 161, 165
Sanghomita, Mumtaz, 189
Sankhya system of philosophy, 11
Sapru, Tej Bahadur, 129
Sarala Devi, 8
'Sare Jahan se Achha Hindustan Hamara', 168
Sarkar, Binoy Kumar, 125
Sarkar, Sumit, 86
Sarkar, Tanika, 6, 7, 13, 95
Sartori, Andrew, 87
Sarwar, Ghulam, 134
Sati (1907), 116
Satpathy, Tathagata, 214
Savarkar, Veer Damodar, 162
science, 35, 202; and development, 79; and politics, 68–69; and reason, 71; and state, 79–80; versus superstition, 67
scientific: consciousness, 20; education, 98; nationalism, 35, 40; rationalism, 35, 40, 68; revolution, 6
sea lanes and land routes, role in creating Asia-sense, 125
sectarian fanaticism, 147
secularism, 86, 195, 198
Sen, Amartya, 62, 74, 76, 77
Sen, Atul Prasad, 12
Sen, Keshub Chandra, 161
Sen, Kshitimohan, 120
Sen, P.C., 116
Sen, Rajanikanta, 13
Sen, Sukumar, 155
Sepoy Mutiny. *See* First War of Indian Independence
Shah, Mian Akbar, 198–99
Shahabadi, Saiduddin, 210
Shahjahan, 192
Shankeranand, 113
Sheikh, Mohsin, 179, 200
Shivaji, 104, 161, 161
Shradhanand, Swami, 131
Sikh Khalsa, 105
Singh, Rajnath, 195, 200, 209
Sinn Fein, 34
space, concept in pre-colonial patriotism, 159
Sriramulu, Potti, 155
Standing Committee on External Affairs, 189–90
Standing Committee system, 190
state power, xii, 20–21, 29, 65, 71–72
state structure and ideology, 25
state, concept of, 28–29
state, nation and, 23–30

Stracey, Cyril John, 198
Suhrawardy, Husain Shaheed, 139–42, 143, 171
suicides among students in elite educational institutions, 201
Sukhdev, 203
Sule, Supriya, 196
Swadeshi, xi, 1, 8, 12–13, 21, 23, 34, 44, 86, 88, 89, 91–93, 95, 115–19, 121–22, 163–64, 176, 192, 206
Swaraj, Sushma, 176, 179

Tagore, Abanindranath, 5, 7, 9, 21, 116
Tagore, Dinendranath, 168
Tagore, Gaganendranath, 116
Tagore, Rabindranath, ix–xi, 3, 15–16, 18–19, 23, 29, 45, 59, 68, 86, 106, 107–9, 116–18, 120–23, 126, 129, 133, 135, 139, 143, 163, 176, 180, 192, 205–8; and our national anthem, 167–70; *Nationalism*, ix–x, 27, 118, 206; analysis of Indian society, xi
territorial nationalism, 114
Thakur, Anurag, 205, 206
Thakur, Ram Singh, 169
Tharoor, Shashi, 189
Thorat Committee, 201
Tilak, Bal Gangadhar, 34, 44
Tipu Sultan, 169
tradition-modernity, dichotomy, 81
Transvaal government, 112
Trevelyan, G.M., 33–34, 36
Trump, Donald, xiv
trusteeship of common property, 69
Tulsidas, 136, 137
Turkey, 46–47

unemployment, 68
Unitarian imperial State, 27, 102, 205–6
United Front, 82
United Nations Security Council, 146
universal brotherhood, 119
universalisms, xiii, 87, 88, 107–26, 161, 163, 176
urban bias, 75
utilitarianism, 160
Uttarpara Hitakari Sabha (1876), 161

Vajpayee, A.B., 191, 210, 212–13
Vedas, 101
Vemula, Rohith, 201–2
Venugopal, 195
Vietnam, 162
Vivekananda, Swami, 16, 88, 113, 116, 205

Walker, Johnny, 154
Wavell, Archibald, 129
West Bengal: Jal Dharo, Jal Bharo, 177; Kanyasree scheme, 177, 185
Wilson, Woodrow, 118
Woolf, Leonard, 53
World War, First, 88, 111, 116, 206
World War, Second, 54, 56, 128

Yokoyama, Taikan, 116, 117, 121
Young India, 46
Yuvajana, Shramika, Rythu (YSR) Congress Party, 213

Zutshi, Chitralekha, 209–10

COPYRIGHT ACKNOWLEDGEMENTS

Grateful acknowledgement is made for permission to reprint the following material:

1. 'The Nation as Mother' first published as 'Nation as Mother' in Sugata Bose and Ayesha Jalal (eds.), *Nationalism, Democracy and Development* (Delhi: Oxford University Press, 1997). Reproduced with permission of Oxford University Press India © Oxford University Press 1997.
2. 'Nation, Reason and Religion', G.M. Trevelyan Lecture, 26 November 1997, University of Cambridge; published in *Economic and Political Weekly*, 1-7 August 1998.
3. 'Instruments and Idioms of Colonial and National Development' first published in Fred Cooper and Randall Packard (eds), *International Development and the Social Sciences: History and Politics of Knowledge* (Berkeley: University of California Press, 1997).
4. 'The Spirit and Form of an Ethical Polity' first published in *Modern Intellectual History*, 4: 1 (2007).
5. 'Different Universalisms, Colorful Cosmopolitanisms' first published in Sugata Bose and Kris Manjapra (eds.), *Cosmopolitan Thought Zones: South Asia and the Global Circulation of Ideas* (London: Palgrave Macmillan, 2010).
6. 'Unity or Partition', B.R. Nanda Memorial Lecture, December 2014, to be published in Naren Nanda (ed.), *Gandhi's Moral Politics* (London: Routledge, 2017).
7. 'Why Jinnah Matters' first published in *The Indian Express*, 25 August 2009. By Sugata Bose, reprinted from *The Indian Express* with permission of The Indian Express (P) Limited © 2017.

8. Track Record of India's Democracy first published as a review of Ramachandra Guha, *India after Gandhi*, in *The Indian Express*, 27 May 2007. By Sugata Bose, reprinted from *The Indian Express* with permission of The Indian Express (P) Limited © 2017.
9. 'Limits of Liberalism' first published as a review of C.A. Bayly, *Recovering Liberties*, in *Britain and the World* 5.2 (2012), pp. 294–313; http://www.euppublishing.com/doi/full/10.3366/brw.2012.0059
10. 'Our National Anthem' first published in *The Indian Express*, 27 December 2016. By Sugata Bose, reprinted from *The Indian Express* with permission of The Indian Express (P) Limited © 2017.